IMAGES
of America

FRANKLIN

On the Cover: A parade approaches the intersection of Twelfth and Liberty Streets in the 1930s. The Salvation Army has always been an important organization in the area. Presently, it has a thrift shop on PA Route 8, just over the Washington Crossing Bridge, and a church located at 737 Elk Street. The first building at left burned in 1981. (Courtesy of Peter Solle.)

IMAGES
of America

FRANKLIN

Sarah Ann Benton
Foreword by Peter Greene

ARCADIA
PUBLISHING

ISBN 978-1-4671-2306-8

Published by Arcadia Publishing
Charleston, South Carolina

Printed in the United States of America

Library of Congress Control Number: 2014948975

For all general information, please contact Arcadia Publishing:
Telephone 843-853-2070
Fax 843-853-0044
E-mail sales@arcadiapublishing.com
For customer service and orders:
Toll-Free 1-888-313-2665

Visit us on the Internet at www.arcadiapublishing.com

I would like to dedicate this book to the citizens of Franklin, Pennsylvania, past, present, and future.

Contents

Foreword

In its past, Franklin, Pennsylvania, has been many versions of the quintessential American small town.

It was a gathering place for Native Americans before Europeans ever intruded on the valley. It was a frontier settlement on the rugged border between the British and French empires. It was the hub of oil-fueled boom and bust.

After the Civil War, Franklin offered any young man the opportunity to become a man of substance and wealth. Big-time robber barons, like John D. Rockefeller, passed through, but other men of lesser wealth stayed and built.

These families did more than build beautiful homes. They invested time and money in building a community and filling it with fine things. The dawn of the 20th century saw the growth of leisure, the nurturing of the arts. Franklin had bands, parks, beautiful homes, and societies devoted to creating a better life for residents. The kind of life later memorialized in *The Music Man* and *Our Town* existed here in the heart of Venango County.

After the Great European War, that life changed a bit. Growth of big cities had outpaced the small places in America, and the young folks moved away in search of opportunity. But they never fully abandoned Franklin. Every five years, the banners would go up, the invitations would go out, and Franklinites would return from all across the nation. They would come home to their own past.

I have called Franklin home for decades. Surrounded by natural beauty, its streets carry the weight of time without being musty or tired. It is still a place where you can walk into town to dine out, see some friends, and listen to a concert in the park. It is still a place where family and history provide a solid richness to life that only time and toughness can bring.

There is something beautiful about images like these, about being able to see the people who once walked these streets, and to see the streets themselves as they looked in an earlier time. It's a good town, a good place to be.

—Peter Greene

ACKNOWLEDGMENTS

First, I must thank Michael Dittman for encouraging me to take a chance and step out of my comfort zone. Without his encouragement, I never would have known that this project was a possibility, let alone it becoming a reality. A special thanks also goes to Peter Greene for the foreword of this publication. His eloquent words are a wonderful and welcomed prologue to this volume.

Next, I would like to thank the following individuals who so graciously lent me photographs from their collections to help me tell the story of our community: Gail Beck, Thomas W. Ross, Kathleen Russo, Gina Staab, Rhonda Steigerwald, and Rebecca Witherup. A huge thanks also goes to Mary Ann Benton and Penny Haylett-Minnick, who not only shared their photographs but also shared their knowledge and time in assisting me with this project. Special thanks and great appreciation also must be extended to the following who shared their information and time with me: Sylvia Coast, Carolee Michener, and Margo Mong. These three ladies, along with Penny, are amazing assets to this town, and I hope this project makes them proud.

I would also like to thank Michael Kline and Anthony Sloss for providing me with information from their respected professions for the creation of this project.

Lastly, I owe a huge thank-you to Jason Bell for helping me stay motivated and focused throughout this entire project. Without his constant supervision and presence, I would not have succeeded.

Thank you all.

Introduction

Franklin was settled in the 1740s and was incorporated as a city in 1868. It was named in honor of Benjamin Franklin. During the time of the American Revolution, the city supported three forts, all strategically situated along the Allegheny River and its confluence with French Creek. Franklin is the seat of Venango County, which was formed on March 12, 1800. The city also greatly benefited from Col. Edwin Drake's discovery of oil in nearby Titusville in 1859. The county was knee-deep in the oil boom, thus bringing much wealth and success.

Few businesses remain in Franklin that have withstood the test of time. The national economic downturn was slow to come to the community and even slower to leave. During the late 1970s and early 1980s, many local industries and companies underwent major layoffs, causing Franklin and its surrounding communities to suffer. When federal and state grants became available once again, the city began to rebuild and rejuvenate itself. The empty storefronts were updated, attracting new business owners. Several business incubators allow crafters and artisans to not only support their families but to also help rebuild the economy and revitalize the business district, bringing people downtown once again.

The total area of Franklin is 4.7 square miles, with 0.1 square miles being water. Situated in a valley formed by the Allegheny River and French Creek, Franklin boasts numerous parks and playgrounds, plus several county and state parks within a short distance. Lush woodlands give outdoor enthusiasts and hunters plenty of room to hunt, trap, and roam. Geocaching, an outdoor activity of searching for hidden objects through the use of GPS coordinates, is also on the rise in the community and surrounding areas. Riverfront Park is the location of the annual Rock in River Festival held every August. The event is a nationally recognized stone-skipping competition that has appeared on ESPN in the past.

The railroad was a fundamental element for economy and business within Franklin and the rest of the Oil Region. Prior to the arrival of the railroad, oil shippers depended on waterways to transport oil barrels to major cities for sale and distribution. The problem with this method was its unreliability. Droughts in the summer brought the water level too low to float a packet boat, and the cold winters only allowed for transportation during a narrow number of months. The railroad allowed for year-round distribution, allowing the local economy as well as the consumer to reap the benefits of the oil boom much more efficiently.

Neighborhood schools were an important part of shaping Franklin. The first school was built in West Park in 1801. The structure was made of logs and used a fireplace for heat. The Union School was erected in the 1860s and accommodated both elementary and secondary classes. Eventually, both a junior and senior high school were built in a centralized area of town to aid the students of the community. Presently, only a handful of elementary schools remains open, including St. Patrick's Catholic School. The current middle and high school resides in Sandycreek Township. The former Seventh Street Elementary building houses the offices for the Franklin Area School District.

Joseph C. Sibley began his life studying medicine and teaching in New York State. He, along with his brother-in-law Gen. Charles Miller, cofounded the Galena Oil Company in Franklin. The company was an early acquirement for John D. Rockefeller's Standard Oil Company. Due to the wealth this transaction allotted him, Sibley was easily able to fuel his political career, as well as entertain other interests and hobbies, including breeding horses. Sibley's home, River Ridge, was completed in 1913. The property included a five-story barn, a gatehouse, a bell tower, and a farm. The mansion is now utilized by the Christian Life Academy.

The original settlers of Franklin were a melting pot of many different religious beliefs and faiths. Presbyterians and Methodists made up the first assemblies in the community. The first established Catholic church came in the 1860s, though records show that Mass had been held prior to that time in a resident's home whenever a priest came through the area. Several churches burned over the years in Franklin and were rebuilt. St. Patrick's, the city's only Catholic church, also houses a Catholic school for kindergarten through eighth grade. First United Methodist Church provides preschool services. Several community churches offer youth groups and adult groups, as well as multipurpose rooms for social groups to hold meetings.

The establishment of the Kinzua Dam in 1965 brought an end to the major floods and ice jams that wreaked havoc on Franklin and its surrounding riverfront communities. The worst occurred in 1926. That season, the ice jams on the Allegheny River and French Creek took out a section of the Big Rock Bridge in the First Ward of town. Once the weather and water began to warm up, the riverbanks were breached, allowing floodwaters to encroach on the low-lying regions of Franklin and those in the rest of Venango County. Several less severe floods also occurred during the 1910s.

The citizens of Franklin gained much from the oil boom of the 1860s. The Pennsylvania oil boom caused Franklin and other towns, such as Oil City and Titusville near Oil Creek, to expand quickly as wells and refineries appeared throughout the region. Oil rapidly became one of the most valuable assets in the entire country and railroads spread into western Pennsylvania to send out petroleum to the rest of the United States. The Pennsylvania oil rush was very similar to the California Gold Rush. Nearby Pithole grew from four modest homes to a large city with over 50 hotels and boardinghouses and the third largest post office in the state (behind Philadelphia and Pittsburgh) in just five months in 1865. The Pennsylvania oil rush not only put places like Franklin on the national map but on the international map as well. More wealth came to the city and region, as Pennsylvania was the first commercial-sized extraction of oil in the country. The Galena Oil Company of Franklin was an early addition to the Standard Oil Company.

Businesses flourished during much of the 1800s and 1900s. Of the businesses from the latter century, gas and service stations were a huge portion of the town's economy. During the mid-20th century, there were approximately 20 family-owned stations within the three wards of the city. This was a time when few national chains or named businesses had invaded small, rural towns. Mom-and-pop neighborhood shops still existed, and everyone knew each other. Presently, only two family-owned businesses still exist that have been in business for over 100 years. The business district has been rebooting itself for the last five years.

Industry has been the backbone of Franklin and its surrounding communities for almost 200 years. Oil was the first major industry to hit Venango County and Franklin. Many products came from the various companies and refineries that have dotted town, such as engines, mining machinery, motor oil and automotive lubricants, building materials, and steel and bronze articles. Joy Global has been a very important company in Franklin for almost 100 years and is still going strong. Johns Manville also had a large influence on the city's economy. Franklin Steel and Franklin Bronze are still in operation. These companies gave the men and women of Franklin stability for themselves and their families.

One

The Victorian City

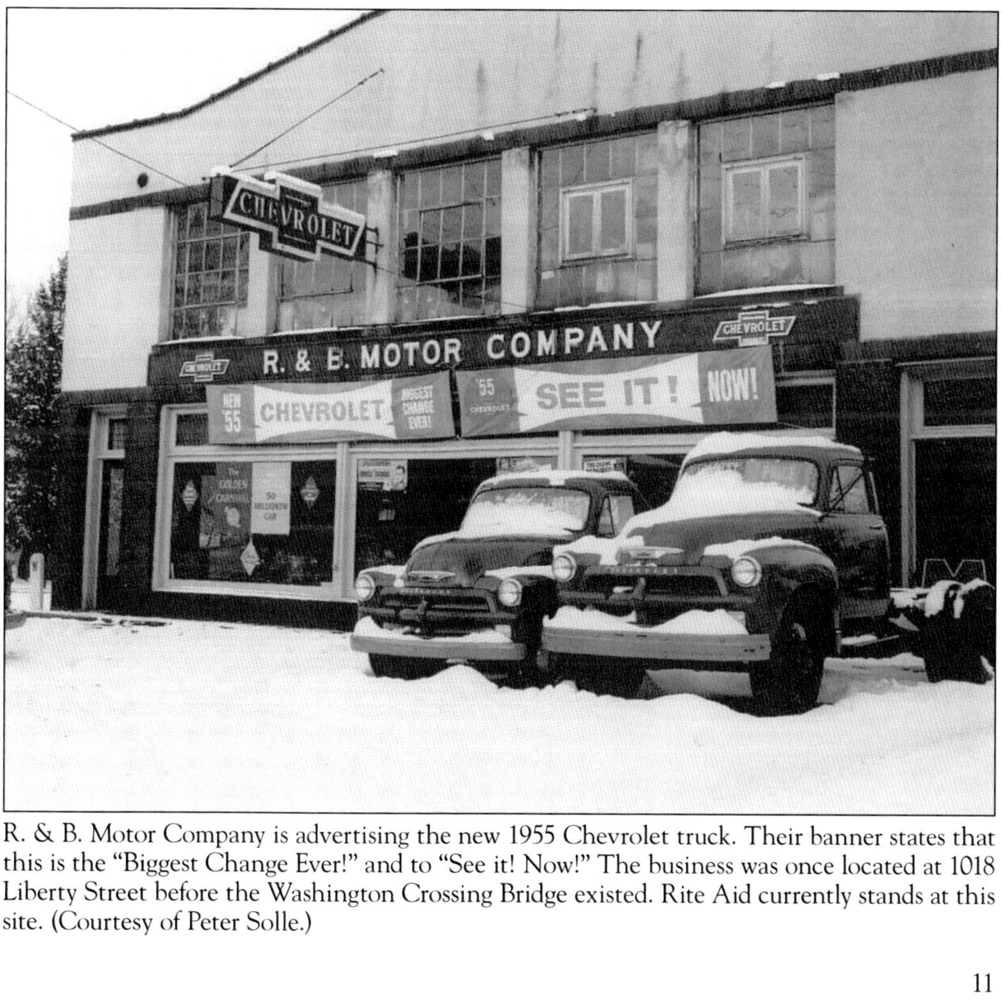

R. & B. Motor Company is advertising the new 1955 Chevrolet truck. Their banner states that this is the "Biggest Change Ever!" and to "See it! Now!" The business was once located at 1018 Liberty Street before the Washington Crossing Bridge existed. Rite Aid currently stands at this site. (Courtesy of Peter Solle.)

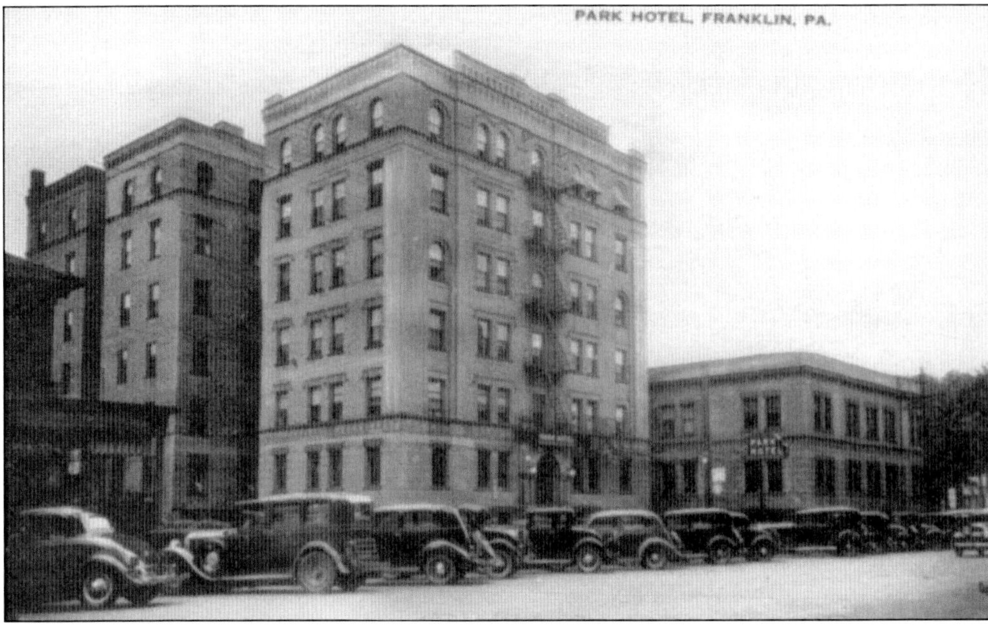

The Park Hotel sat on the corner of Twelfth and Liberty Streets for almost 50 years. Built in 1902 by Gen. Charles Miller, it was originally named the Alsace for the region of France where General Miller was born. On the night of January 2, 1944, an explosion occurred in a dumbwaiter, and the hotel was destroyed by fire with no injuries or deaths. (Courtesy of Penny Haylett-Minnick.)

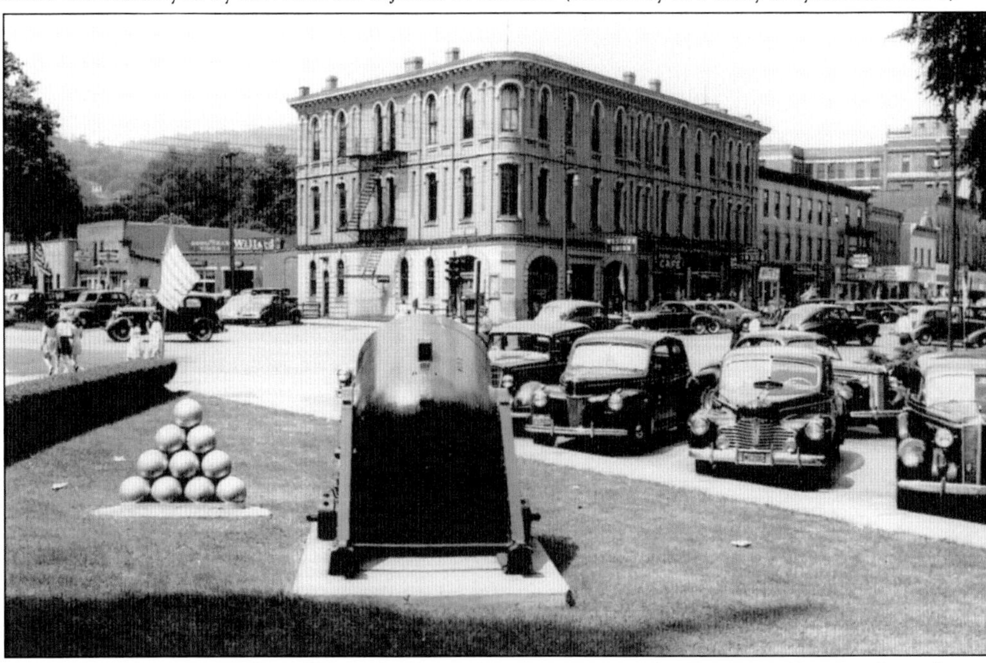

Located on the corner of Twelfth and Liberty Streets opposite the Venango County Courthouse the Plumer-Hancock Block was opened in November 1868. For over 100 years, various businesses called the block their home, including restaurants, music stores, grocery stores, banks, and drugstores, along with Western Union. The building was lost to fire in 1981. The cannon in the foreground was used in World War I. (Courtesy of Peter Solle.)

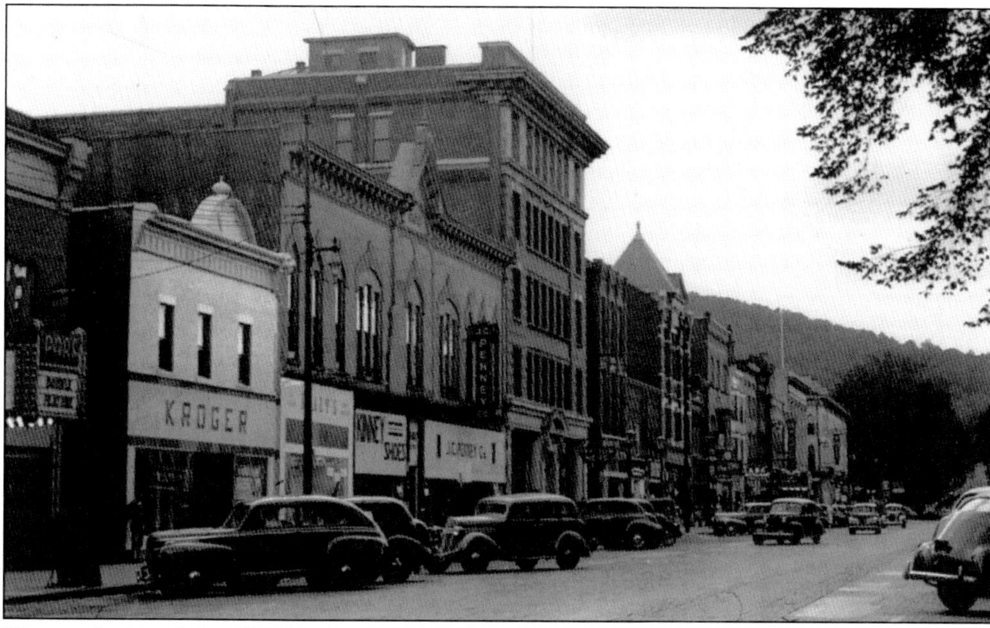

The south side of the 1200 block of Liberty Street has not changed much at all. The facades are the same, but the signs and businesses are different. From left to right are the Park Theatre, the former International Bank Building, the Bleakley Block, the Franklin Trust Building, the Dodd-Osmer Building, the Raymond Buildings, and the Masonic Building. (Courtesy of Peter Solle.)

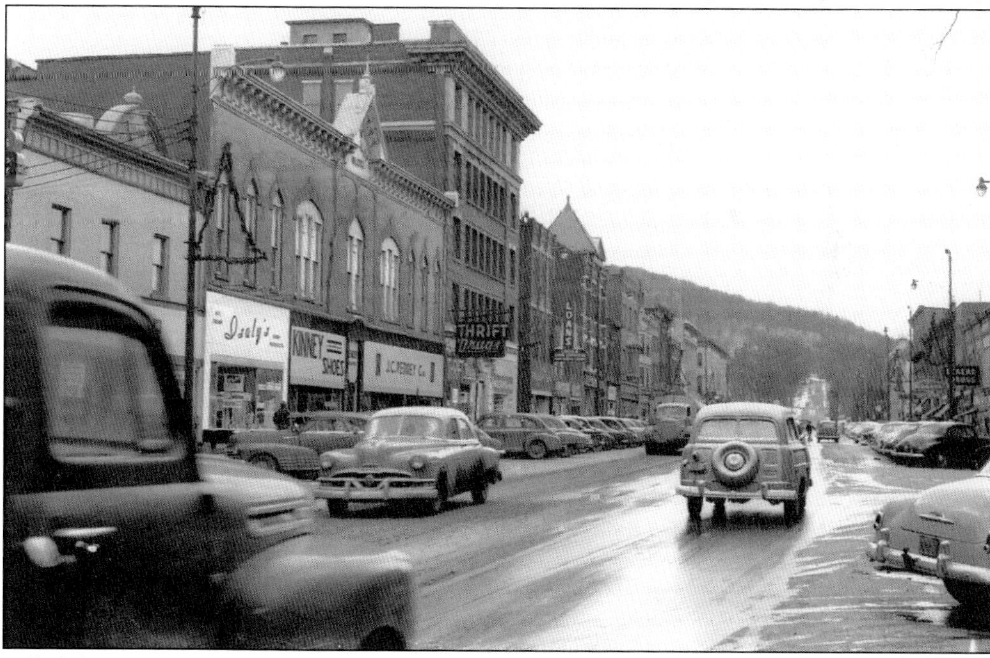

A holiday view of Franklin's business district shows, from left to right, Isaly's Ice Cream and Soda Fountain, Kinney Shoes, J.C. Penney Company, and Thrift Drugs. Note the Christmas tree ornaments on the lampposts. Every year on the Saturday before Thanksgiving, the city celebrates Light-Up Night with the Electric Lights Parade, which includes floats constructed by local businesses, schools, churches, and other organizations. (Courtesy of Peter Solle.)

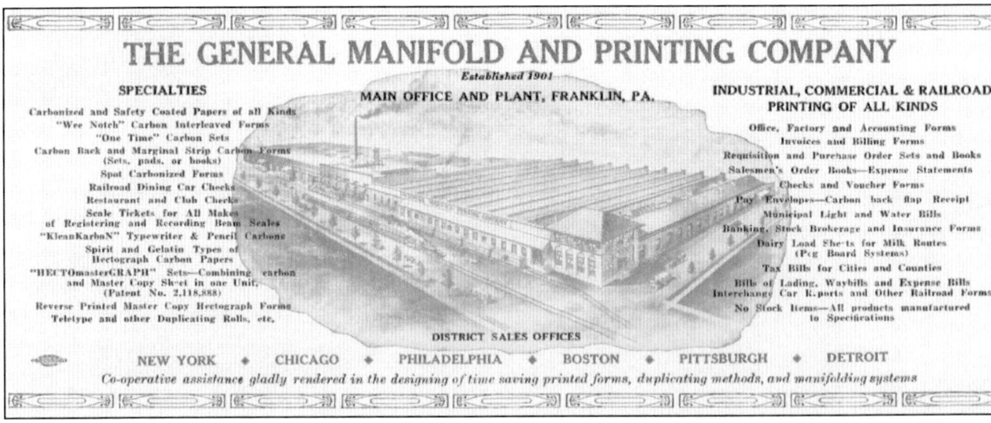

The General Manifold and Printing Company was a core business in Franklin starting in 1901 and continuing throughout the war years. Many women worked here to create war ration books, as well as other paper products. The building no longer exists. The former site is now a shipping and receiving area for Joy Global. (Author's collection.)

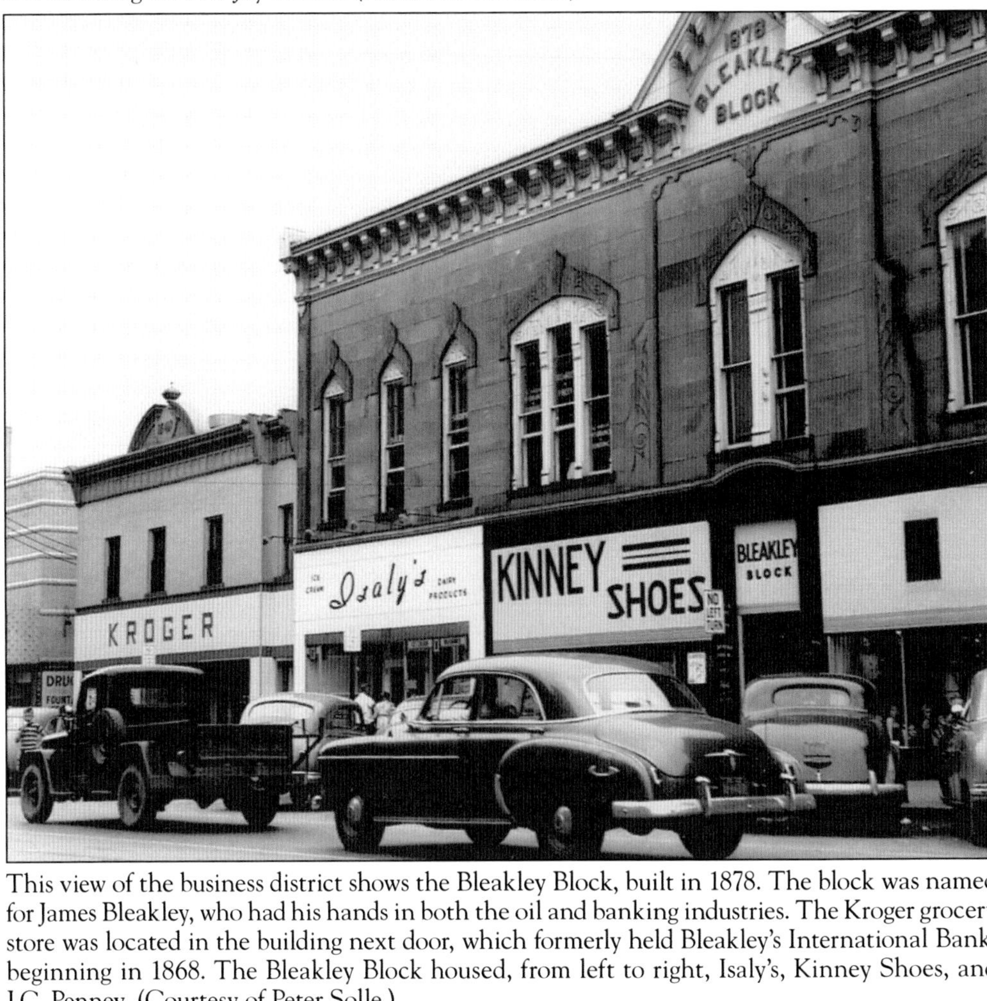

This view of the business district shows the Bleakley Block, built in 1878. The block was named for James Bleakley, who had his hands in both the oil and banking industries. The Kroger grocery store was located in the building next door, which formerly held Bleakley's International Bank, beginning in 1868. The Bleakley Block housed, from left to right, Isaly's, Kinney Shoes, and J.C. Penney. (Courtesy of Peter Solle.)

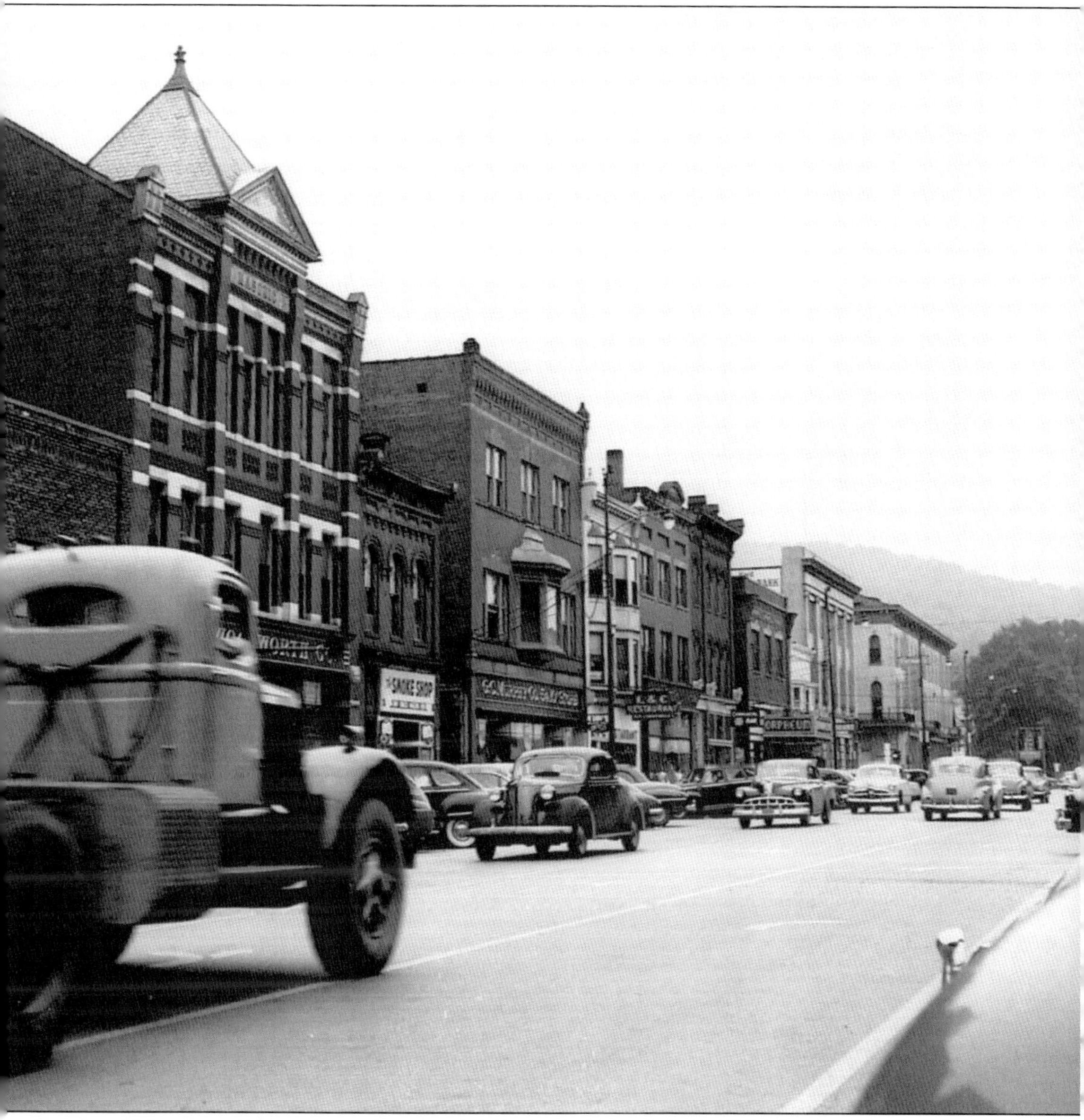

Farther down the south side of the 1200 block of Liberty Street, the buildings include, from left to right, the Masonic Building, the Thomas Moore and Sons Building, the Gearing Building, the Lambros and Conomikes Building, the Bacharach Building, the Commercial Hotel Building, the old Orpheum Theatre Building, and the old Exchange Bank Building. One of the oldest groups of Masons is the Myrtle Lodge, founded on February 21, 1858. The lodge bought the building, where it held meetings on the second and third floors, while the first-floor storefront was home to several other businesses over the years, including F.W. Woolworth Company five-and-ten store, Thrift Drugs, and Bensinger, Smith & Company's stationery and bookstore. The Orpheum Theatre was built in 1916 and provided the residents of the community with the best in entertainment, including both talking and silent films, plays, vaudeville acts, and musicals. (Courtesy of Peter Solle.)

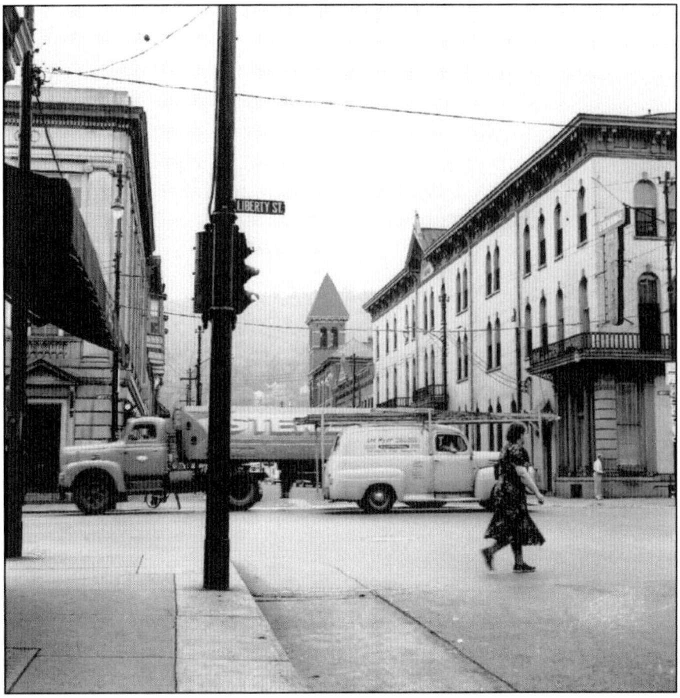

The tower of Franklin City Hall is seen in the background of this photograph taken from the corner of Thirteenth and Liberty Streets. The building was constructed in 1883 and housed the fire department and the police station, along with various city offices and council chambers. Because of expensive renovations, the building was razed. The present building was erected in the 1970s. (Courtesy of Peter Solle.)

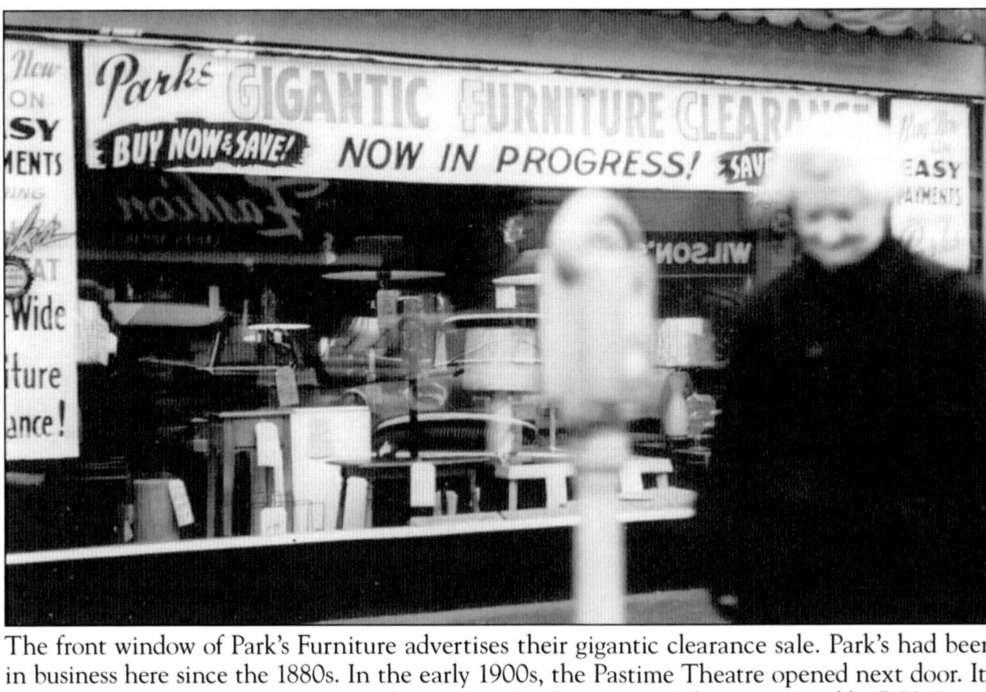

The front window of Park's Furniture advertises their gigantic clearance sale. Park's had been in business here since the 1880s. In the early 1900s, the Pastime Theatre opened next door. Its beautiful, whimsical facade was torn down in 1913. The Princess Theatre, owned by B.H. Printz of Printz's clothing store, was built in its place. As Printz's clothing store grew next door, he closed the Princess to make more room. (Courtesy of Peter Solle.)

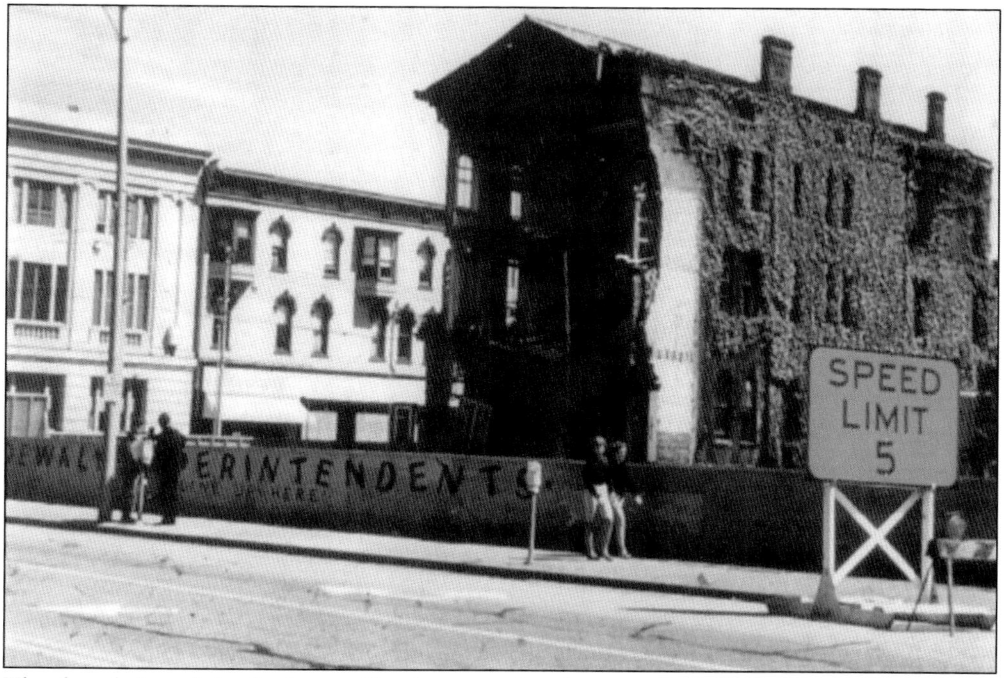

The demolition of the Exchange Hotel occurred in January 1965. With the exception of the lobby's marble floor, the establishment was dated and past its prime. The carpet was worn, the hallways were narrow, and the paint was chipped. In June 1964, an auction was held to dispose of any remaining furniture, goods, and equipment. (Courtesy of Penny Haylett-Minnick.)

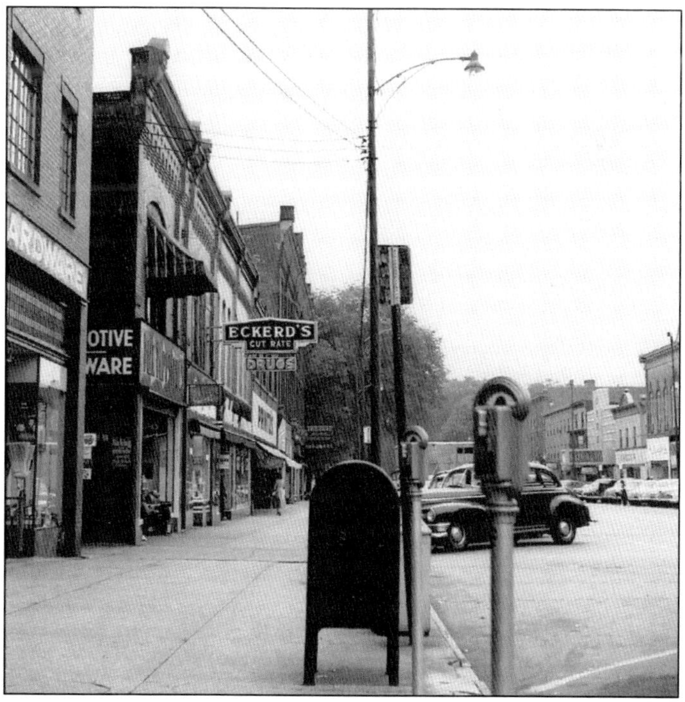

The north side of the 1200 block of Liberty Street also remains unchanged in structure, though it has new tenants. From left to right are the Evening News Building, the Boyd N. Park Building, the Printz Building, and the Snook Block. The Boyd N. Park Building had been the home of Park's Furniture and Undertaking business since the 1880s. (Courtesy of Peter Solle.)

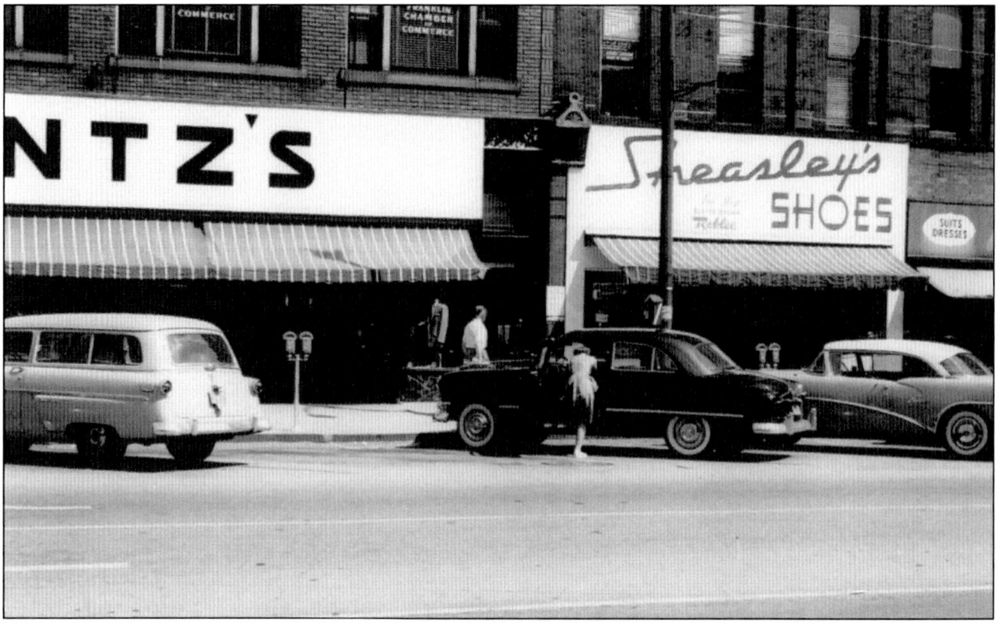

Printz's was a popular clothing store in the 1950s. Having been a fixture in Franklin's business district for several decades, the store specialized in men's and boys' clothing as well as Boy Scout uniforms and all related accessories. When patrons made purchases, their money and the bill of sale would be taken by means of a tube system to the business office on the second floor. (Courtesy of Peter Solle.)

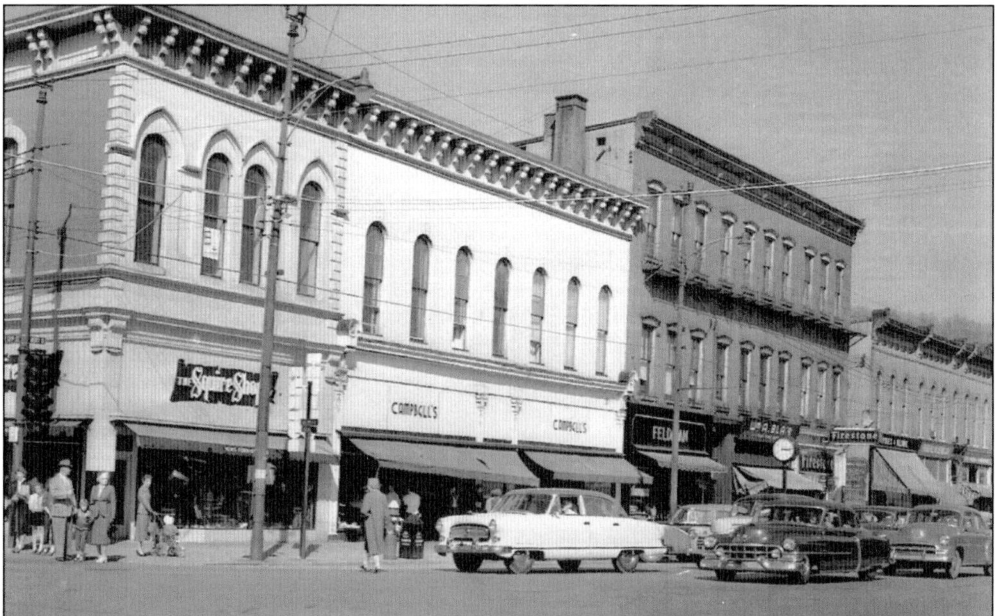

Farther up the north side of the 1200 block of Liberty Street, the buildings are, from left to right, the former First National Bank Building, the Whitmer Building, and the Centre Block. Built in 1872, the Centre Block was the hub of downtown Franklin. It housed numerous services over time, including physicians, lawyers, tailors, and photographers. (Courtesy of Peter Solle.)

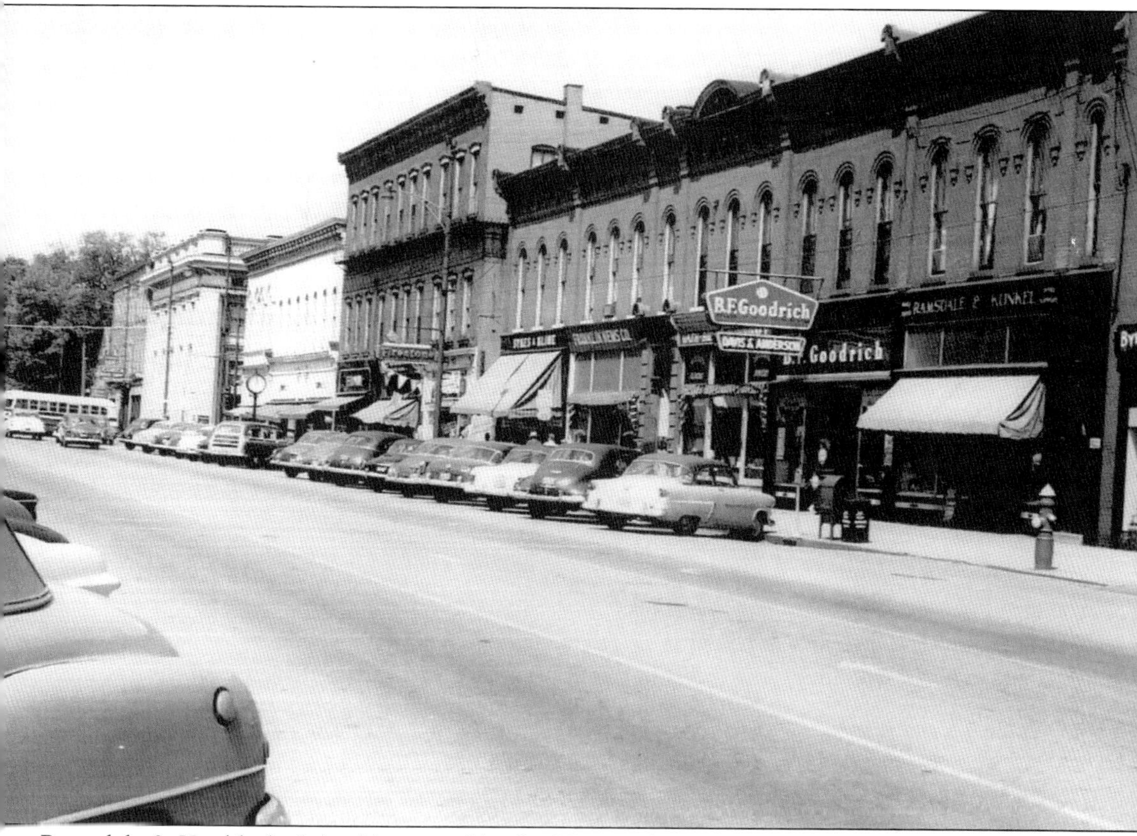

Ramsdale & Kunkle (right) sold toys and books. Next is the Davis & Anderson B.F. Goodrich store. Continuing down the street are Vath, Burns & Mawhinney, one of two jewelry stores located in this block, which was known as the Centre Block; the Franklin News Company a magazine and newspaper retailer; and Sykes & Kline, a boys' and men's clothier. Finally, Feldman Jewelers (left) is seen with its recognizable clock. Feldman Jewelers stands on the former site of Huling's boardinghouse, which was an old frame building erected during the early years of the community. The Feldman Building was damaged during a fire in 1886. The building was originally home to businesses such as Martin and Epley Drugstore, Byrer Hardware, and Myron Park's general store. It was rebuilt in 1900 and has housed the jewelry store ever since. B.J. Feldman first opened his business in 1871. (Courtesy of Peter Solle.)

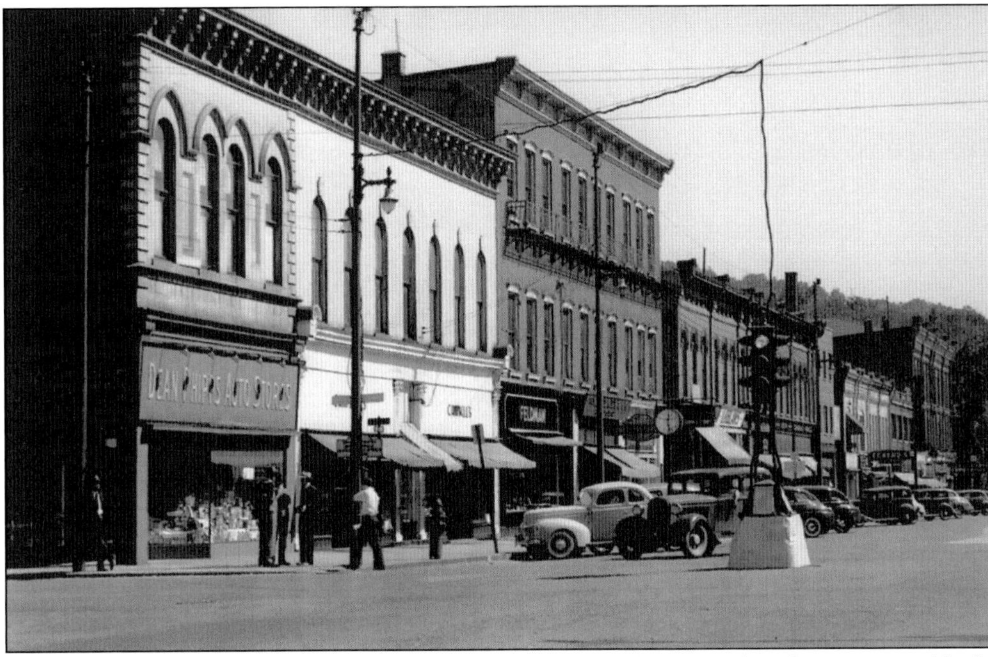

In downtown Franklin in the 1930s and 1940s, the traffic lights were placed on concrete blocks in the middle of intersections. Looking down Liberty Street from its intersection at Thirteenth Street, the businesses are, from left to right, Dean Phipps Auto Stores, Campbell's dress shop, and Feldman Jewelers, with its famous clock out front. (Courtesy of Peter Solle.)

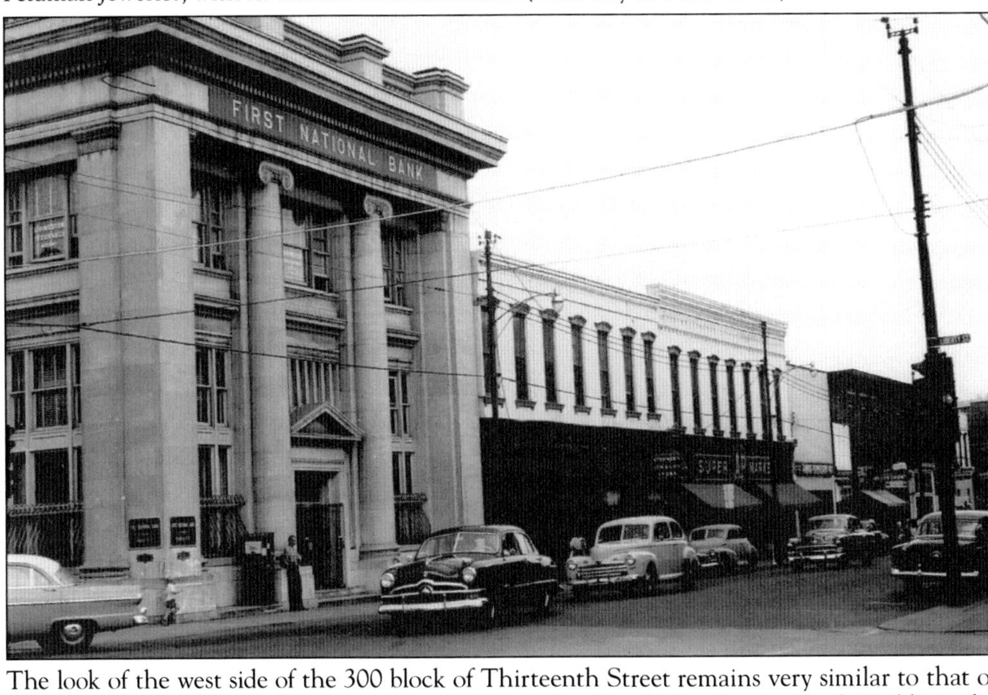

The look of the west side of the 300 block of Thirteenth Street remains very similar to that of over 50 years ago. The buildings are, from left to right, the old Lamberton Bank Building, the old Butler-Wick Building, the Woodburn Cone and Company Building, and the old Salvation Army Building. (Courtesy of Peter Solle.)

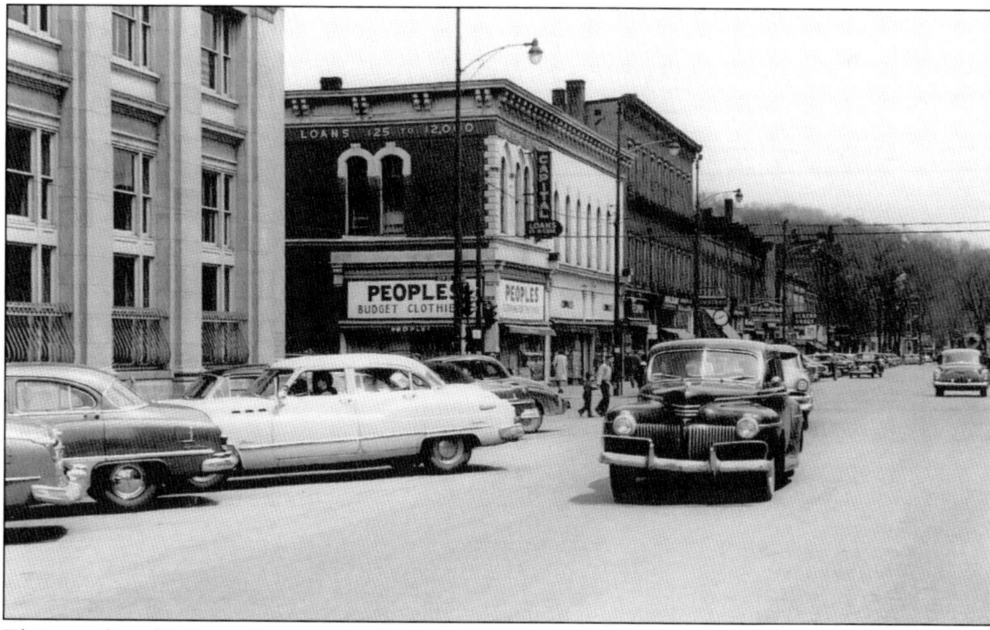

Thirteenth and Liberty Streets was the main intersection of the business district. The Lamberton National Bank (left) was run by Chess Lamberton, the original namesake of the county airport. This building was constructed of white marble and concrete. Across Thirteenth Street was Peoples Budget Clothing. The second floor housed Capital Loans. The sign along the roofline states, "Loans $25 to $2,000." (Courtesy of Peter Solle.)

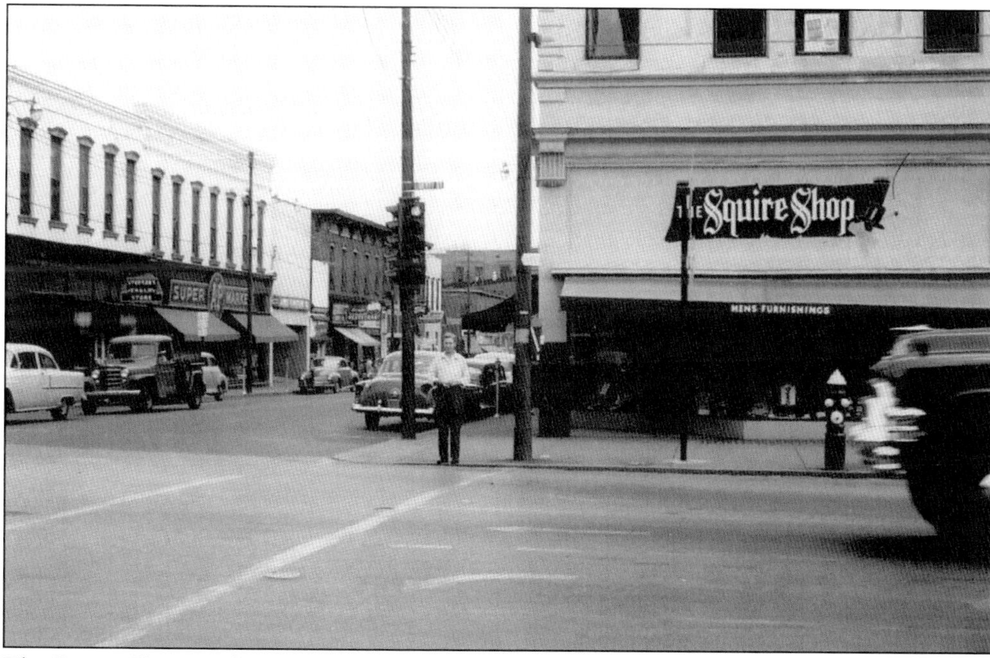

The Squire Shop was located on the corner of Thirteenth and Liberty Streets in the late 1950s. The shop specialized in men's furnishings and clothing. At left, Stephen's Jewelry Store and the A&P Super Market can be seen on Thirteenth Street. By this time, the traffic lights had been moved from the middle of the intersections to poles on the corners. (Courtesy of Peter Solle.)

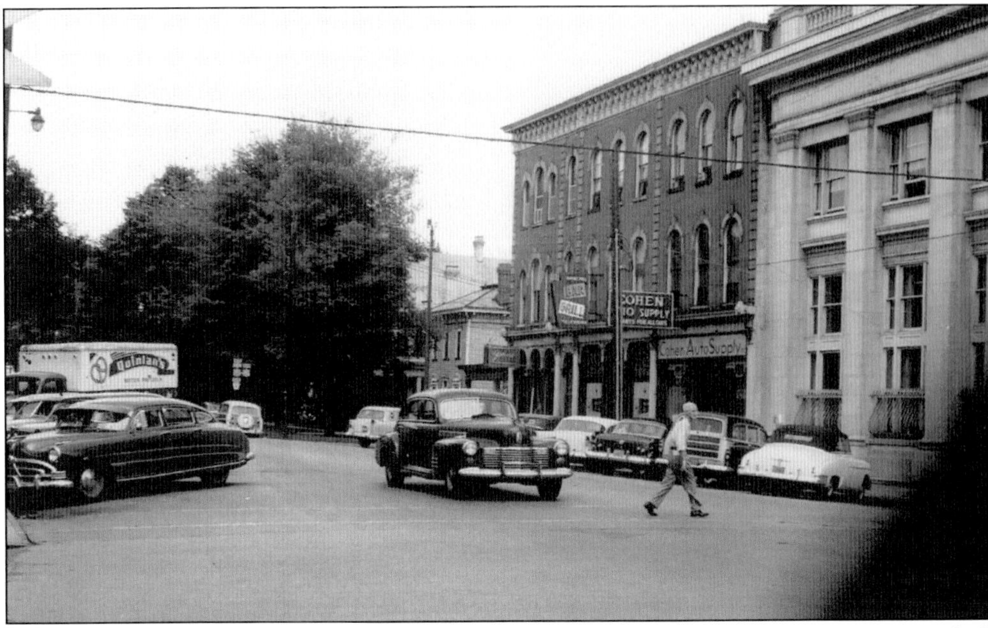

Just west of Thirteenth Street on Liberty Street is the Mitchell Block, built by Forster Mitchell. Mitchell resided in the Exchange Hotel, also his creation, which sat across Liberty Street from the block. Seen here in the 1950s, the block housed Cohen Auto Supply and a bar and grill for which the sign also advertised dancing and television. The block was razed in 1968. (Courtesy of Peter Solle.)

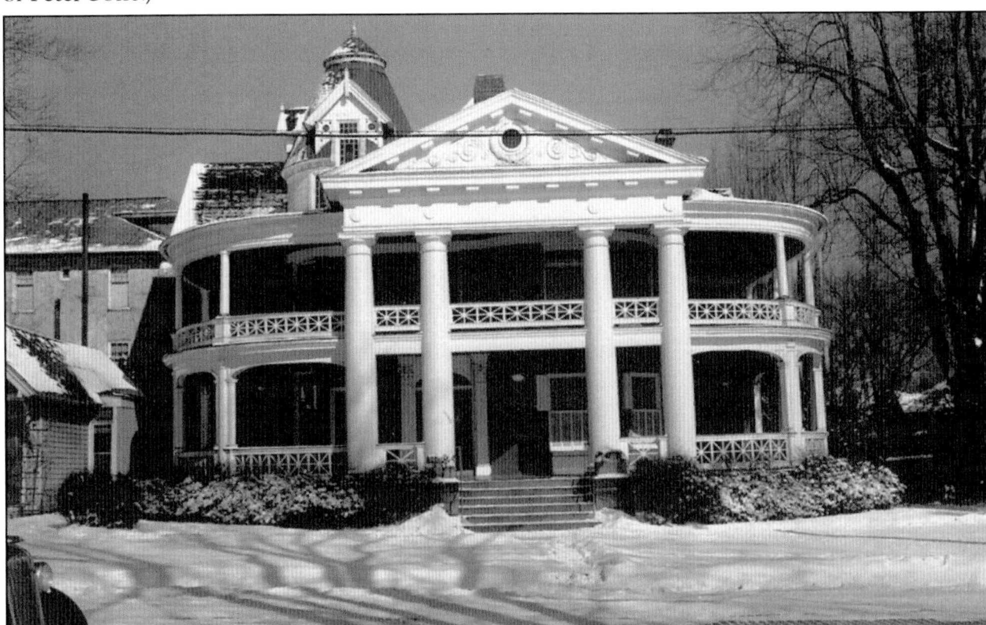

In December 1877, a group of college students started the Nursery Club, later known as a young businessmen's group. Original membership was reserved for unmarried men only, but by the late 1880s, married men were permitted. The club purchased this building in 1889, adding the ballroom. In 1913, the Nursery Club changed its name to the Franklin Club. (Courtesy of Peter Solle.)

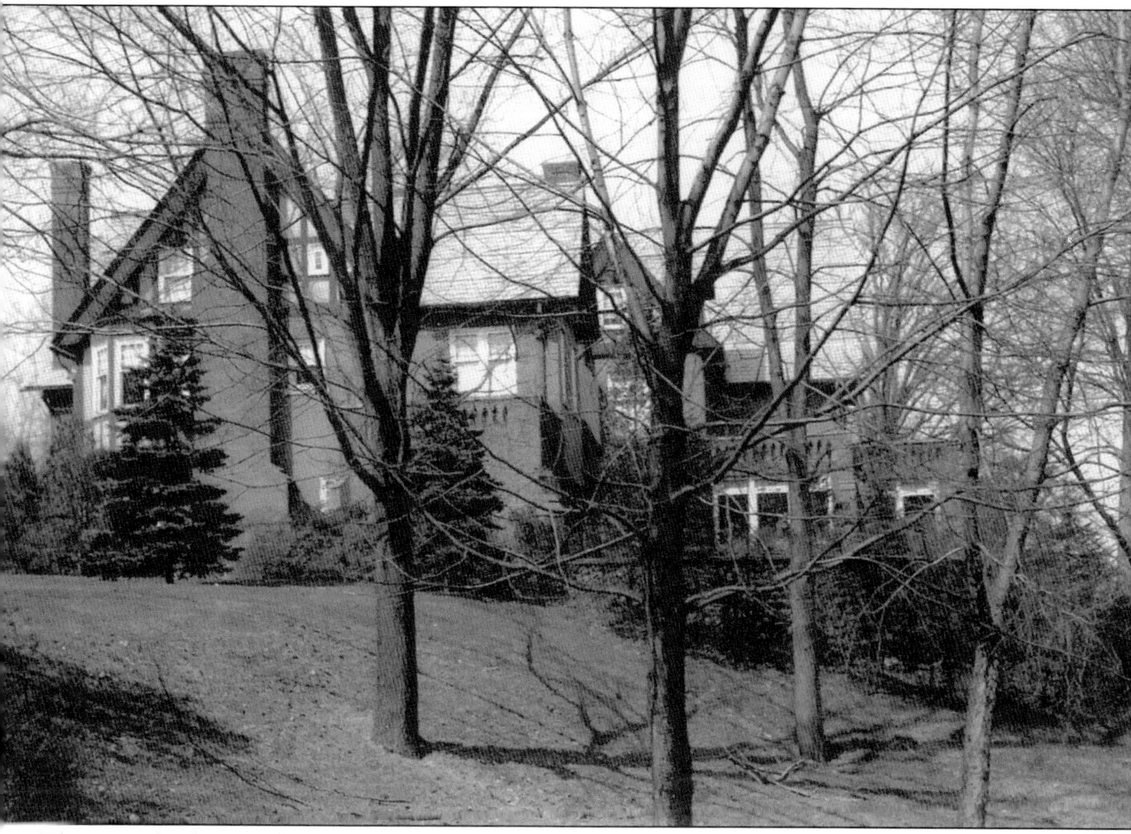

This was the home of Gen. Charles Miller and his wife, Ann. Charles began constructing his 17-acre neighborhood, Miller Park, in 1898. His neighbors consisted of family, friends, and colleagues. Keeping with his French roots, Miller designed his mansion in the Tudor style with a brick facade, a slate roof, and three chimneys. The home has since been converted to beautiful apartments. W.E. and Josephine (Sibley) Heathcote, neighbors of the Millers, also built their home in Miller Park. Located on Adelaide Avenue, the Heathcote home was built in the Colonial Revival/Neoclassical style with columns and a full-height portico entryway, which also enclosed a rounded second-floor balcony. W.E. served as the second vice president of the Galena-Signal Oil Company. His wife was the niece of Gen. Charles Miller, who was one of the founders of the oil company, along with Joseph C. Sibley, her father. (Courtesy of Peter Solle.)

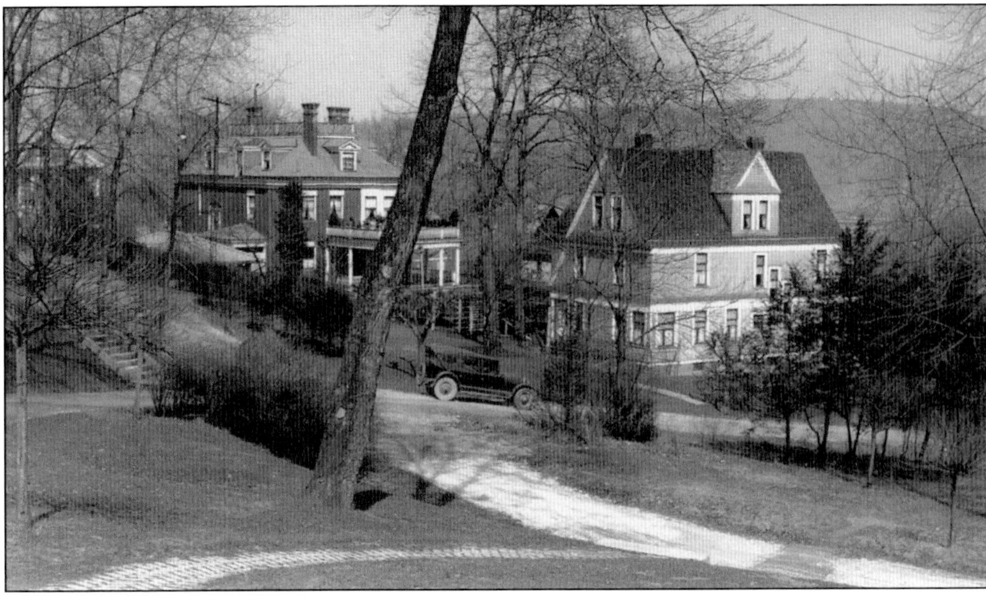

Seen in this view of Miller Park are the Queen Anne–style home of Joel Stephen Coffin Sr. and Emily Frances Baxter Coffin (left) and that of William Miller and Katherine Anna Schlegel Miller. William was the brother of Gen. Charles Miller. A matching house was built across the street, resulting in their nickname of "the twins" or "the sisters." Both homes were built in 1900. (Courtesy of Peter Solle.)

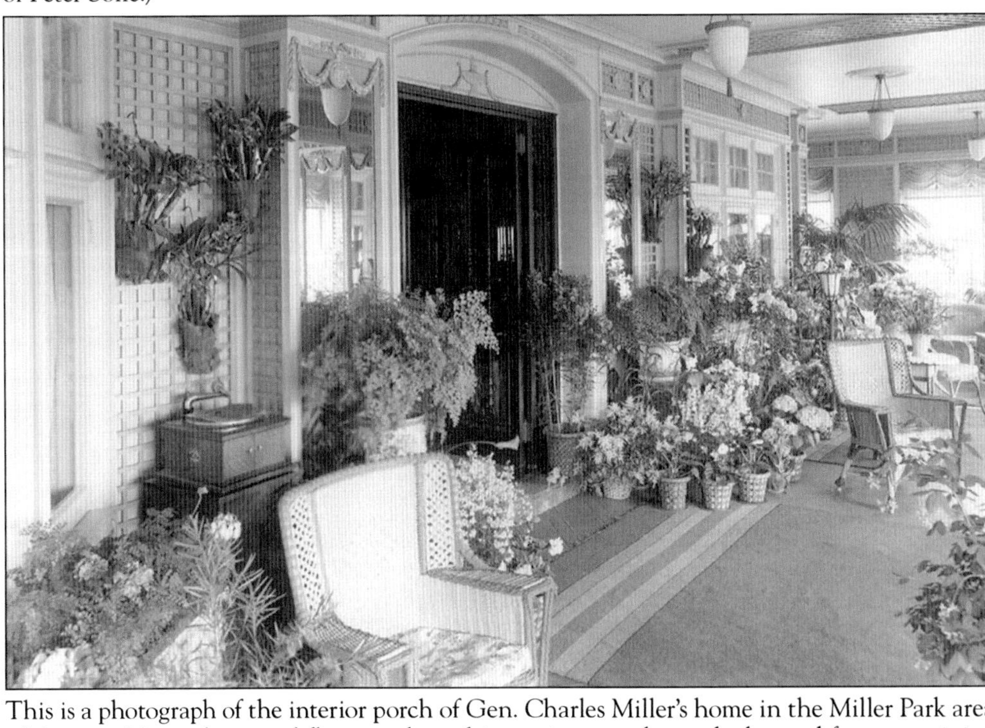

This is a photograph of the interior porch of Gen. Charles Miller's home in the Miller Park area of the city. Many plants and flowers adorn this spacious porch, no doubt used for entertaining guests. A Victrola is located to the left of the doorway leading into the residence. General Miller passed away in 1927. (Courtesy of Penny Haylett-Minnick.)

This view was taken from the corner of Buffalo Street, looking up Seventh Street. Note the bricked streets with the trolley tracks running down the middle. The houses shown on the right still stand and look almost exactly the same. Seventh Street continues up the hillside seen in the distance. Presently, this hillside is grown over with trees, and a single house sits near its base. (Courtesy of Peter Solle.)

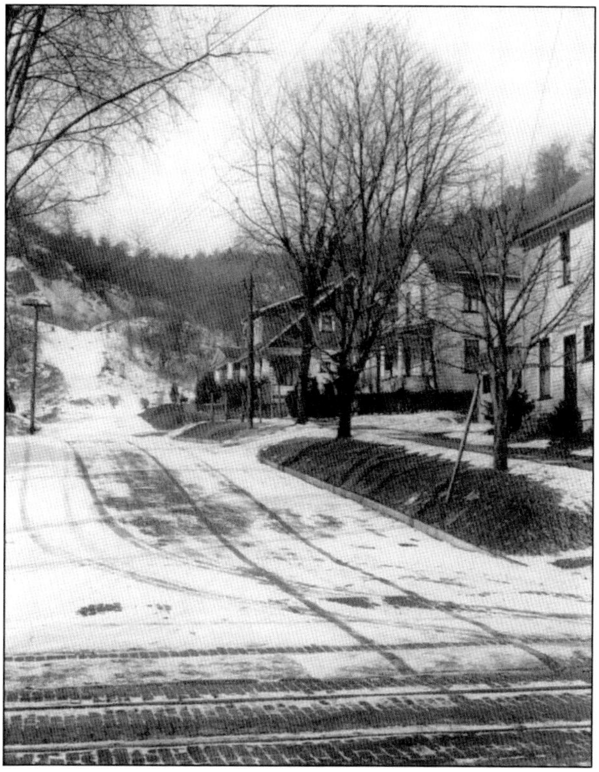

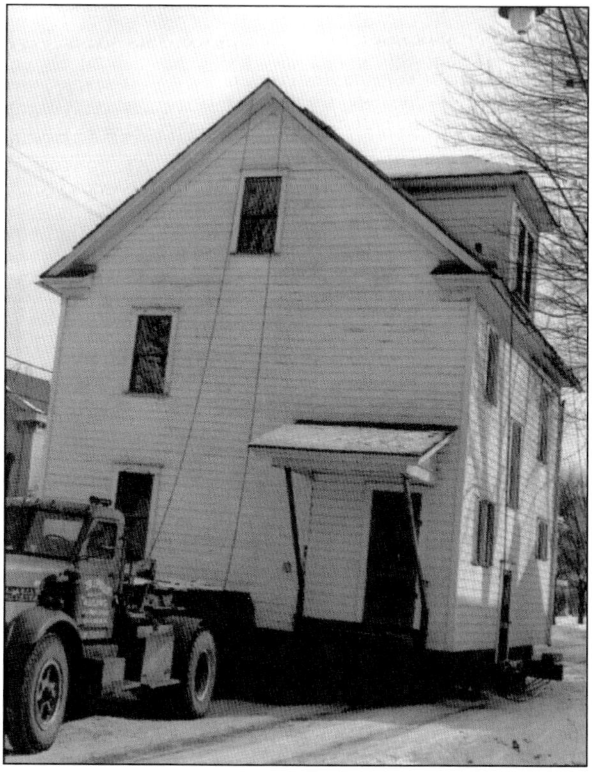

Phillips Hauling is shown moving a house down a snow-covered Liberty Street in the 800 block during the late 1940s or early 1950s. Many houses were brought from other areas of Franklin and placed on empty lots at the lower end of town, especially on Buffalo Street, where the author's birth (and current) residence was relocated. (Courtesy of Peter Solle.)

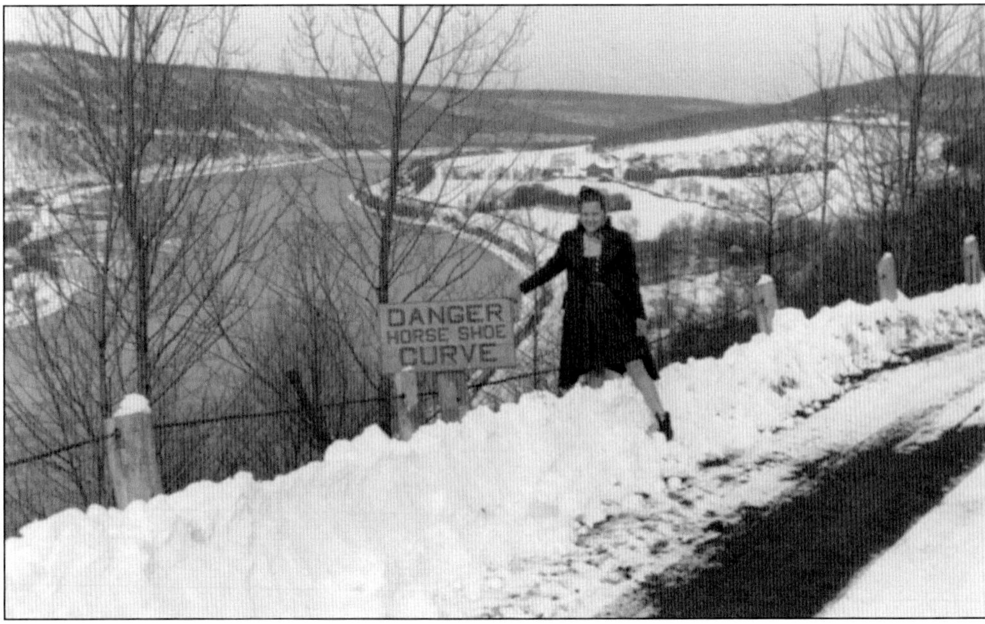

A young lady shows the "Danger Horse Shoe Curve" sign located on Lower River Ridge Road, with the Sibley mansion on the hillside in the background to the right. The Allegheny River is shown in the background at left, winding its way toward Reno and Oil City. Many of the smaller outbuildings are now gone from the property. (Courtesy of Peter Solle.)

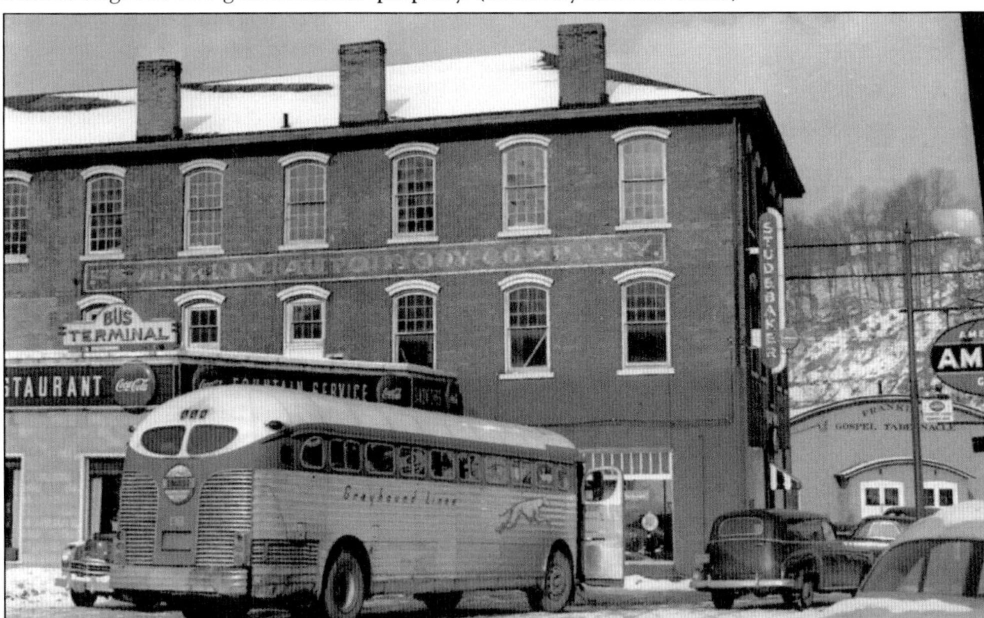

A Greyhound Lines bus awaits riders at the bus terminal on Twelfth Street, between Elk and Otter Streets. In the background are the Franklin Auto Body Company, displaying a neon Studebaker sign, and the Franklin Gospel Tabernacle Church. The Franklin Auto Body Company and bus terminal building is now home to Provide Medical and Vixen Vapors, while the church now houses the congregation of the Christian Missionary Alliance. (Courtesy of Peter Solle.)

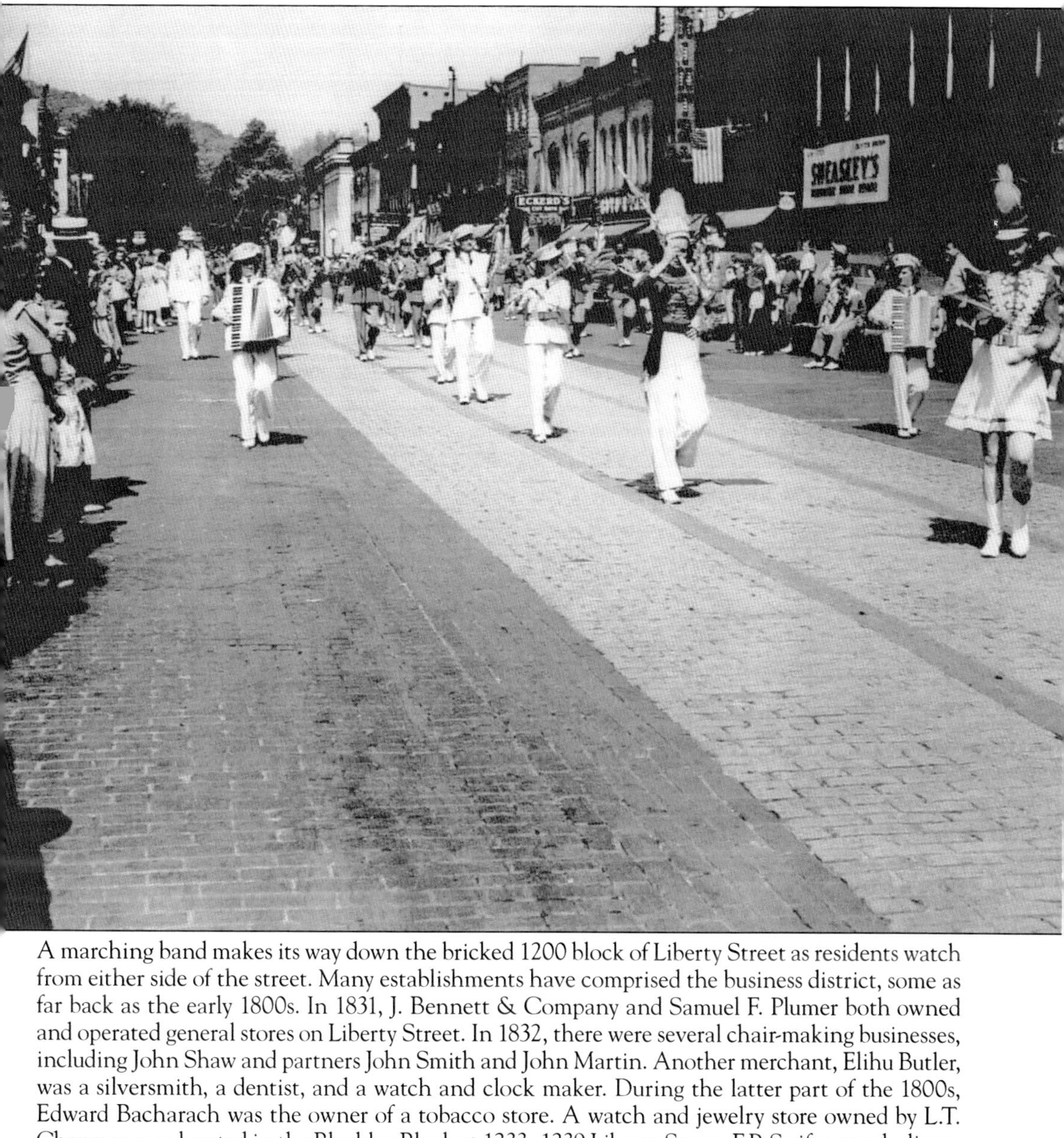

A marching band makes its way down the bricked 1200 block of Liberty Street as residents watch from either side of the street. Many establishments have comprised the business district, some as far back as the early 1800s. In 1831, J. Bennett & Company and Samuel F. Plumer both owned and operated general stores on Liberty Street. In 1832, there were several chair-making businesses, including John Shaw and partners John Smith and John Martin. Another merchant, Elihu Butler, was a silversmith, a dentist, and a watch and clock maker. During the latter part of the 1800s, Edward Bacharach was the owner of a tobacco store. A watch and jewelry store owned by L.T. Chapman was located in the Bleakley Block at 1233–1239 Liberty Street. F.P. Swift owned a livery at the back of the Snook Building, facing West Park Street. (Courtesy of Peter Solle.)

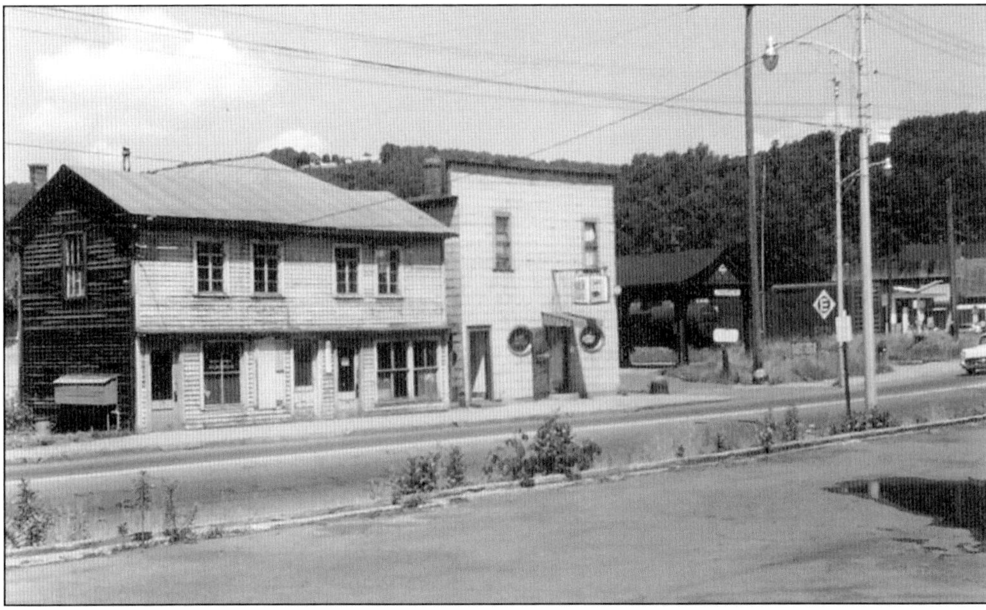

This photograph shows a few buildings that stood on the west side of North Thirteenth Street, just past the Thirteenth Street Bridge in the Third Ward section of the city. To the right of these buildings, the Erie Railroad depot can be seen near the tracks. Across Atlantic Avenue is a gas station, now the present location of Kwik Fill. (Courtesy of Penny Haylett-Minnick.)

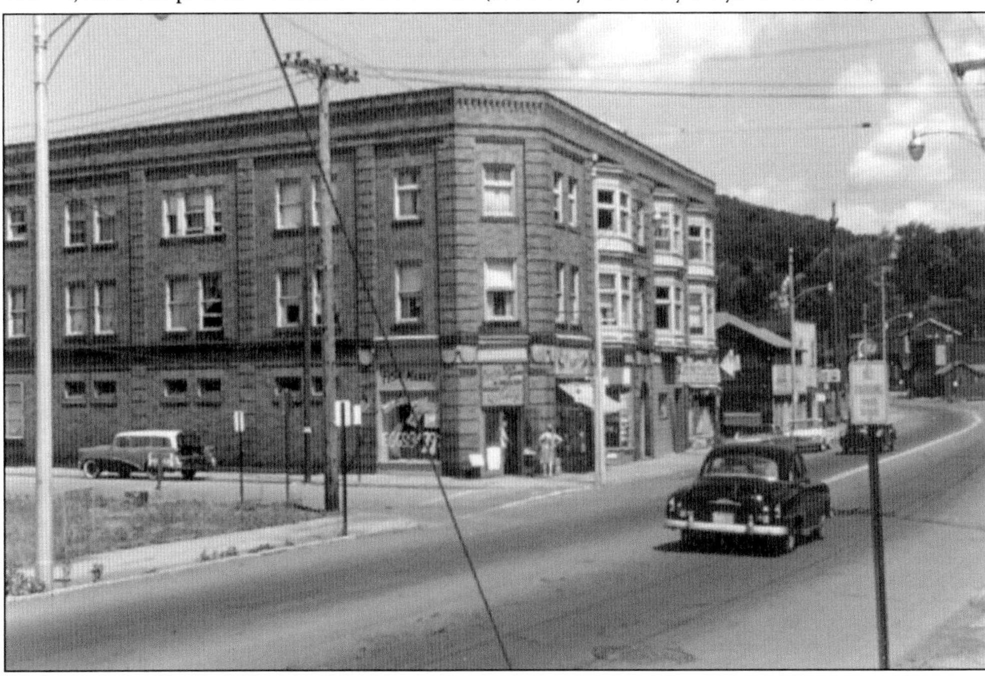

The Grimm Building stood beside the Erie Railroad station and yard in the 100 block of North Thirteenth Street, between Howard Street and Atlantic Avenue. McGinty's Drugstore was on the corner of this building, along with McGinty-Jones Market and Sykes Café. The top two floors housed apartments. The building was razed, and the Caring Place is now located on the lot. (Courtesy of Penny Haylett-Minnick.)

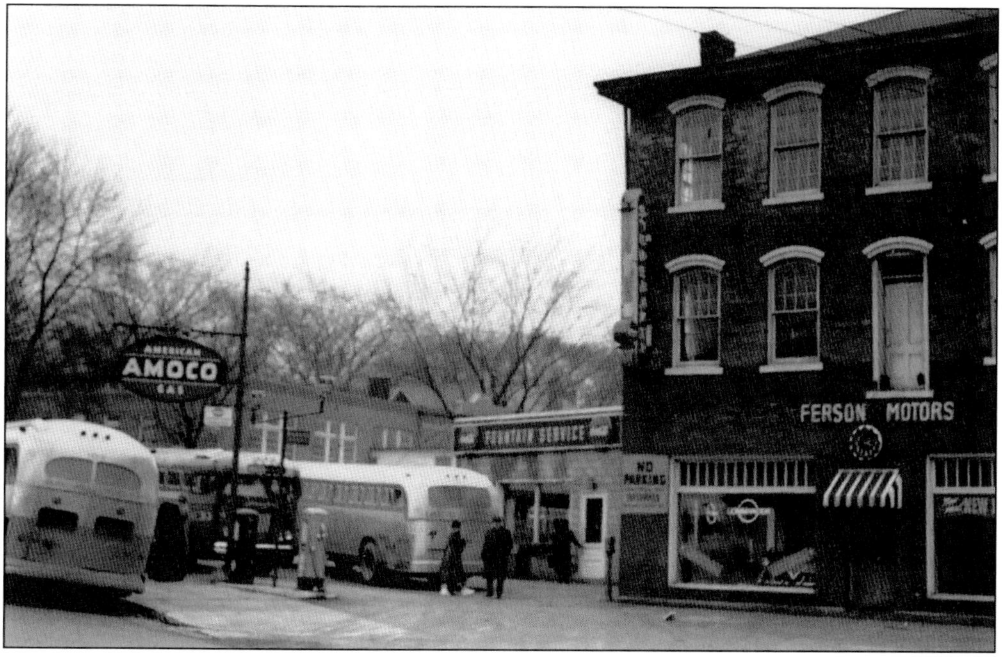

Ferson Motors was located on the corner of Twelfth and Otter Streets in the 1950s, with the Fountain Service connected to it. The Amoco gas pumps serviced the bus station provided for travelers. In the background, the city's post office can be seen on the corner of Twelfth and Elk Streets. (Courtesy of Peter Solle.)

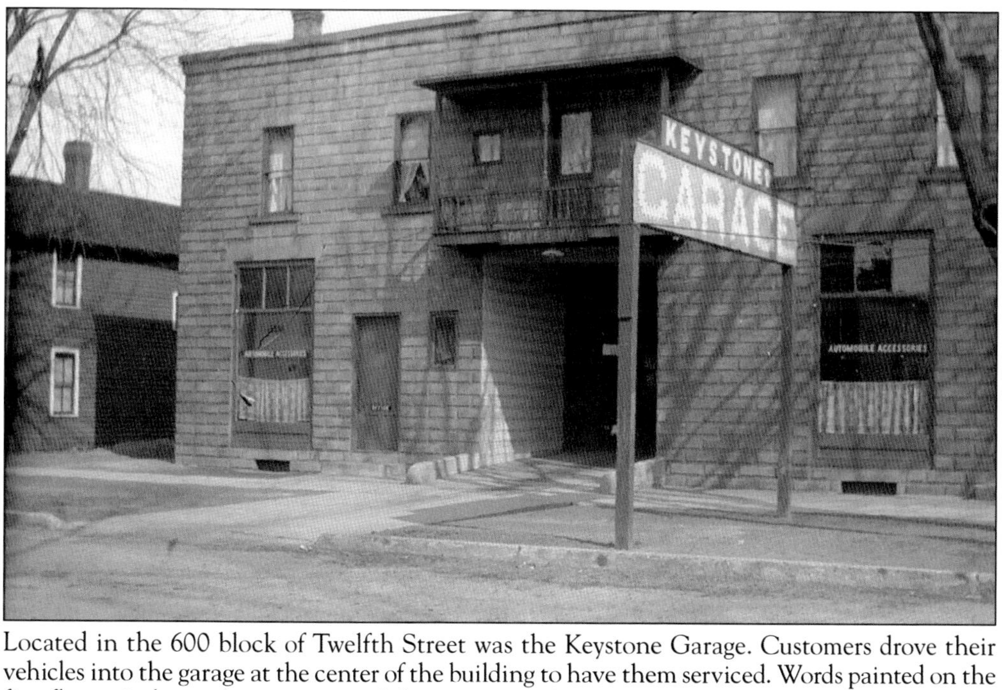

Located in the 600 block of Twelfth Street was the Keystone Garage. Customers drove their vehicles into the garage at the center of the building to have them serviced. Words painted on the first-floor windows advertise automobile accessories. In more recent years, Venango Newspapers used the building, which now provides storage for the Barrow-Civic Theatre. (Courtesy of Penny Haylett-Minnick.)

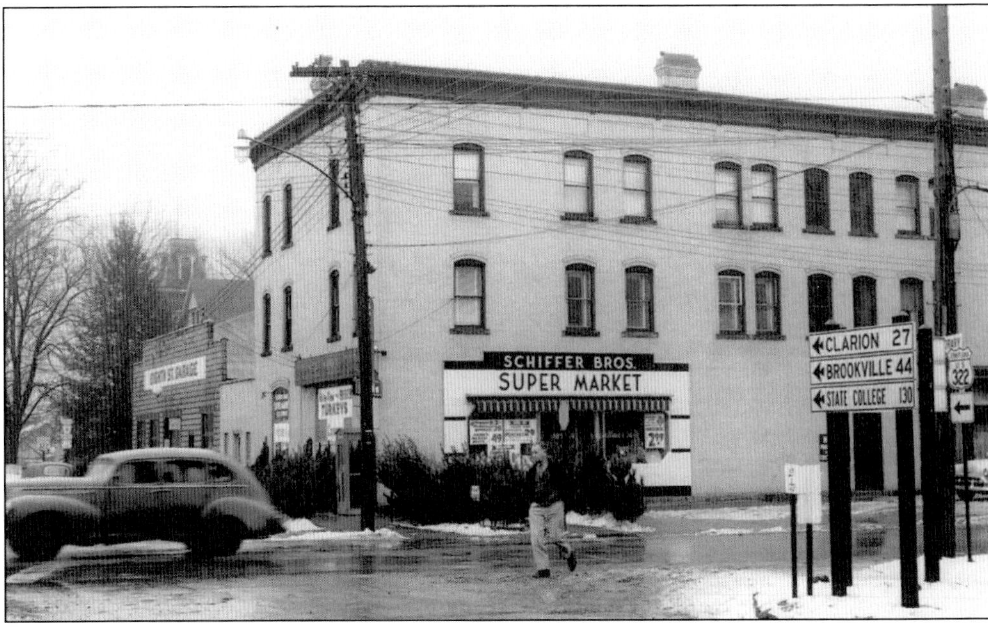

Schiffer Brothers Super Market was located on the corner of Eighth and Liberty Streets. Along with carrying regular grocery products, the business also sold Christmas trees during the holiday season. This storefront now houses the Venango County Humane Society Thrift Shop, which serves those in need while helping to raise money for the society. A new building is currently being constructed in nearby Seneca to house the animals. (Courtesy of Peter Solle.)

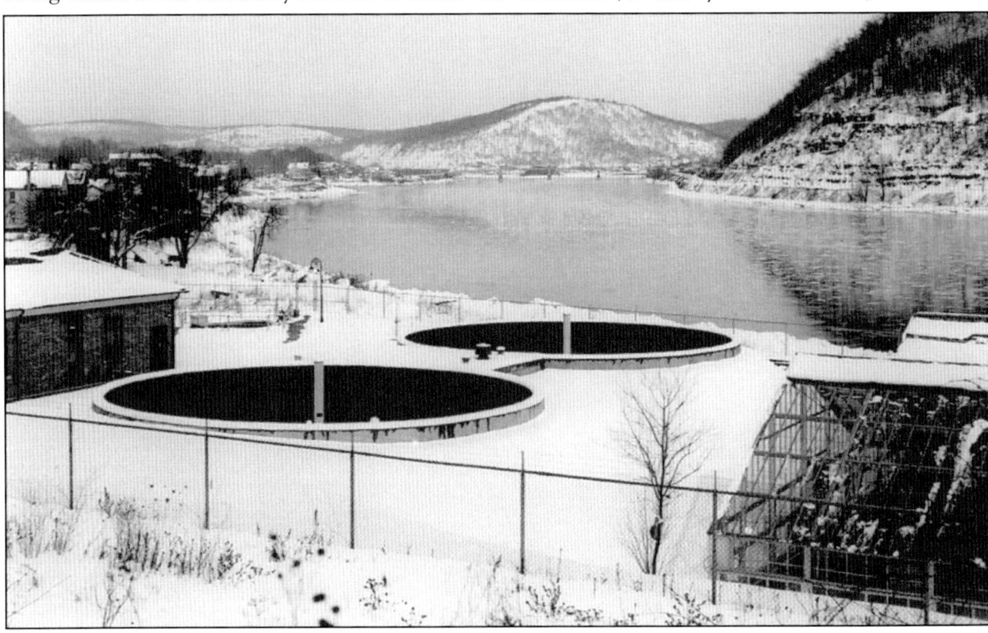

Referred to as the Glen Fern Plant when it was built in 1939, the city's wastewater treatment plant was upgraded in 1975 according to the Federal Clean Water Act of 1972. A secondary treatment status was added to meet the new biological treatment standards. The plant can treat up to six million gallons of wastewater per day and can double its capacity when stormwater runs high. (Courtesy of Peter Solle.)

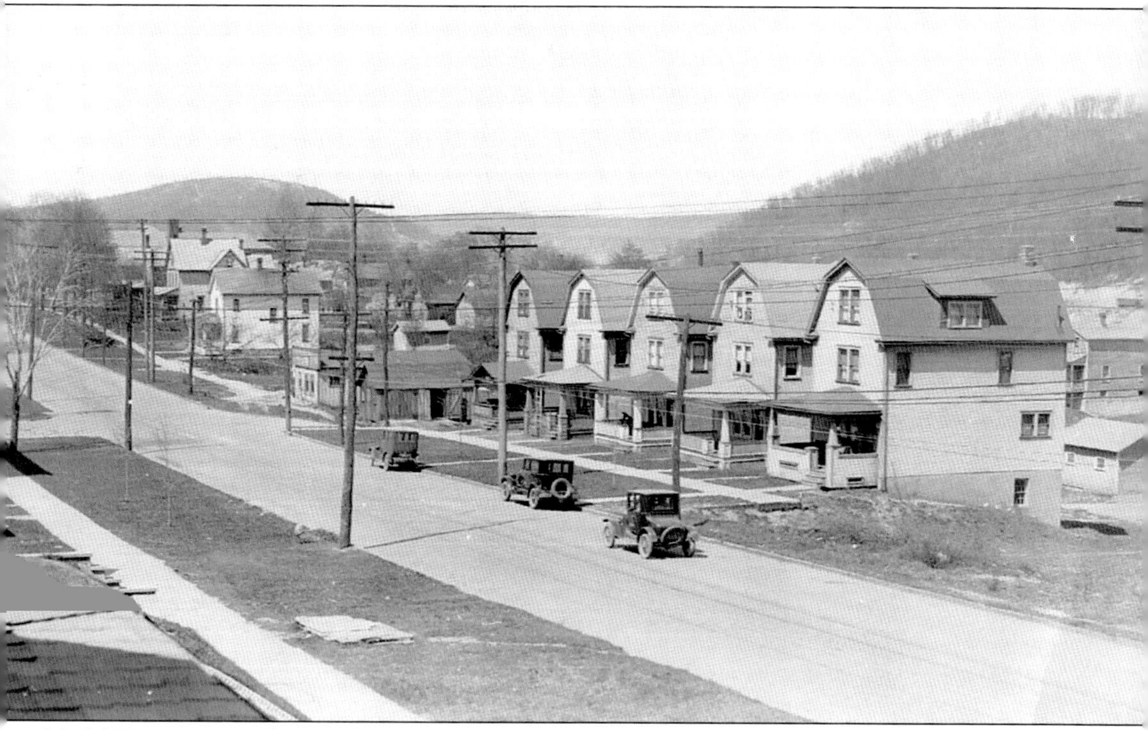

Model Ts are seen in front of five identical houses built along the 200 block of Liberty Street in the early 1920s. Related families tended to live in the same area, sometimes even the same city block, and contracted the same developers for their houses. These houses still stand today, almost 100 years later. An early landmark just a few miles downstream from these houses is Indian God Rock. Located eight miles south of Franklin along the Allegheny River, Indian God Rock displays early Native American petroglyphs from as early as 1200 CE. Steamboat travelers would often rush to the side of the boat to view the landmark when crew members announced its proximity. The rock, 22 feet tall and composed of sandstone, was added to the National Register of Historic Places in 1984. (Courtesy of Peter Solle.)

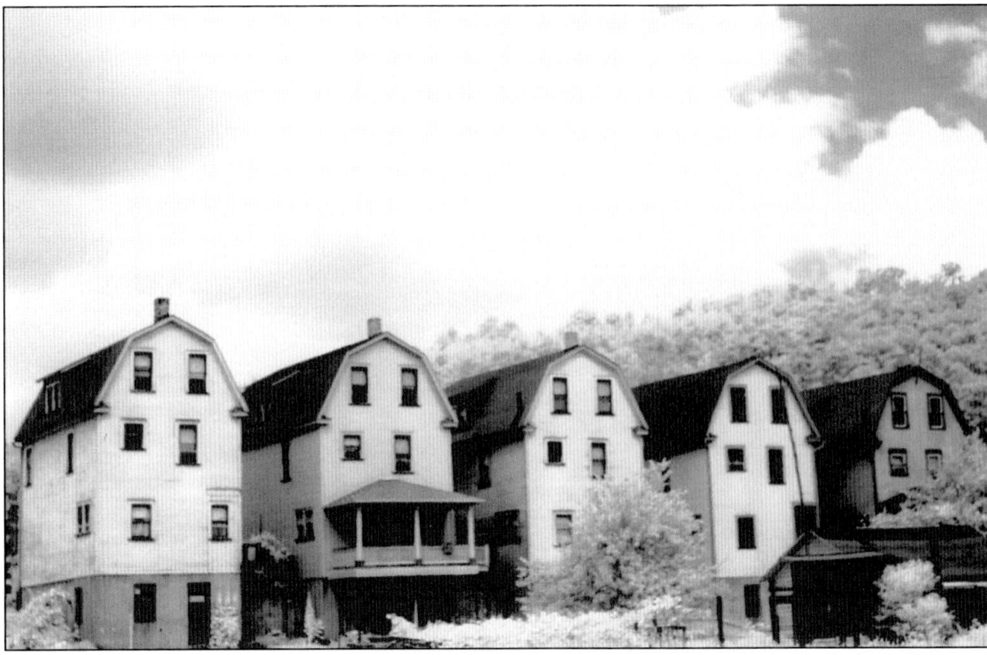

The rear view of the five identical houses in the 200 block of Liberty Street reveals slight differences, particularly with the addition of a porch on the second house. The last house looks to have a porch as well, but a tree is blocking the view. These houses are still easily identifiable today from either side. (Courtesy of Peter Solle.)

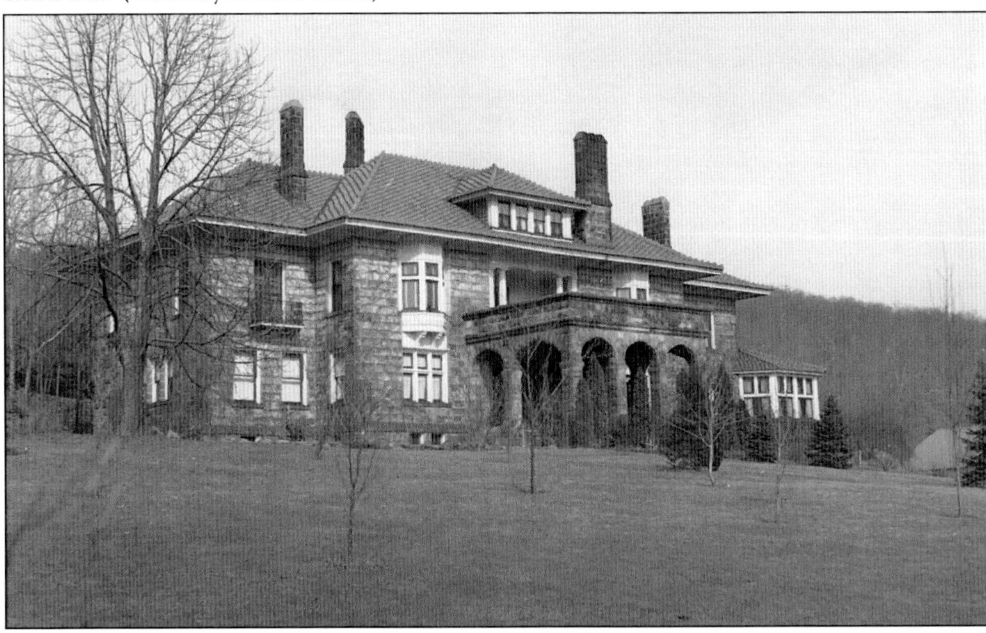

Glen Moy was the home of Duncan McIntosh. Born in Cleveland, Ohio, McIntosh was employed as an office boy by John D. Rockefeller before the Standard Oil Company was formed. He later transferred to Oil City to run the Imperial Refinery. After 10 years, he was named the general manager of the Eclipse Refinery in Franklin. Glen Moy now houses the Turning Point Treatment Center. (Courtesy of Peter Solle.)

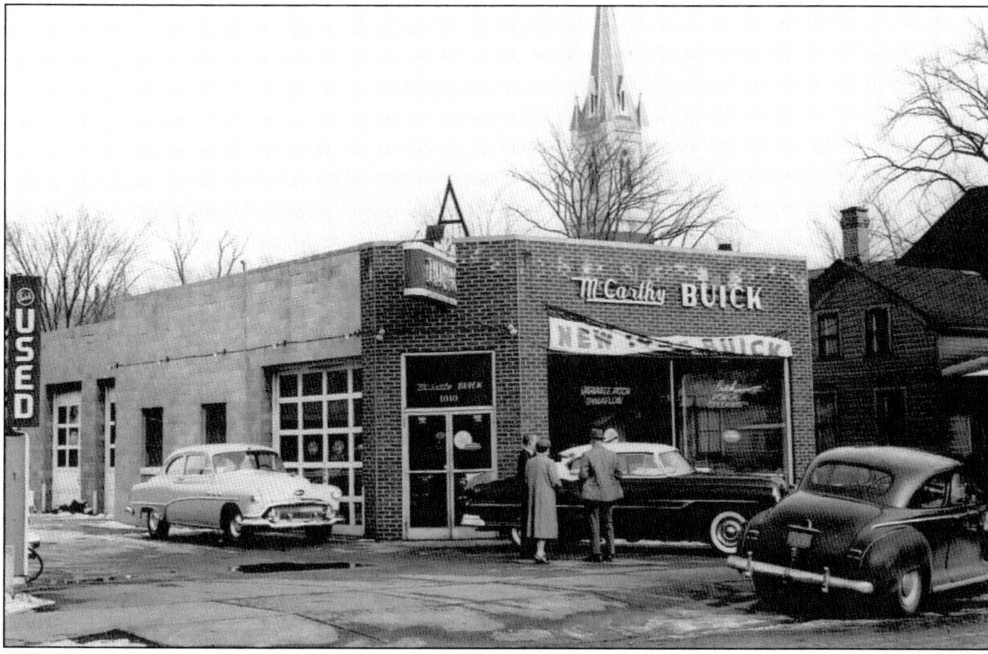

McCarthy Buick was one of Franklin's car dealerships and garages. The banner on the building reads, "New 1955 Buick." A salesman shows a couple one of the dealership's newest vehicles. McCarthy Buick was located at 1010 Buffalo Street until the 1980s, when the building was renovated. It now houses Community Ambulance Service, Inc. (Courtesy of Peter Solle.)

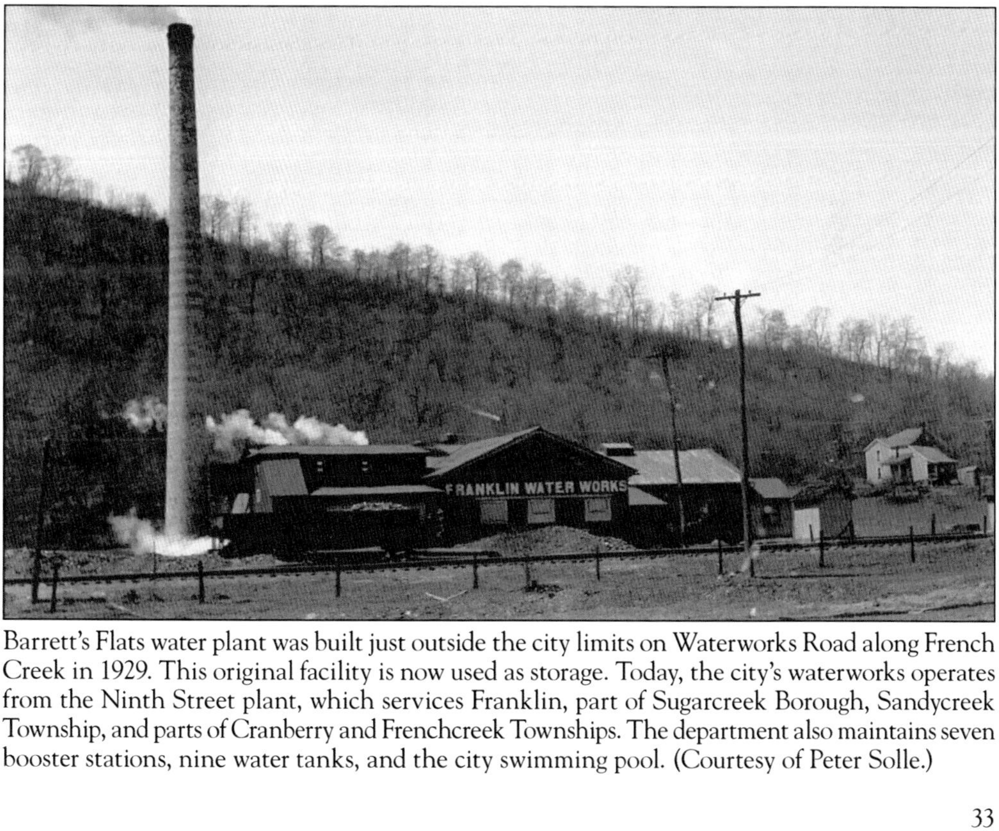

Barrett's Flats water plant was built just outside the city limits on Waterworks Road along French Creek in 1929. This original facility is now used as storage. Today, the city's waterworks operates from the Ninth Street plant, which services Franklin, part of Sugarcreek Borough, Sandycreek Township, and parts of Cranberry and Frenchcreek Townships. The department also maintains seven booster stations, nine water tanks, and the city swimming pool. (Courtesy of Peter Solle.)

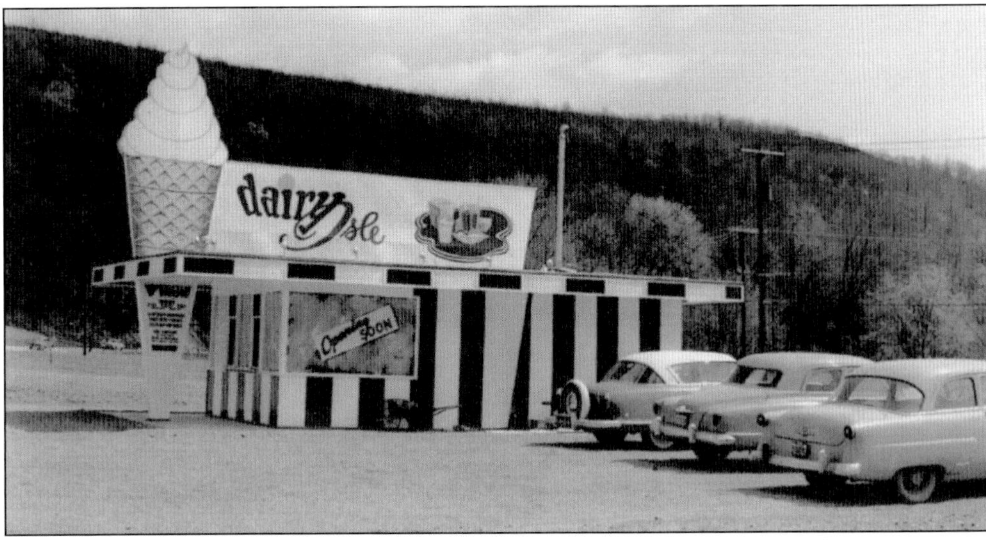

The Dairy Isle, originally owned by Ted Bear and his wife, was the place to go for ice cream and Coney dogs in the Third Ward. The business still exists today, though it has changed hands and is now known as Polly's. With just a few minor adjustments, the original shape of the building is still recognizable. (Courtesy of Peter Solle.)

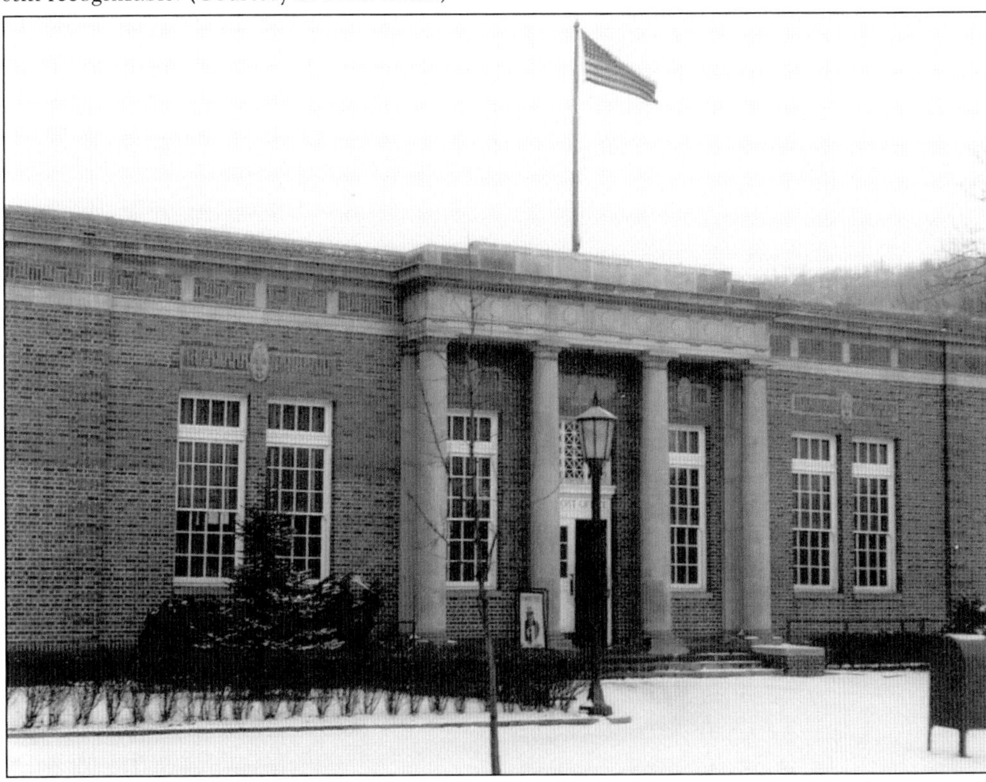

The Franklin Post Office is located on the corner of Twelfth and Elk Streets. The federal government chose this site in the early 1910s, and construction was set to begin upon the close of World War I. In 1925, the construction contract was finally awarded to A.M. Lundberg of St. Louis, Missouri. The project was completed approximately one year later. (Courtesy of Peter Solle.)

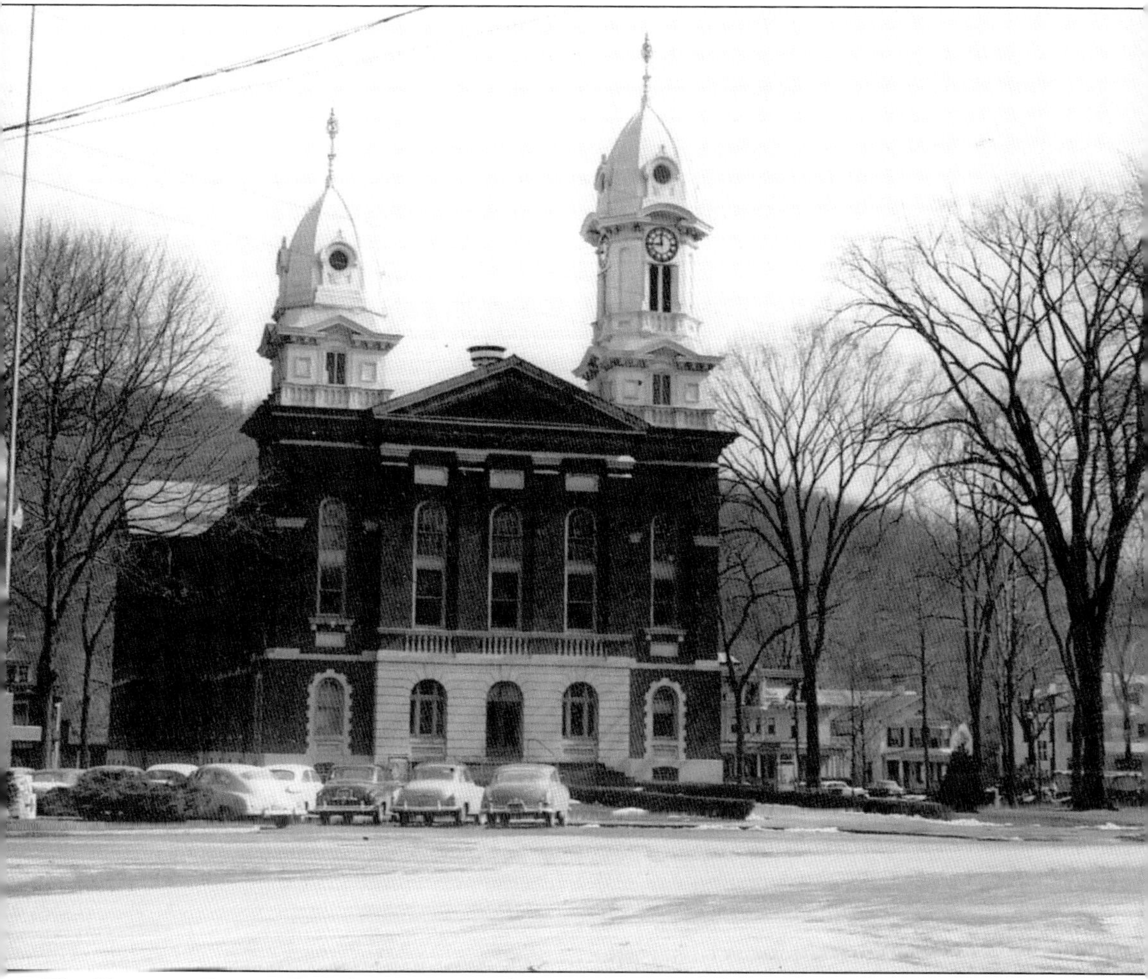

The Venango County Courthouse is one of two most recognizable buildings in Franklin, the other being the Franklin Public Library. The clock, located on the right spire, chimes on the hour and half hour. Behind the courthouse is Elk Street, lined with great old houses to the right of the Venango County Jail seen at left. Located on the corner of South Park and Elk Streets one block down is the Old Stone House. It is one of the oldest buildings in the city, having been built in 1843 by Edward Pearce. In its heyday, the home was thought of as the best and most stylish in the eastern part of the United States. John McConnell completed the stonework. Pearce was a Revolutionary War soldier, as well as an innkeeper and wagon maker. He owned the Rising Sun Hotel. (Courtesy of Peter Solle.)

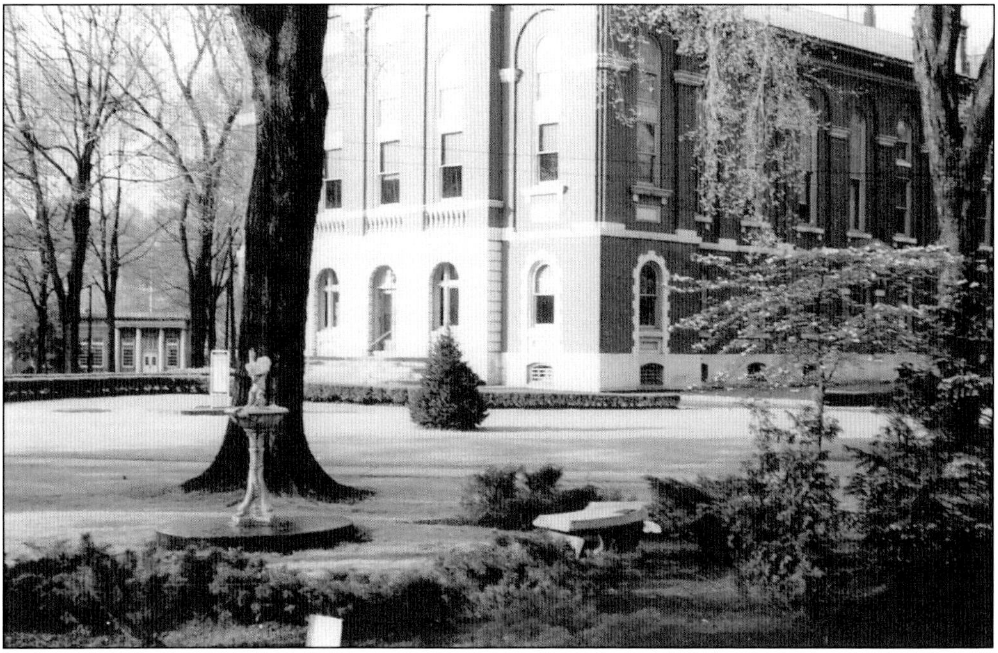

The bird font is located near the corner of Twelfth and Liberty Streets in the city's South Park. The Venango County Courthouse is seen in the background. South Park is also home to the city's bandstand, the Civil War monument, and the new Vietnam Honor Roll, which was dedicated on November 11, 2011. (Courtesy of Peter Solle.)

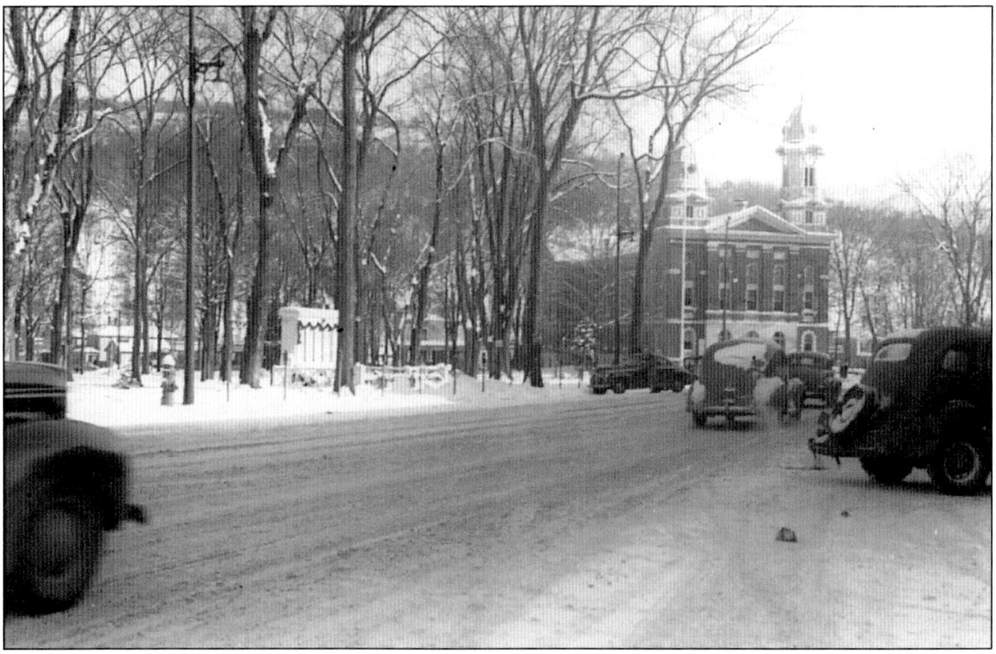

Looking down Liberty Street, the Venango County Courthouse is seen at the intersection of Twelfth Street. As the seat of Venango County, the courthouse has been the most photographed building in Franklin. This was the county's third edifice, built in 1868–1869 by Samuel Sloan and Addison Hutton, both of Philadelphia. (Courtesy of Peter Solle.)

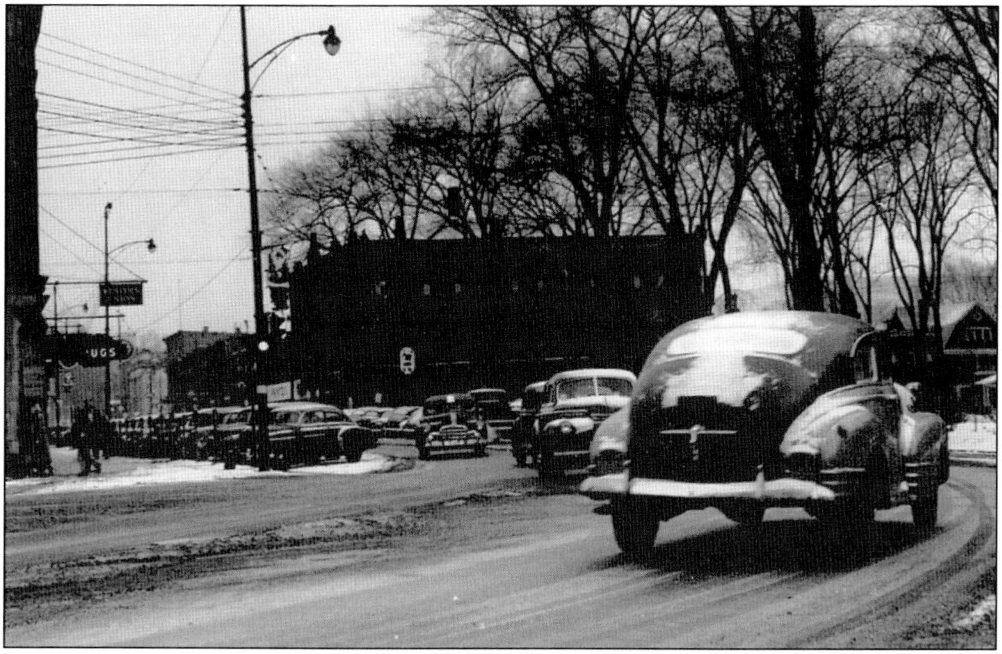

The Snook Block is seen at center of this photograph. Before 1860, temporary structures stood on this lot. The area was referred to as "Rat Hole Row." Construction of the Snook Block began in 1883 and finished in 1888. The top two floors have housed the YMCA, Knights of Columbus, and the Franklin Library, along with offices, clubs, and small businesses. (Courtesy of Peter Solle.)

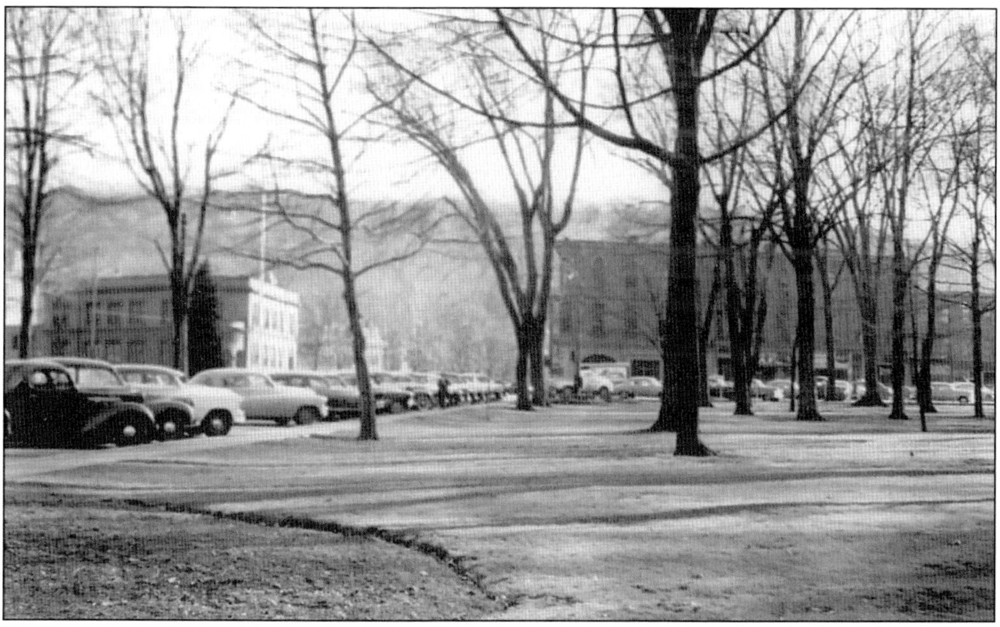

Looking out toward Liberty Street from the intersection of Twelfth and Elk Streets, most of the buildings in this photograph have been gone for decades, whether from fire or urban renewal. From left to right, the News-Herald Building was razed in 1964, the Franklin Public Library still stands as it did in 1849 with some additions, and the Hancock Building burned in November 1980. (Courtesy of Peter Solle.)

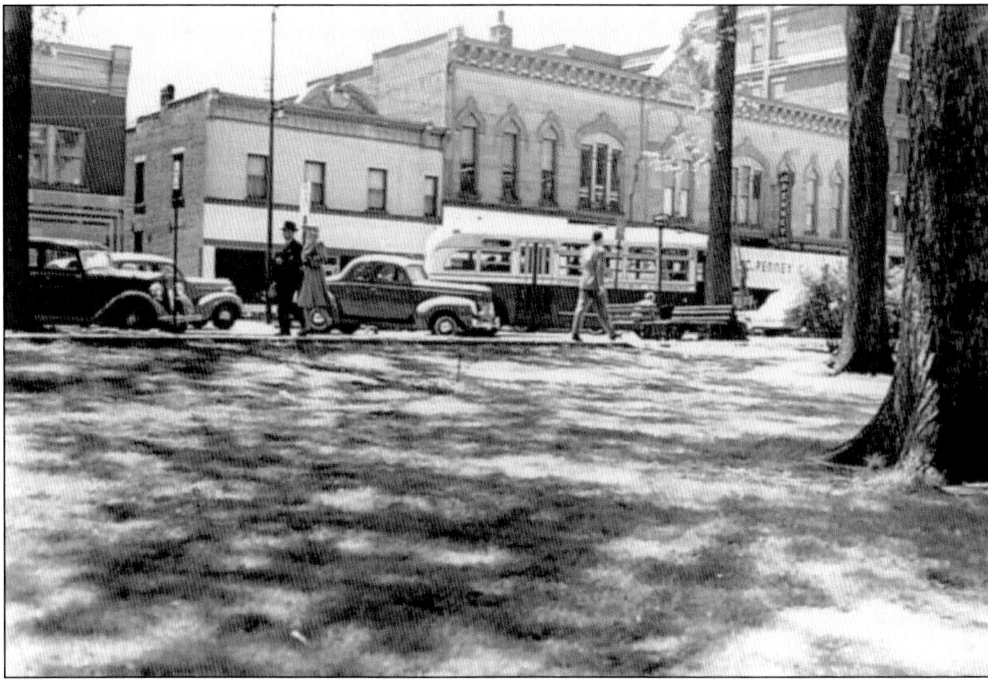

Above is the business district as viewed from West Park. Both West and South Parks, complete with gardens and playgrounds, were originally used as gathering places, pastures, and training grounds for the military. Men arrested and charged with public drunkenness were often sentenced to removing tree stumps from the grounds. In 1852, the community held a tree-planting day in the parks to help improve the landscape. (Courtesy of Peter Solle.)

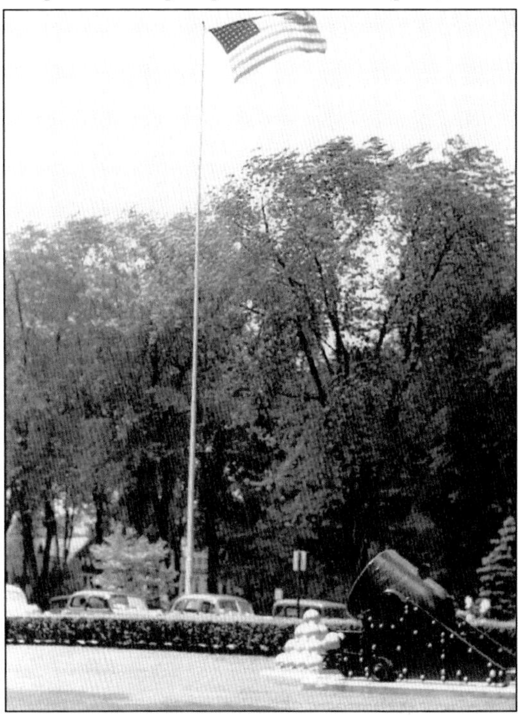

Dating from World War I, the Howitzer cannon and its stack of cannonballs once stood proudly in front of the Venango County Courthouse in the area of Twelfth and Liberty Streets. With the start of World War II and the United States' involvement, the entire display was sacrificed for the cause, melted down and transformed into items for use in the war. (Courtesy of Peter Solle.)

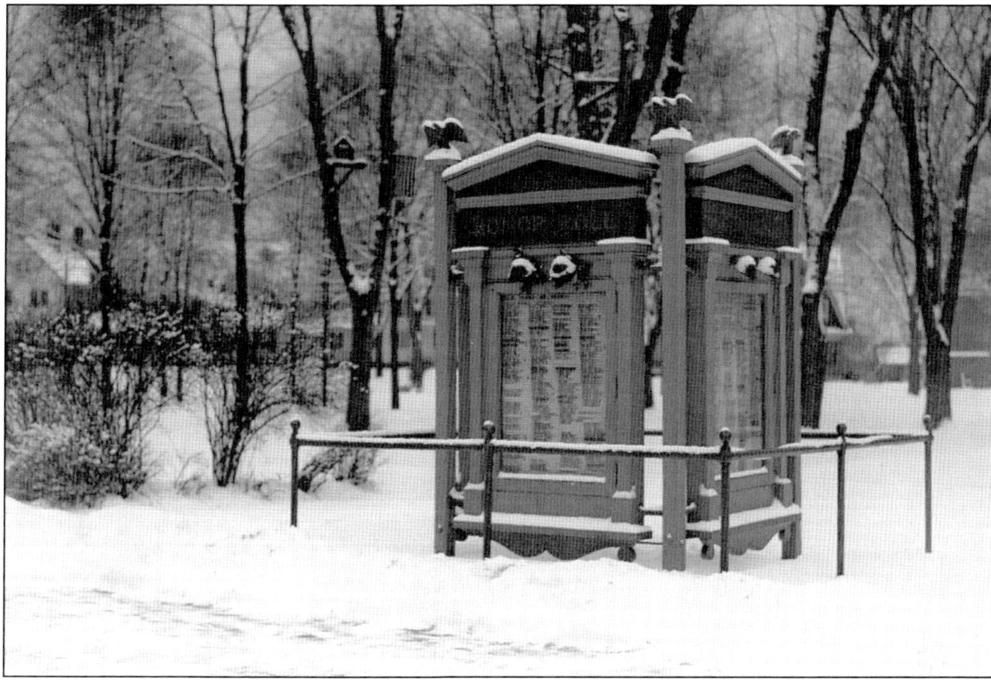

Once located in West Park, the honor roll included the names of soldiers killed in World War I. Placed in the early 1920s, the monument was later removed to add those killed in World War II. During this process, the monument was misplaced, then stolen—never to be recovered. Presently, the downtown parks contain monuments for both World Wars I and II, the Civil War, and Vietnam War. (Courtesy of Peter Solle.)

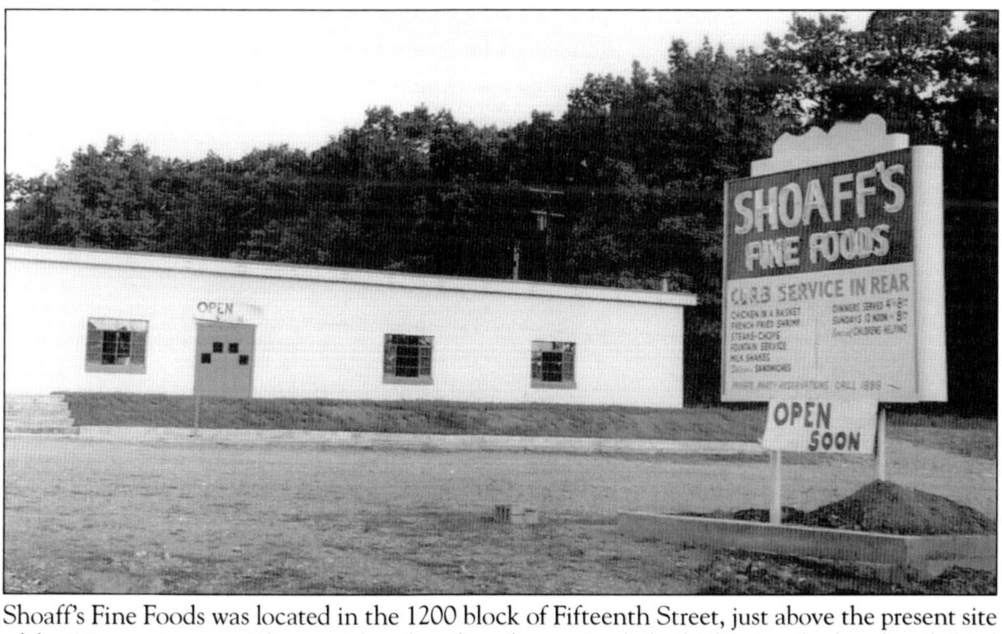

Shoaff's Fine Foods was located in the 1200 block of Fifteenth Street, just above the present site of the Airways Lounge. The specialties listed on the sign include chicken in a basket, french fried shrimp, steaks and chops, milk shakes, and "delicious" sandwiches. Unfortunately, the restaurant, which offered curb and fountain service, was only open a short time. (Courtesy of Peter Solle.)

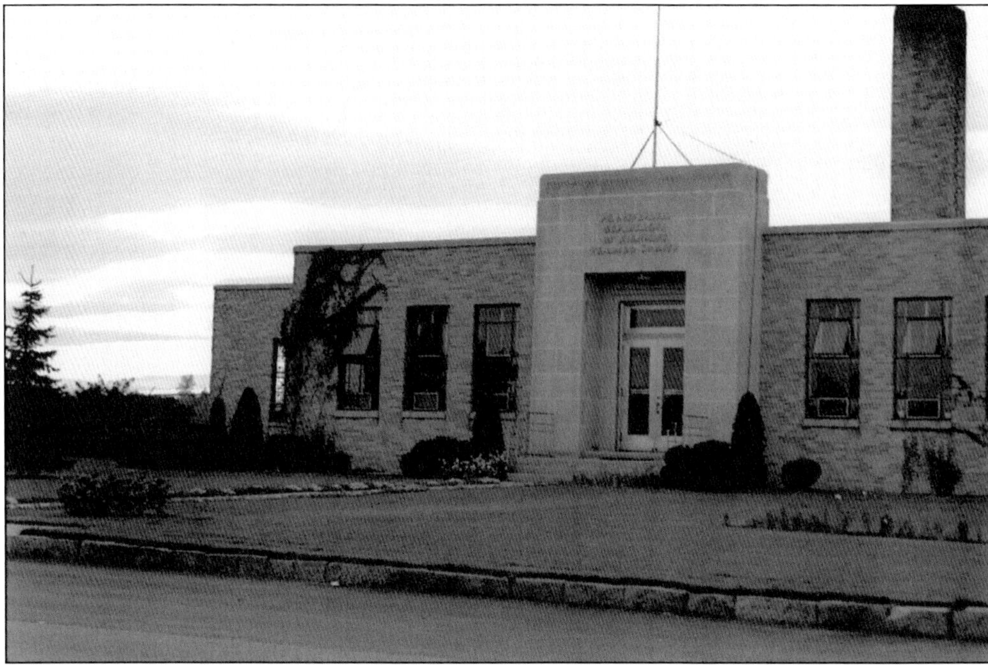

The Pennsylvania Department of Highways Venango County is located at 1460 Pittsburgh Road. The construction of this building was finished on November 9, 1937. The Pennsylvania Department of Transportation (PennDOT) was created from this department by Pennsylvania Act 120, which was approved on May 6, 1970. The department oversees more than 41,000 miles of roadway throughout the Commonwealth of Pennsylvania. (Courtesy of Peter Solle.)

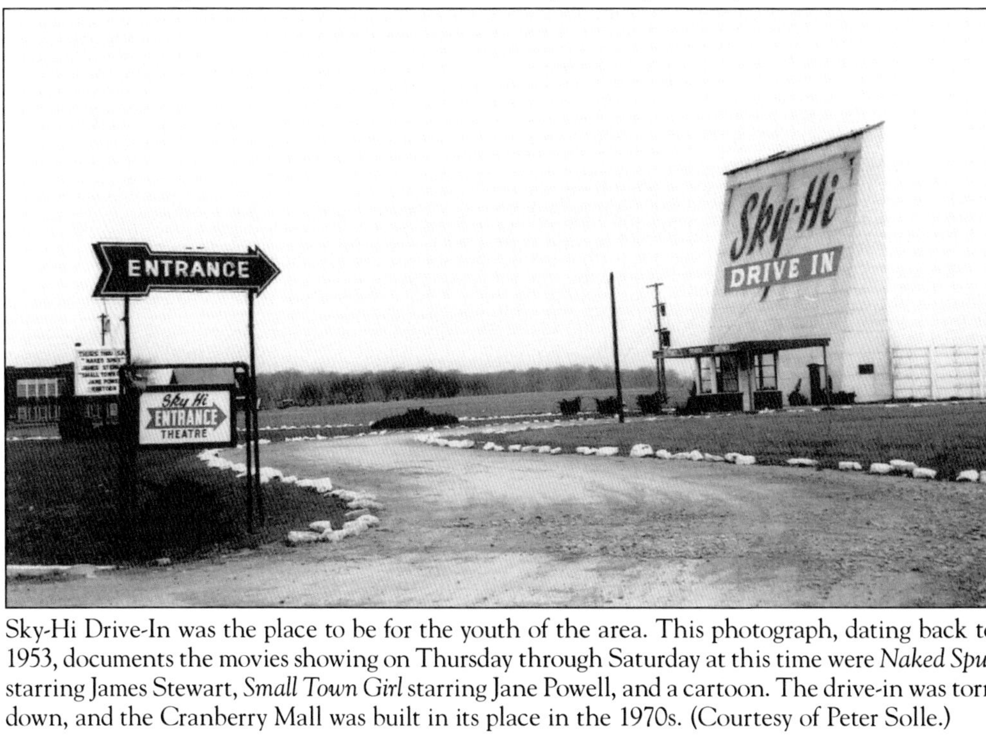

Sky-Hi Drive-In was the place to be for the youth of the area. This photograph, dating back to 1953, documents the movies showing on Thursday through Saturday at this time were *Naked Spur* starring James Stewart, *Small Town Girl* starring Jane Powell, and a cartoon. The drive-in was torn down, and the Cranberry Mall was built in its place in the 1970s. (Courtesy of Peter Solle.)

Two

The Faces of Franklin

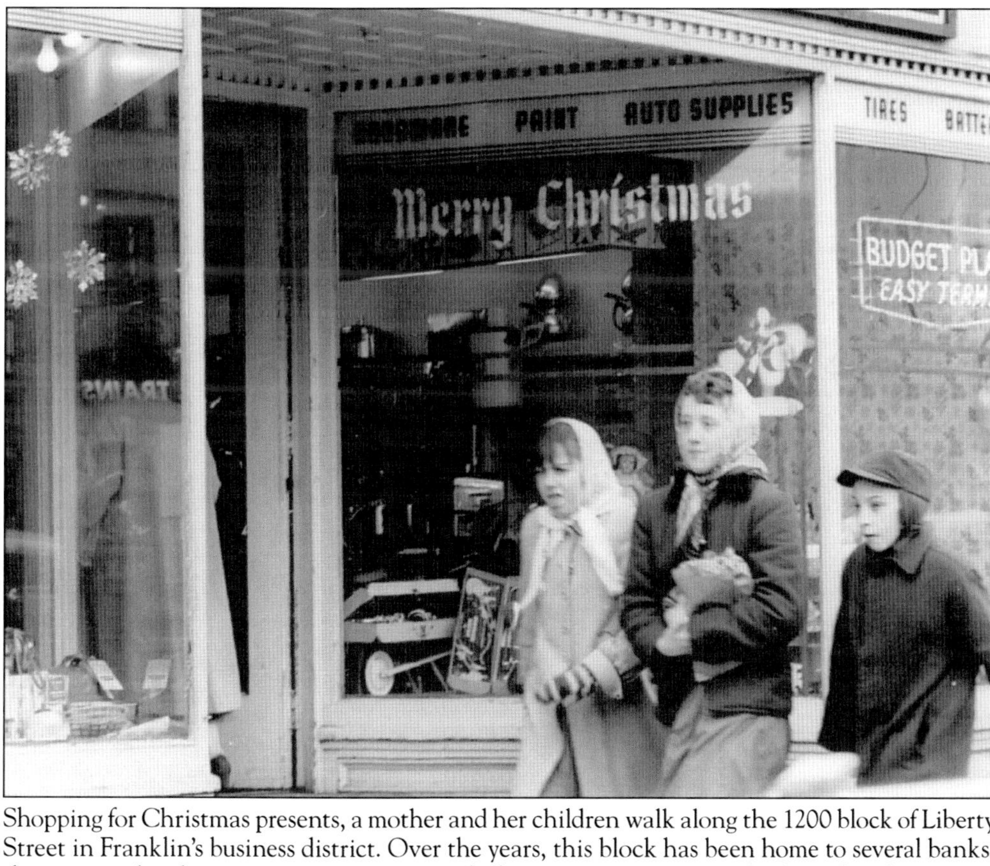

Shopping for Christmas presents, a mother and her children walk along the 1200 block of Liberty Street in Franklin's business district. Over the years, this block has been home to several banks, shoe stores, hardware stores, restaurants, clothing stores, insurance brokers, butcher stores, department stores, theaters, and hotels. (Courtesy of Peter Solle)

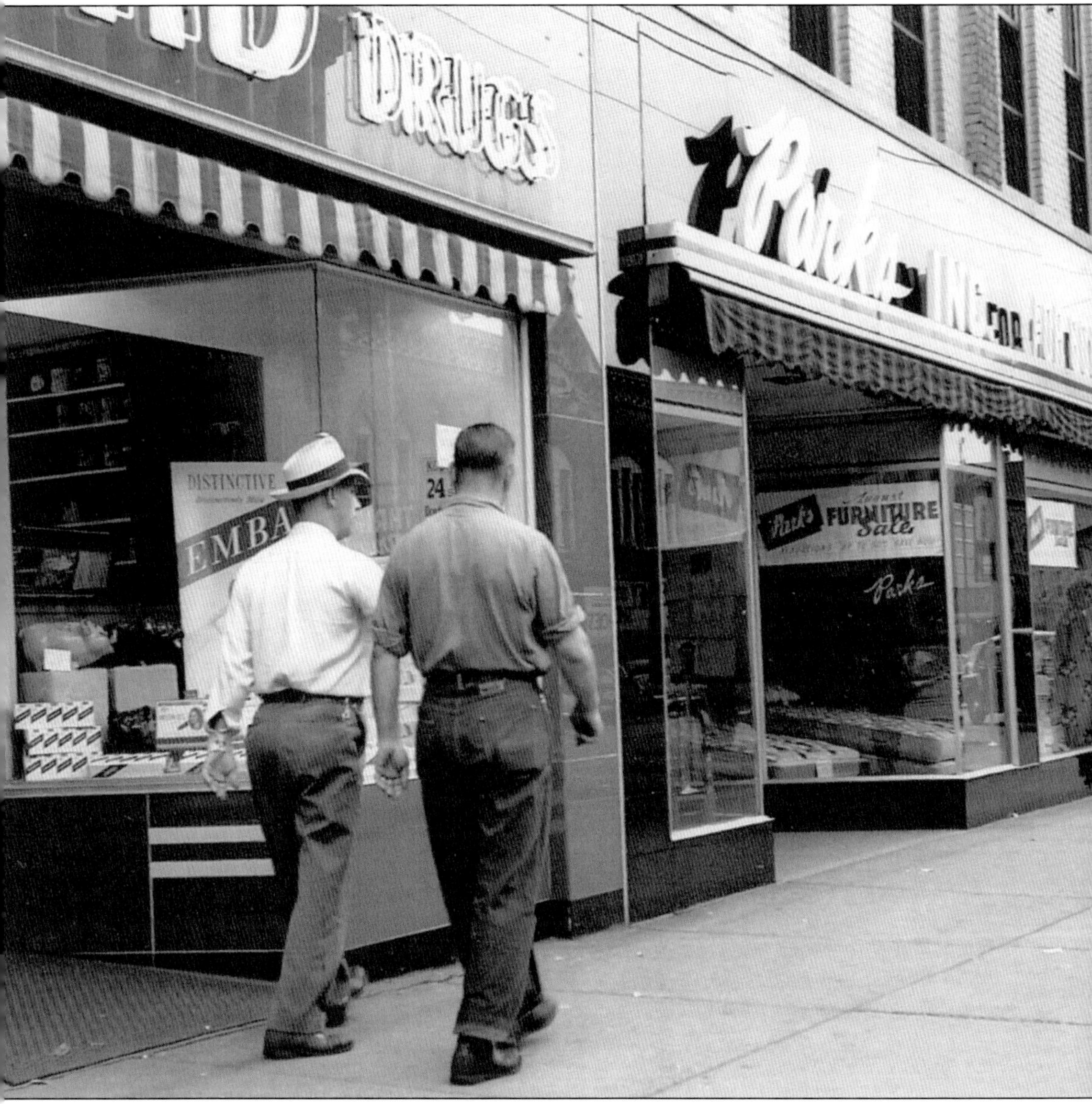

Here, two men walk past Eckerd Drugs and Park's Furniture on Liberty Street in downtown Franklin. Many of the stores were staples to the business district, thriving for numerous decades. Two of the lasting businesses are Anderson's Furniture, located at 225 Thirteenth Street, and Feldman Jewelers, located at 1260 Liberty Street. Both have been in business for approximately 100 years. During the late 1800s, the Hotel Seanor occupied the Anderson's Furniture building. B.D. McClure then purchased the building in 1897 and renovated it at a cost of $25,000. The remodel took a total of two years to complete, including the addition of a 34-foot bar. The building reopened in March 1900 as the McClure Hotel. The hotel claimed that it was "not the biggest but the best." Robert Anderson purchased the building in 1915 as the home of his furniture store, and it has remained as such ever since. (Courtesy of Peter Solle.)

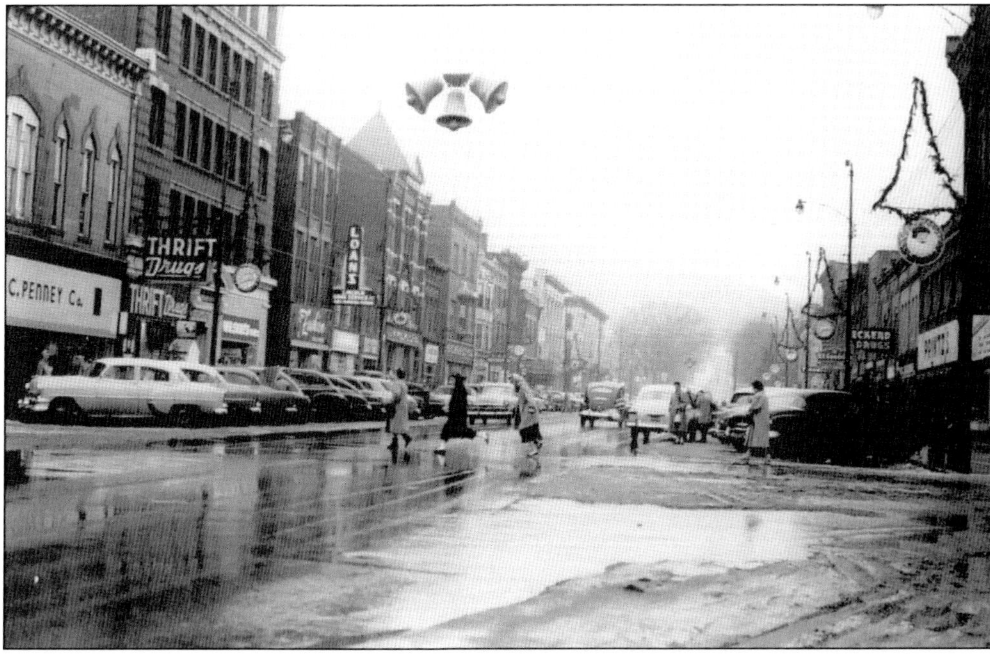

Christmastime in downtown Franklin has always been a busy and bustling time. Ladies rush to cross the street to shop in the many stores, including J.C. Penney, the Fashion, Wilson's Shoes, Thrift Drugs, Printz's, and Eckerd Drugs, just to name a few. This photograph, dating to the late 1940s to early 1950s, shows that street parking was diagonal at the time. (Courtesy of Peter Solle.)

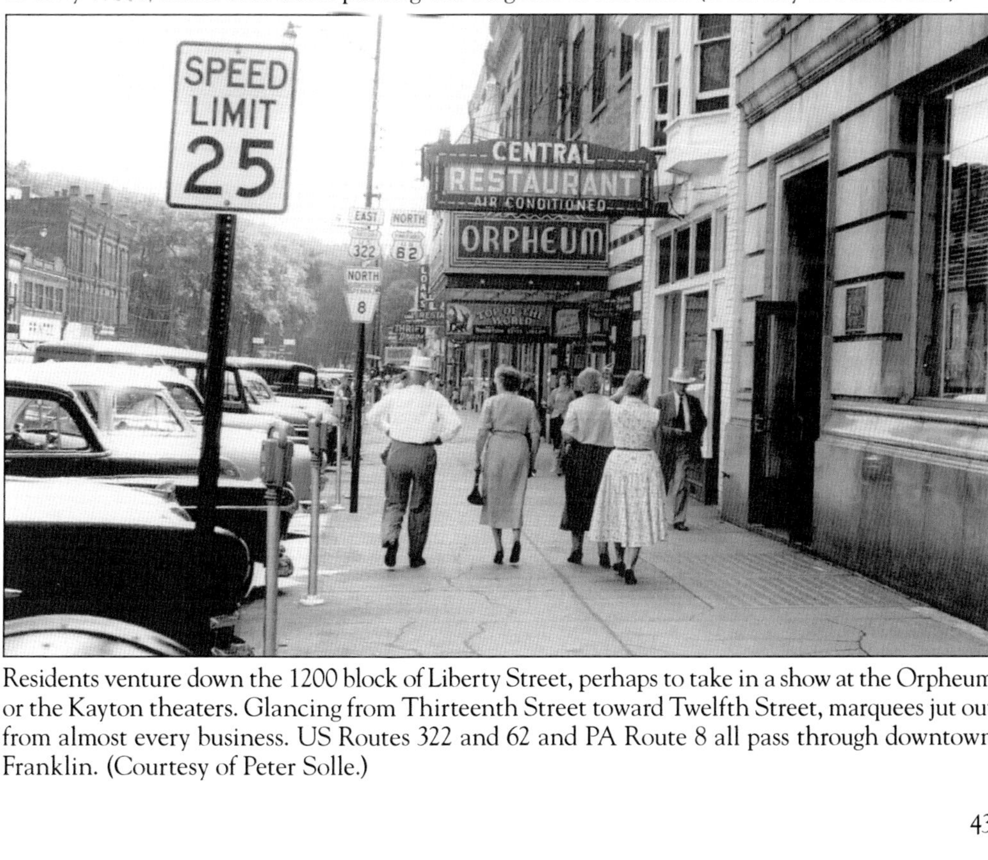

Residents venture down the 1200 block of Liberty Street, perhaps to take in a show at the Orpheum or the Kayton theaters. Glancing from Thirteenth Street toward Twelfth Street, marquees jut out from almost every business. US Routes 322 and 62 and PA Route 8 all pass through downtown Franklin. (Courtesy of Peter Solle.)

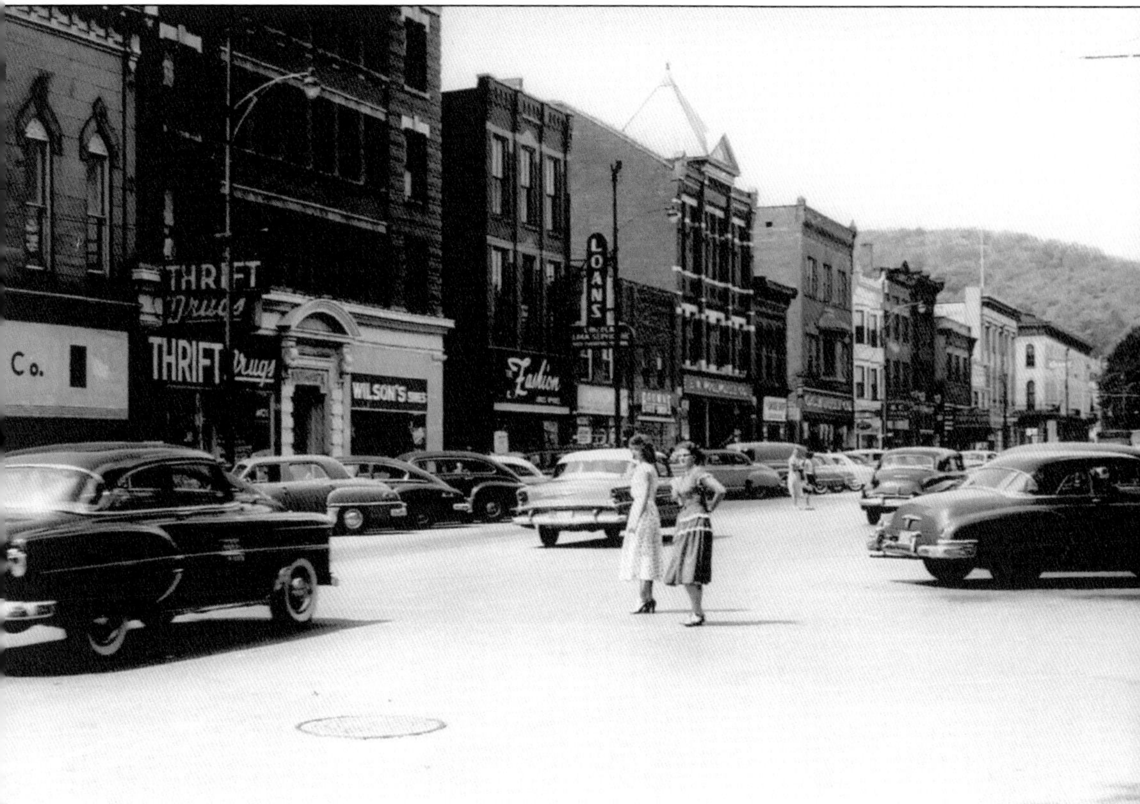

A couple of ladies wait to cross the street in the business district. Thrift Drugs had a soda shop, which served many drinks to the youth of Franklin and the surrounding communities for decades. The residents of Venango County, both past and present, treasure memories like these. To the right of Thrift Drugs and Wilson's Shoes is the Fashion, a women's clothing store. Located in the Dodd-Osmer Building, the business flourished for almost 60 years under the direction of owner Jerome Silverman. The building itself was constructed in the 1880s for attorney Samuel C.T. Dodd, who authored the Standard Oil Trust. The building also housed the law offices of James H. Osmer and his sons. To the right are the Raymond Buildings, which are a few of the oldest structures in the business district. William Raymond built his home and shop here in the early 1800s. (Courtesy of Peter Solle.)

Two men cross the 1200 block of Liberty Street in the 1950s. Cars used to park at an angle in the business district. The businesses shown are, from left to right, the National Meat Specialists, Brown's Boot Shop, F.W. Woolworth Company, the Smoke Shop, L&C Restaurant, and the Orpheum Theatre. (Courtesy of Peter Solle.)

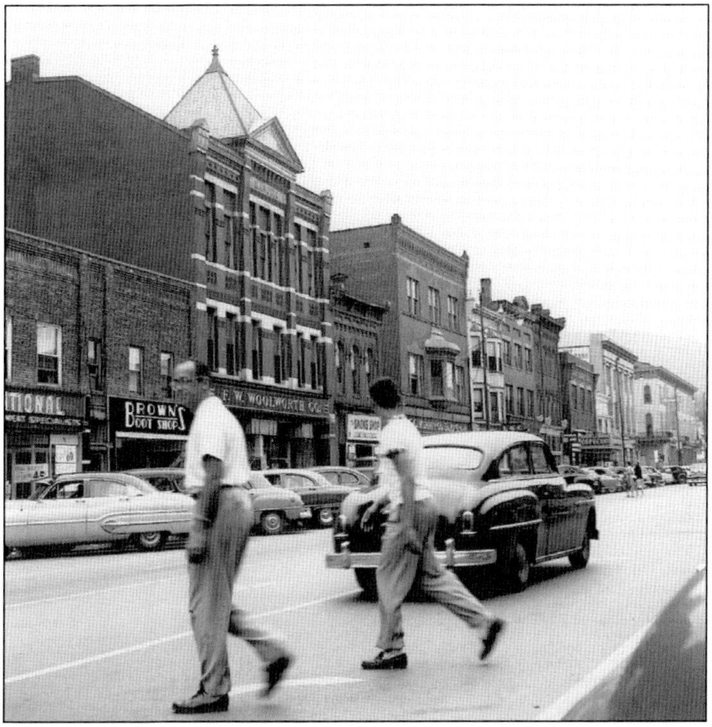

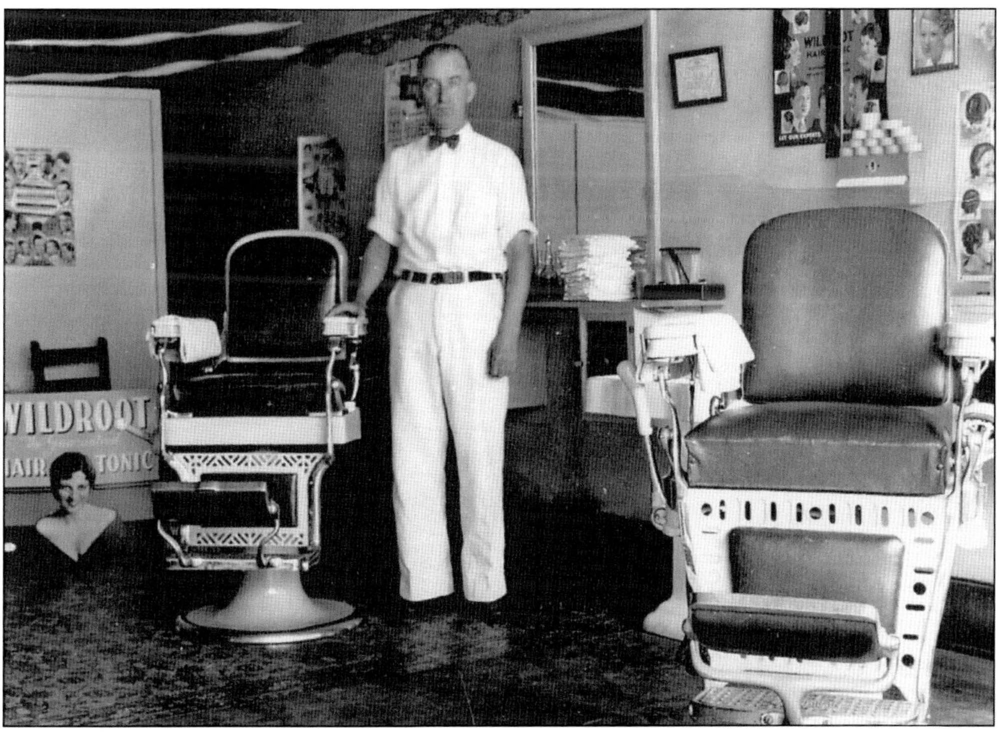

In the 1930s, Willis Andrew Baker owned a barbershop, located in the 200 block of Thirteenth Street. As a young man, Baker's first job was taking care of a horse. In this photograph, Baker was in his 40s. The First National Bank now stands at this site. (Courtesy of Gail Beck.)

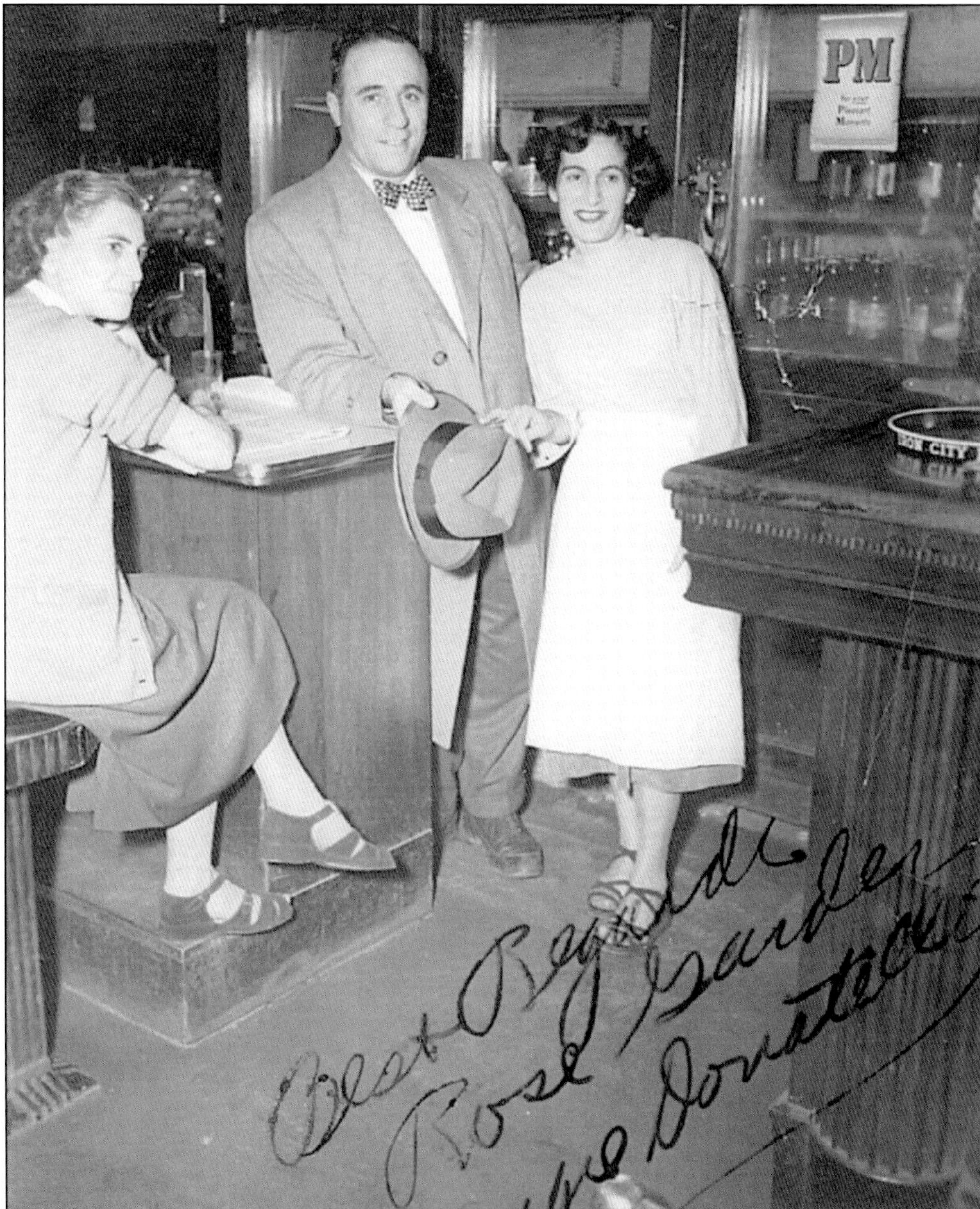

Frances Serge Eakin and her sister Julia Serge pose around the counter with Augie Donatelli at the Rose Garden restaurant in the early 1940s. The restaurant was located in the 500 block of Thirteenth Street. Born in 1914 in Heilwood, Pennsylvania, Indiana County, Donatelli served in the 8th Air Force of the US Army Air Forces during World War II and as an American umpire for Major League Baseball. Diagonally across from the Rose Garden restaurant is the Elks Club, which was constructed in the early 1950s. Prior to the club, Adam and Sarah Smith Webber had built their house on the property in the 1840s. Adam was the postmaster of Franklin for approximately 20 years. He died in 1860. Sarah Smith Webber, then a widow, converted their home into a boardinghouse, where John Wilkes Booth stayed from the spring of 1864 until that September. (Courtesy of Frances Serge Eakin.)

Frances Serge Eakin is shown posing in front of the cash register at the Rose Garden restaurant in Franklin in the early 1940s. To her left and right are various bottles of liquor, and above her head are the signs "We reserve the right to refuse service to anyone!" and "Please don't use profane language." (Courtesy of Frances Serge Eakin.)

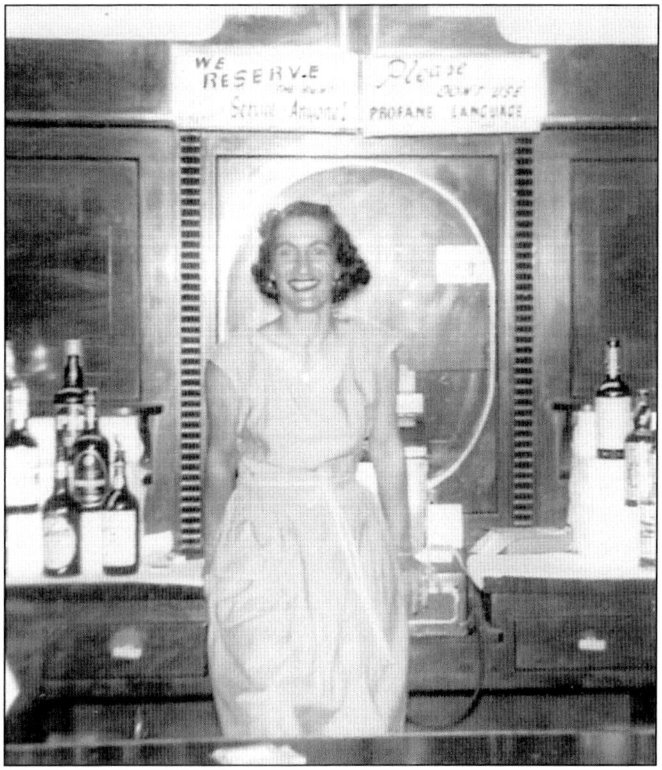

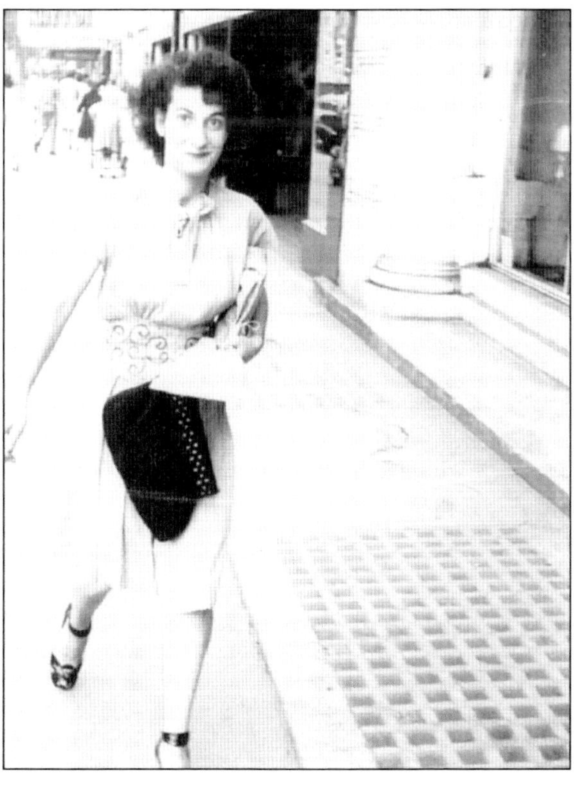

Frances Serge Eakin is shown walking up Liberty Street toward the intersection of Thirteenth Street in the 1940s. She worked as a waitress at the Rose Garden restaurant, which was located in the 500 block of Thirteenth Street. A gentleman approached Eakin on her walk and asked her if he could take her picture. She permitted him to do so. (Courtesy of Frances Serge Eakin.)

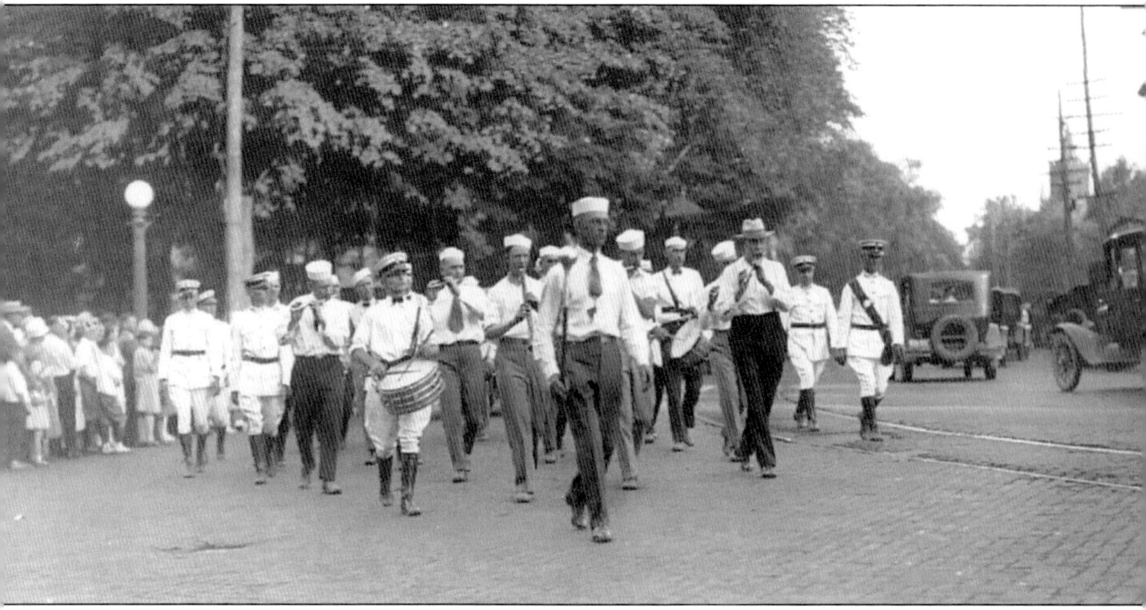

A military band marches in a parade during the summer of 1926. Franklin boasts many parades, celebrations, and events throughout the year. On the first Saturday in February is the Franklin on Ice competition for professional ice carvers, and a chili cook-off is judged as well. The first weekend in May is reserved for Franklin's May Garden Mart, with over 50 vendors offering plants ranging from seeds and flowers to bushes and trees, as well as garden furniture, yard decorations, and other handmade items. The Thursday Nights in the Park concert series is held in the bandstand between May and August, featuring the Silver Cornet Band and other performers. A Taste of Franklin occurs on the first Sunday of August and features cuisine from the top restaurants in the city. Finally, early fall signals the Taste of Talent singing contest sponsored by the University of Pittsburgh Medical Center (UPMC) Northwest hospital. The contest is the city's own *American Idol*esque competition. (Courtesy of Peter Solle.)

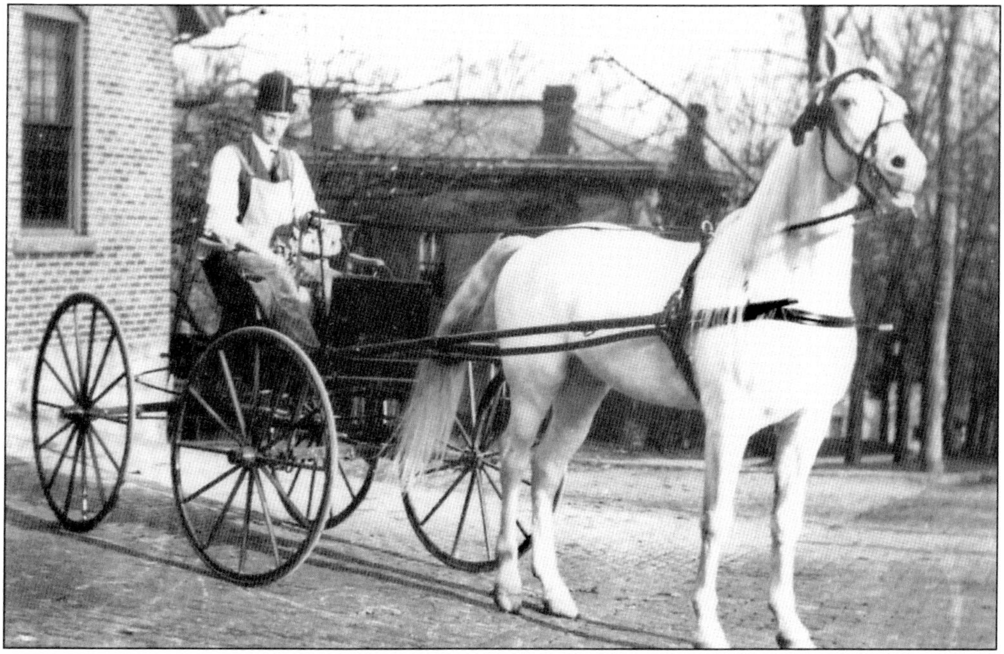

Shown here at the age of 18 or 19 in 1906 or 1907, Willis Andrew Baker is seated in a carriage being pulled by Rabe. Baker's first job was taking care of Rabe. He took great pride in caring for Rabe and would lead parades while on horseback. This photograph was taken from the corner of Sixteenth and Elk Streets (Courtesy of Gail Beck.)

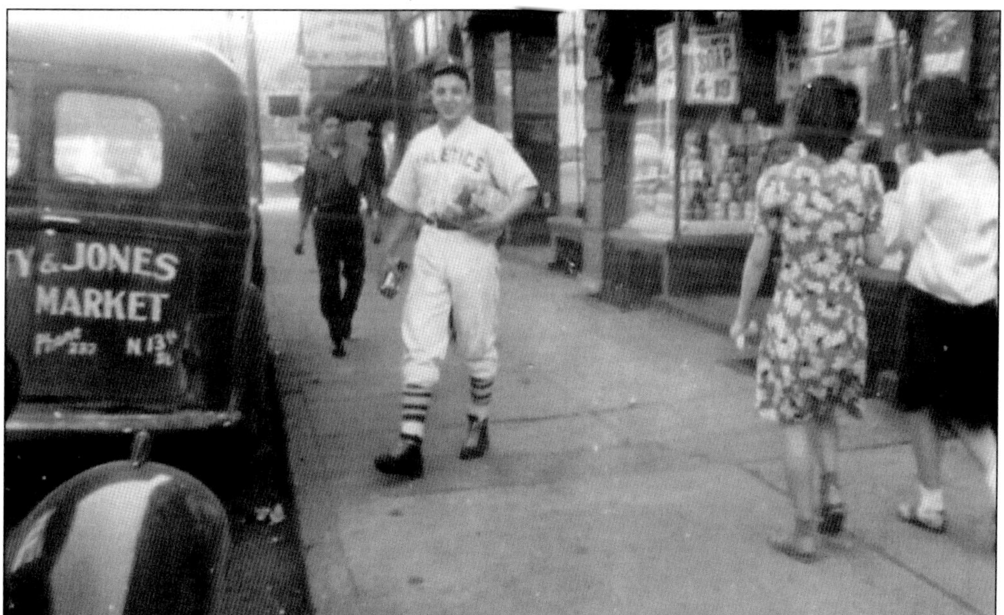

Suited up in his baseball uniform, a member of the Athletics walks by McGinty & Jones Market on North Thirteenth Street, near the Grimm Building, on March 27, 1942. Sports have always been a part of Franklin's history. In December 1903, the Franklin Athletic Club's football team won the World Series of Football. (Courtesy of Frances Serge Eakin.)

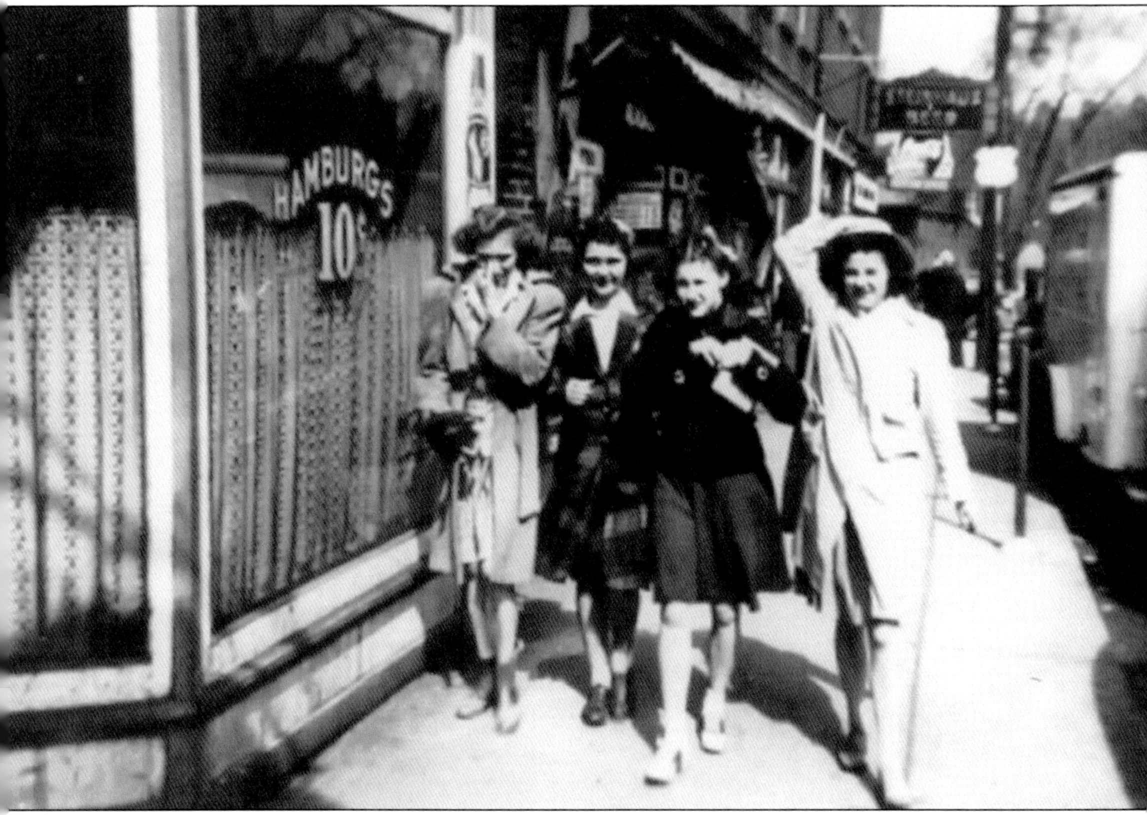

Four high school girls try to stay warm on an early spring day in front of the Washington Lunch. Located in the 100 block of Thirteenth Street, the restaurant was originally owned by the Monarch family. Local folklore often speaks of the family's cat sleeping on the grill at night. A popular menu special was six hot dogs with mustard sauce and onions for a dollar. Earlier shops on Thirteenth Street provided a wide variety of wares and services. Sam Lee's Chinese laundry was located on this street around 1900, and before that, John Quinn Jr. ran a pool hall on Thirteenth Street around 1887. John Coefield managed the Standard Sewing Machine Company in 1887 as well. Peter Emmicke's widow, Margaret, took over her husband's grocery store around 1900. Early Franklin was a melting pot of immigrants, not just the French and British who established Fort Machault and Ford Venango, respectively. (Courtesy of Frances Serge Eakin.)

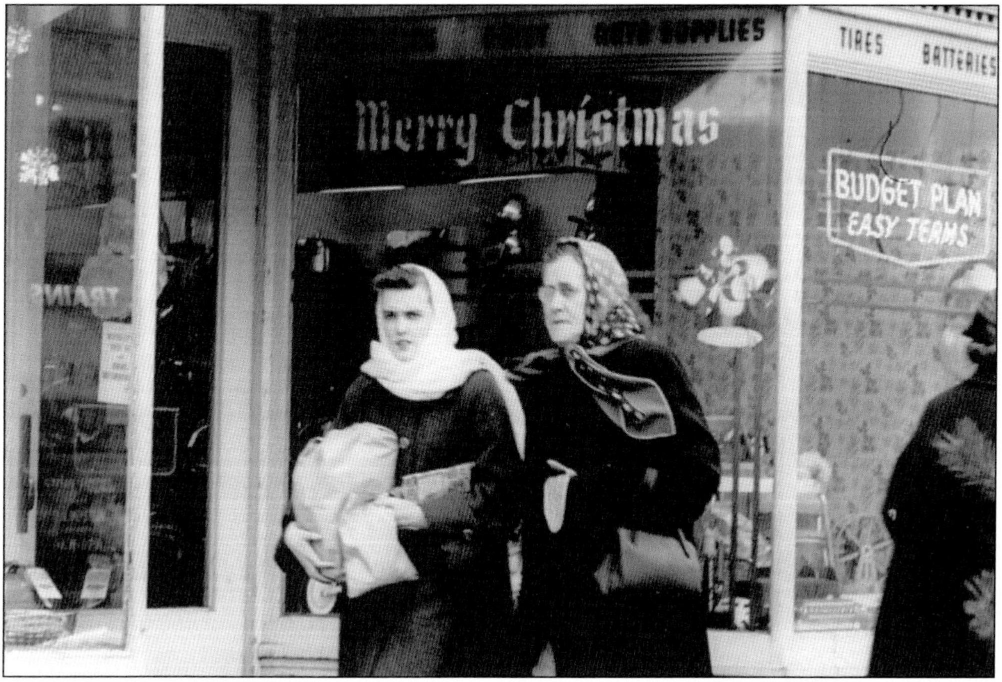

Ladies shop during the holiday season in the business district. With the revitalization of the downtown occurring over the past five years, locals have started returning to shop. In past decades, many young people hung out on the courthouse "circle" in the 300 block of Twelfth Street, around Cherrytree Island. (Courtesy of Peter Solle.)

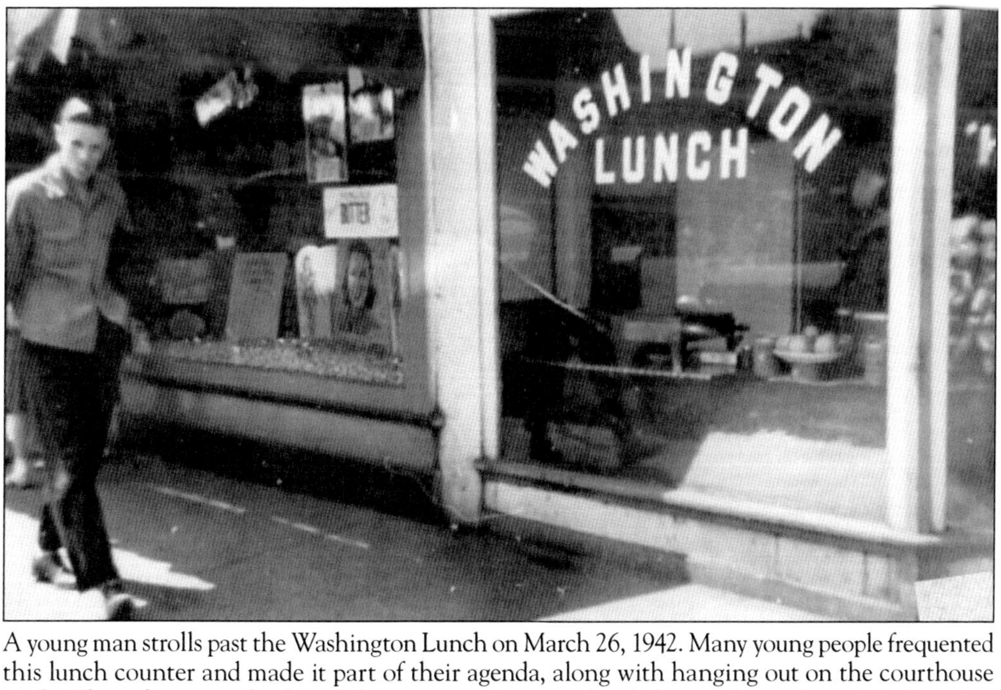

A young man strolls past the Washington Lunch on March 26, 1942. Many young people frequented this lunch counter and made it part of their agenda, along with hanging out on the courthouse circle. The police never bothered the teenagers because they behaved themselves while listening to the new genre of music—rock and roll. (Courtesy of Frances Serge Eakin.)

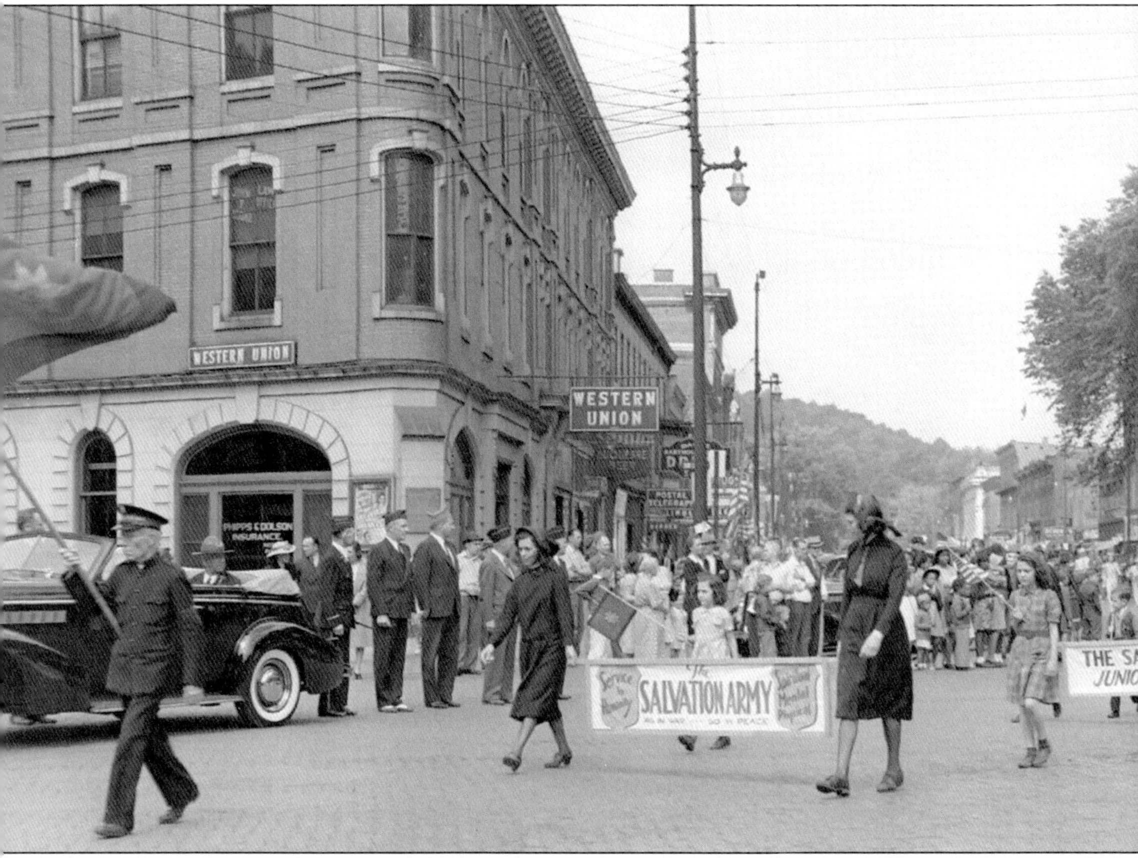

The Salvation Army is seen making their way to the intersection of Twelfth Street on Liberty Street during a parade in the 1930s. The organization serves the community well, always responding to house fires when aid for the family is needed. They often provide transients with a warm bed for the night in the winter as well if money is not had for a hotel room. Just a block from the church that is owned by the organization (at the corner of Seventh and Elk Streets) stood the Old Saltbox House, landmarked as the Mellissa Gildersleeve House. Cyrus Gildersleeve built this beautiful New England saltbox home in 1828. His daughter Melissa was born at the residence in 1840 and became one of the first telegraphers in the community; she also worked as a schoolteacher. In the early 1990s, the house was moved to the Samuel Justus bike trail, across Eighth Street Bridge. It serves as an information center for the region. (Courtesy of Peter Solle.)

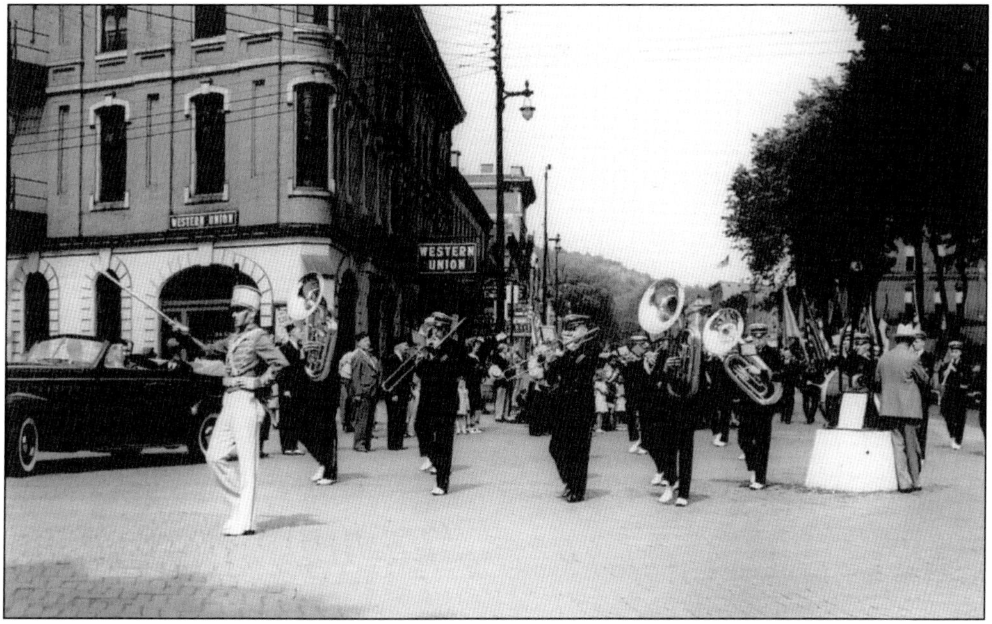

A marching band participates in a parade through downtown Franklin. The Silver Cornet Band is one of the oldest volunteer community bands in the country, having formed in 1856. The band incorporated in 1873 with 17 members, which included veterans from the Civil War. The longest-serving director was Edwin Frye, who retired from the bandmaster position in 2000. (Courtesy of Peter Solle.)

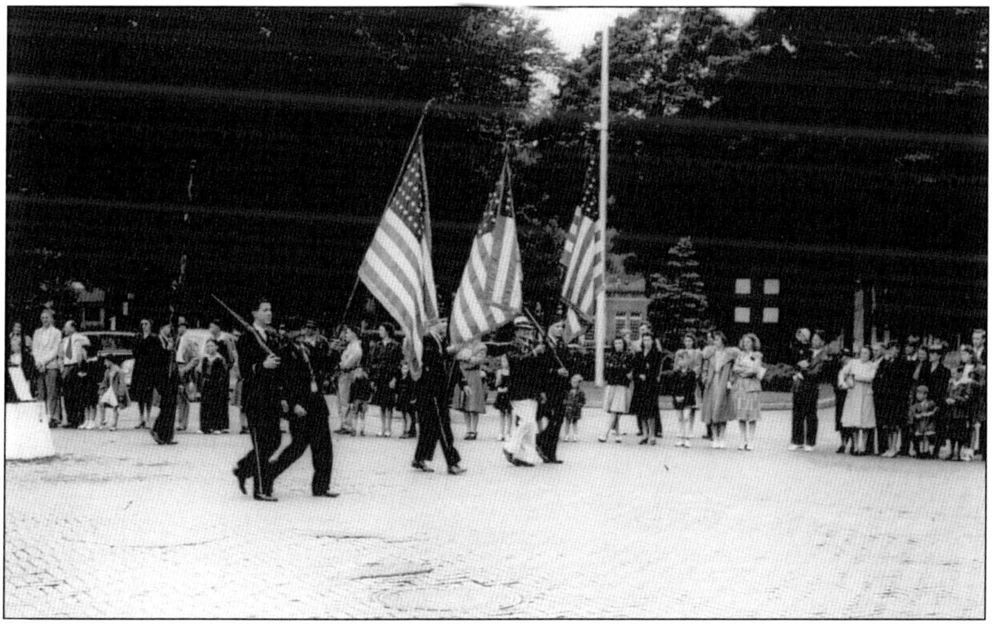

As spectators look on, servicemen carry American flags to signal the start of a parade at the intersection of Twelfth and Liberty Streets in Franklin. Cherrytree Island and the post office are visible in the background. The Libertyfest parade, aiding in the city's Fourth of July celebration, is the largest parade every year, extending from Eighth Street to Thirteenth Street on Liberty Street. (Courtesy of Peter Solle.)

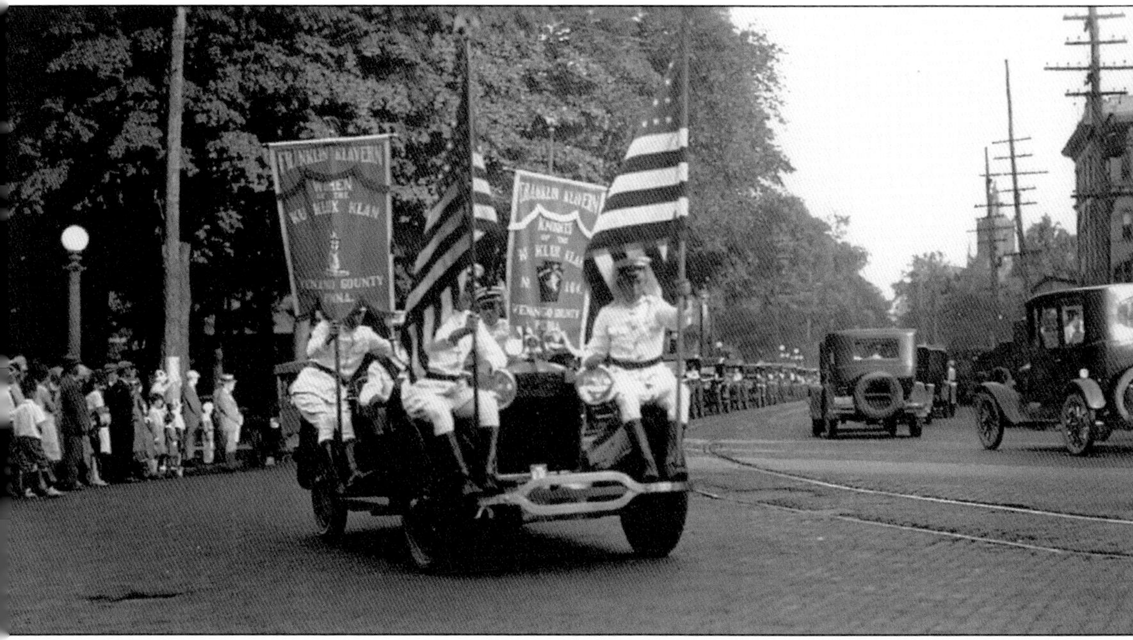

On July 24, 1926, Franklin was the site of a Ku Klux Klan parade. Approaching the intersection of Twelfth Street, cars can be seen bumper to bumper far down Liberty Street. Members are not wearing hoods. The banners being held on the lead car are for both the Knights and the Women of the Franklin Klavern. Behind the long line of cars and the lush trees lining the edge of South Park is the Galena-Dockery Building (not pictured). Originally the site of the Rural House hotel destroyed by fire in 1891, the present building was erected in 1901 to house the Galena Oil Works, which specialized in lubricating oil for the railroad industry. Gen. Charles Miller developed the company. The building was used for offices. Its outer walls are 16 to 20 inches thick, and the structure itself is equipped with 11 walk-in vaults. (Courtesy of Peter Solle.)

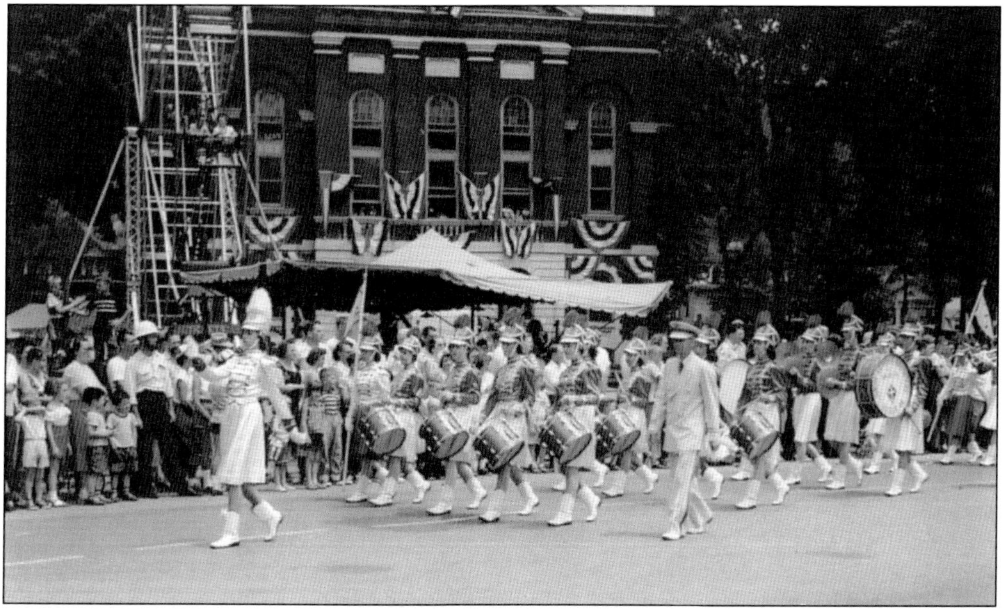

A marching band from Butler performs in a parade during the celebration of America's bicentennial. Note the bunting draping the Venango County Courthouse and the Ferris wheel in the background. The city organizes several parades and celebrations each year for national holidays and local festivals, such as Applefest, Franklin on Ice, and Rock in River. (Courtesy of Peter Solle.)

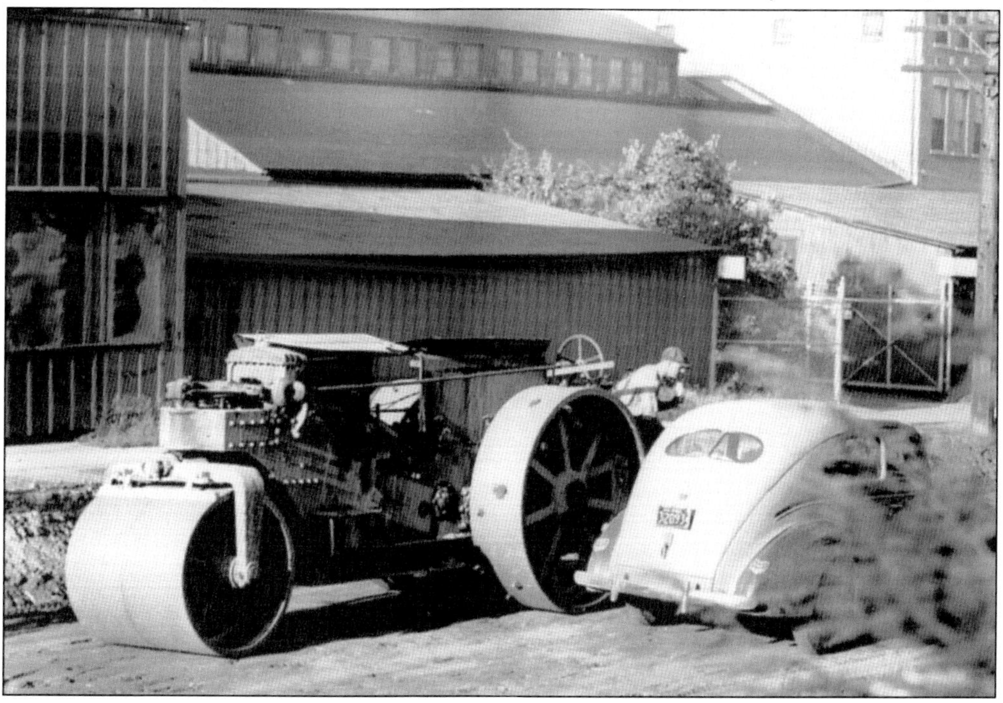

A steamroller operator pauses to speak to a passing driver on the Joy Manufacturing Company grounds in the 1940s. There were many innovations happening in the world during these times that helped change what once was primitive to a more modern practice, including transistors, Velcro, and the microwave oven. Much was changing in Franklin as well. (Courtesy of Peter Solle.)

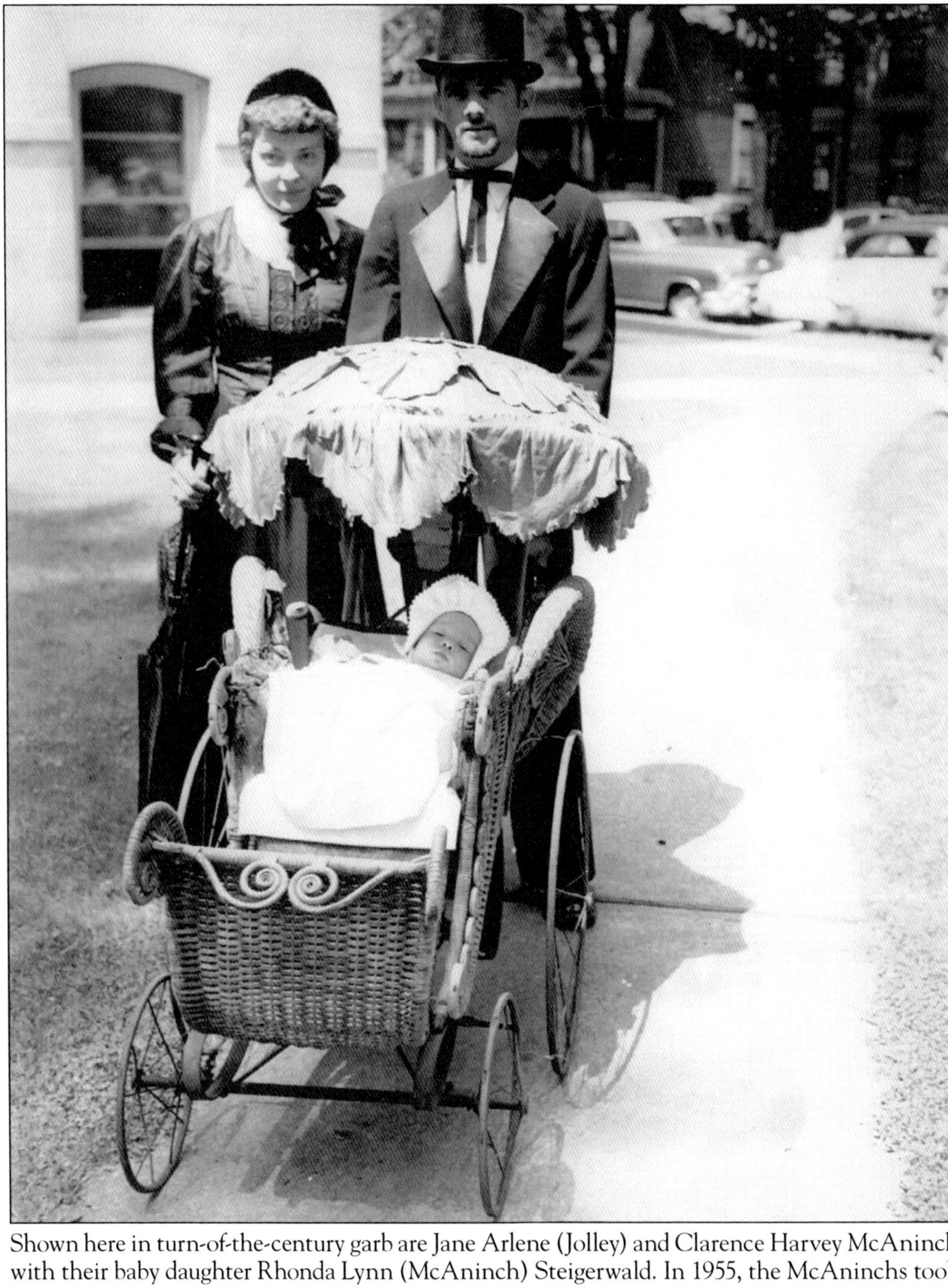

Shown here in turn-of-the-century garb are Jane Arlene (Jolley) and Clarence Harvey McAninch with their baby daughter Rhonda Lynn (McAninch) Steigerwald. In 1955, the McAninchs took first place in the "Fashions of Yesteryear" contest during the Venango County sesquicentennial celebration held in the downtown parks in Franklin. The first floor of the Venango County Courthouse can be seen in the background. This photograph was taken in the city's South Park. Near the center of the park stands the Civil War monument, constructed in September 1866 and dedicated to the inhabitants of Venango County. At over 150 years old, the engraved names of the 400 fallen soldiers from Venango County are barely legible. The first Civil War reunion for the county was held in Franklin on October 12, 1876. (Courtesy of Rhonda Steigerwald.)

Three

Landscapes

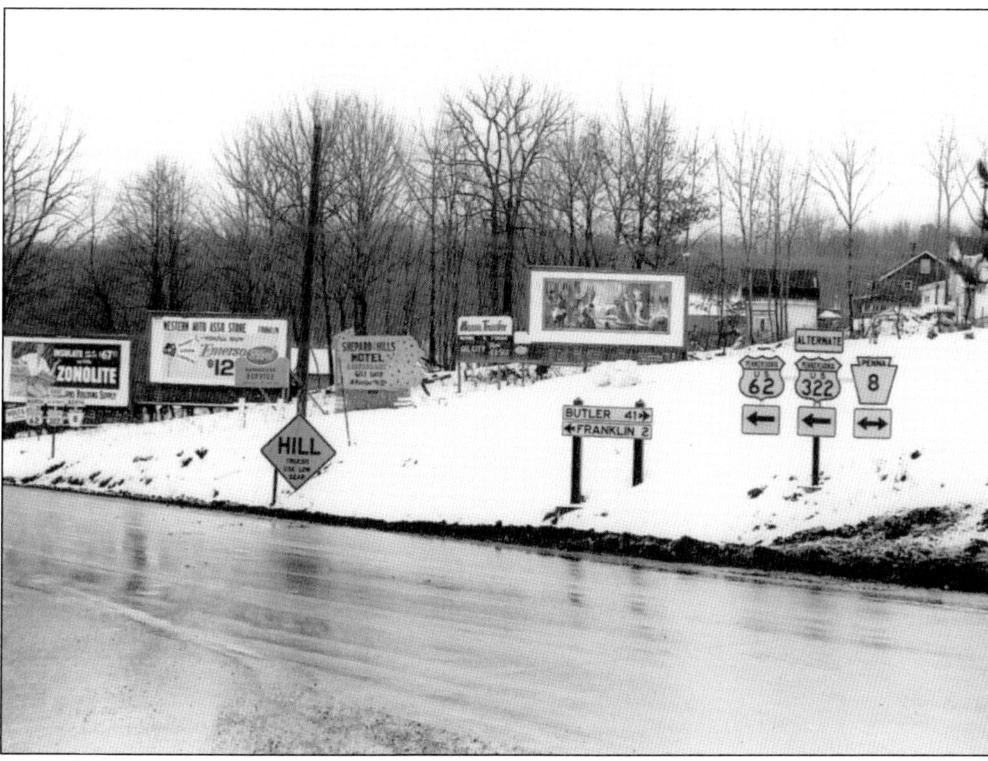

Located three-quarters of the way up Fifteenth Street Hill is the intersection of PA Routes 8 and 62. Using Route 8 South, one can get to Pittsburgh by way of Butler, while Route 8 North takes one into Franklin and communities farther north. The billboards in the background no longer exist, and the hill is now equipped with a runaway truck ramp for tractor trailers. (Courtesy of Peter Solle.)

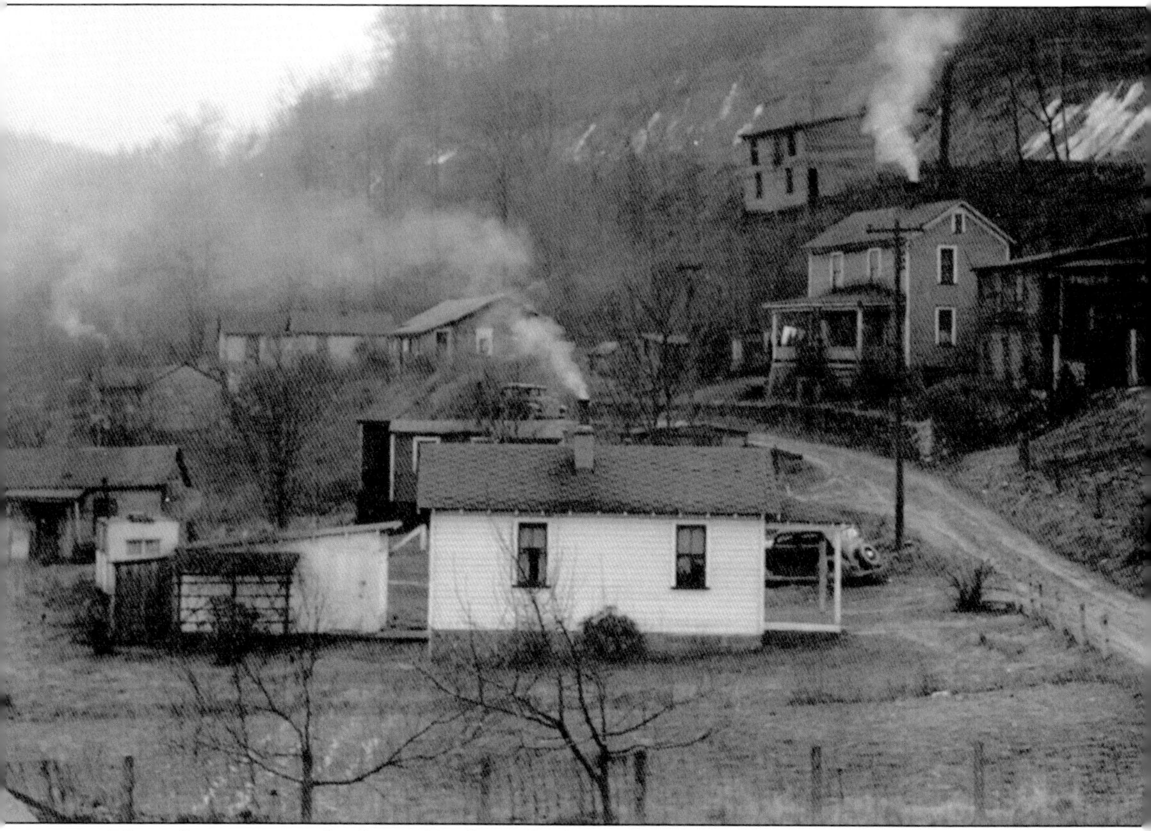

These houses sit at the foot of Bully Hill off Third Street at the eastern end of the city. With Joy Manufacturing dominating this area of town, many employees lived nearby. Bully Hill, now covered in trees, was once covered in derricks during the Oil Boom of the late 1800s. Col. Edwin Drake struck oil in nearby Titusville in 1859, a first for the country. A second well was drilled in the region months after Drake's and was located at the bottom of High Street (now Twelfth Street) where it meets with Otter Street in Franklin. James Evans was a blacksmith in Franklin. He and his sons decided to drill down an old water well. Upon reaching a depth of 70 feet, oil was struck near the shoreline along French Creek in November 1859. Evans Well was situated on the southern tier of the Franklin Heavy Crude District. (Courtesy of Peter Solle.)

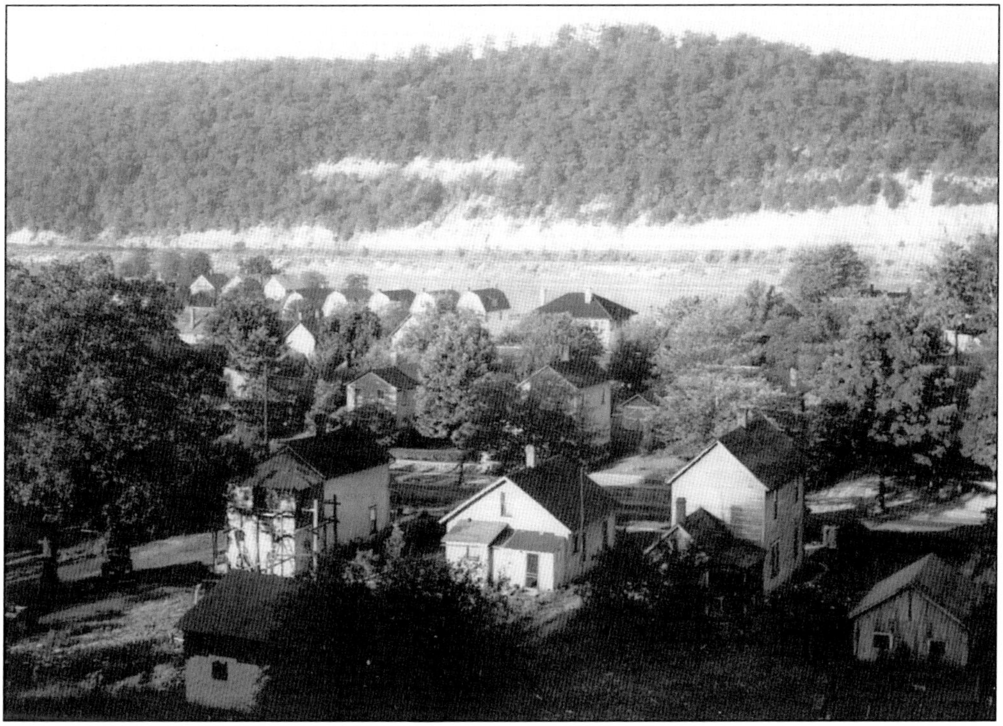

Here is a summer view from Gurney Hill in the area of Second Street, looking toward the Allegheny River. This area has been home to Joy Mining and Manufacturing for 90 years. The author's father, Charles Benton, worked for the company for six years as a tow motor operator until the plant underwent a huge layoff in 1982. (Courtesy of Peter Solle.)

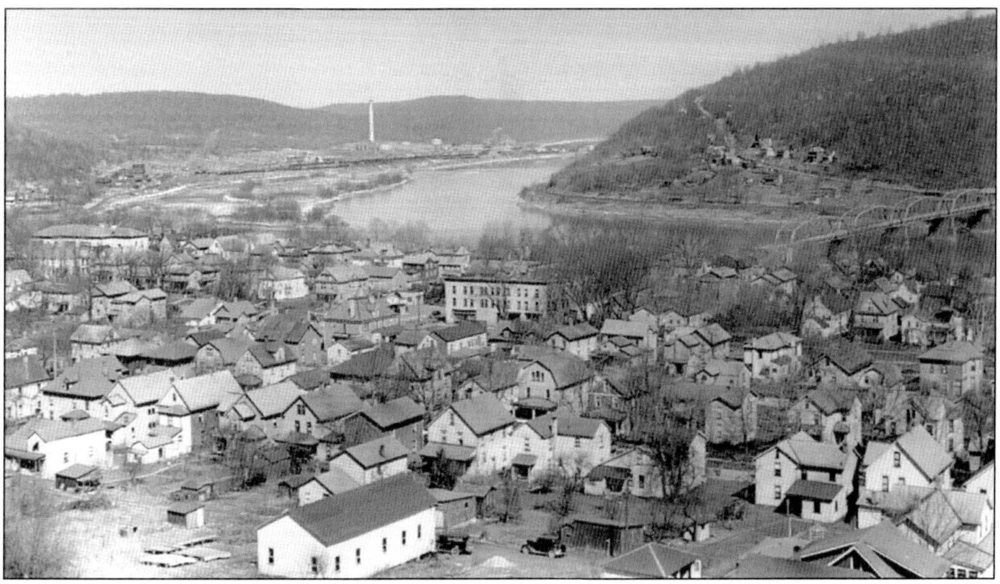

Taken from the hillside, this view shows the lower end of town. The large building at center is Schiffer Brothers Super Market, located on the corner of Eighth and Liberty Streets, with the Eighth Street Bridge extending over the Allegheny River in the background. Near the horizon is a smokestack from the Eclipse Refinery on PA Route 8. (Courtesy of Peter Solle.)

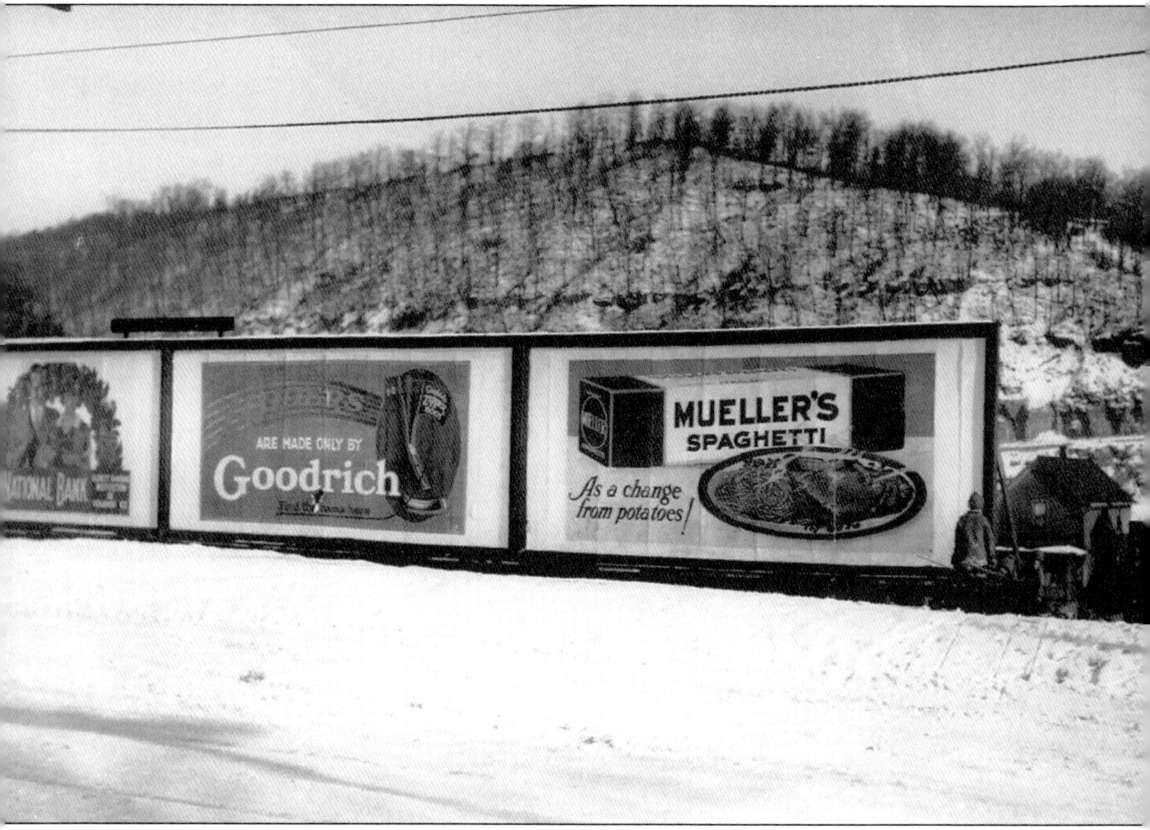

Billboards once stood at the lower end of town near the Joy Manufacturing Company. This particular sign advertises the Lamberton National Bank, B.F. Goodrich zipper galoshes, and Mueller's spaghetti. The Hookless Fastener Company held the rights to Gideon Sundback's invention of the "modern zipper" in Meadville, Pennsylvania, in 1913. The Lamberton National Bank stood on the corner of Thirteenth and Liberty Streets starting in 1899. Prior to its residency, an earlier building at that location burned in 1866. Next, a book and stationery store owned by Rally and Griffin opened there in 1871. The bank was later razed and replaced by the current structure in the early 1970s. The C.F. Mueller Company was formed in 1867 in Jersey City, New Jersey. At the time of its inception, the company built the most state-of-the-art and largest facility in the country. (Courtesy of Peter Solle.)

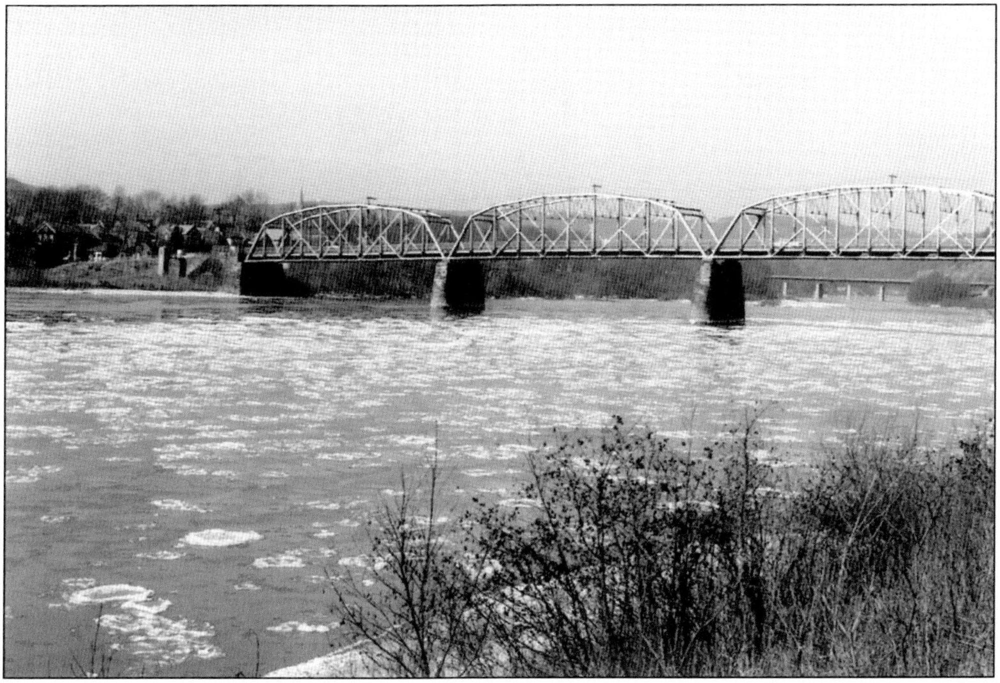

Taken from US Route 322 East, the Eighth Street Bridge (formerly known as the Valley Bridge) stands in the foreground while Washington Crossing Bridge is visible in the background. St. Patrick's Church spire can also be seen at left above the Valley Bridge. (Courtesy of Peter Solle.)

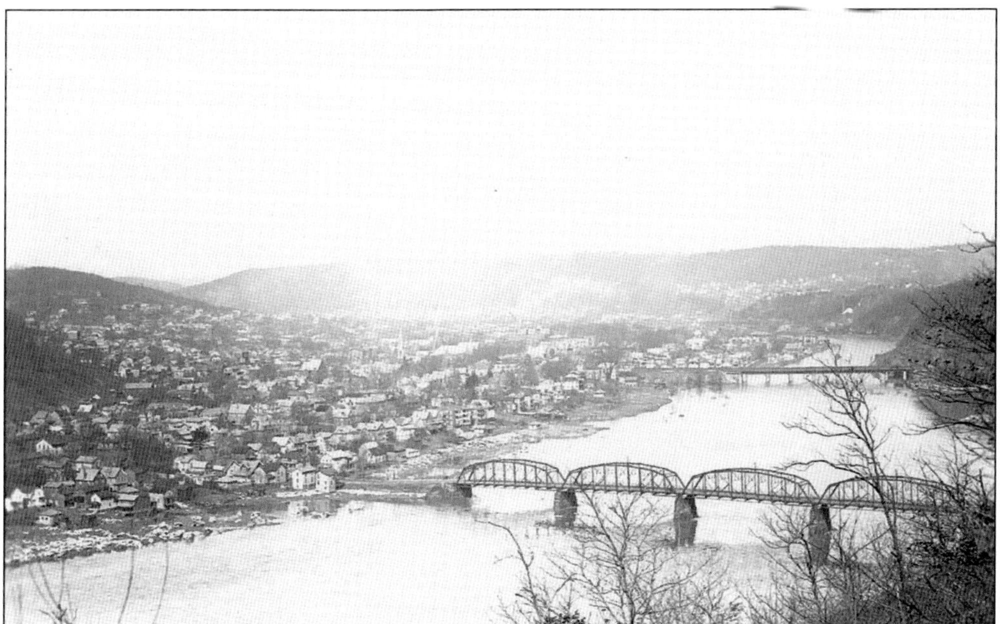

In this aerial view of Franklin, the Eighth Street Bridge is seen in the foreground while Washington Crossing Bridge and the railroad bridge stand in the background. Spring thaw is occurring, causing some flooding and ice chunks along the shoreline of the Allegheny River in the lower portion of town. Gurney Hill can be seen at left and Point Hill at right. (Courtesy of Peter Solle.)

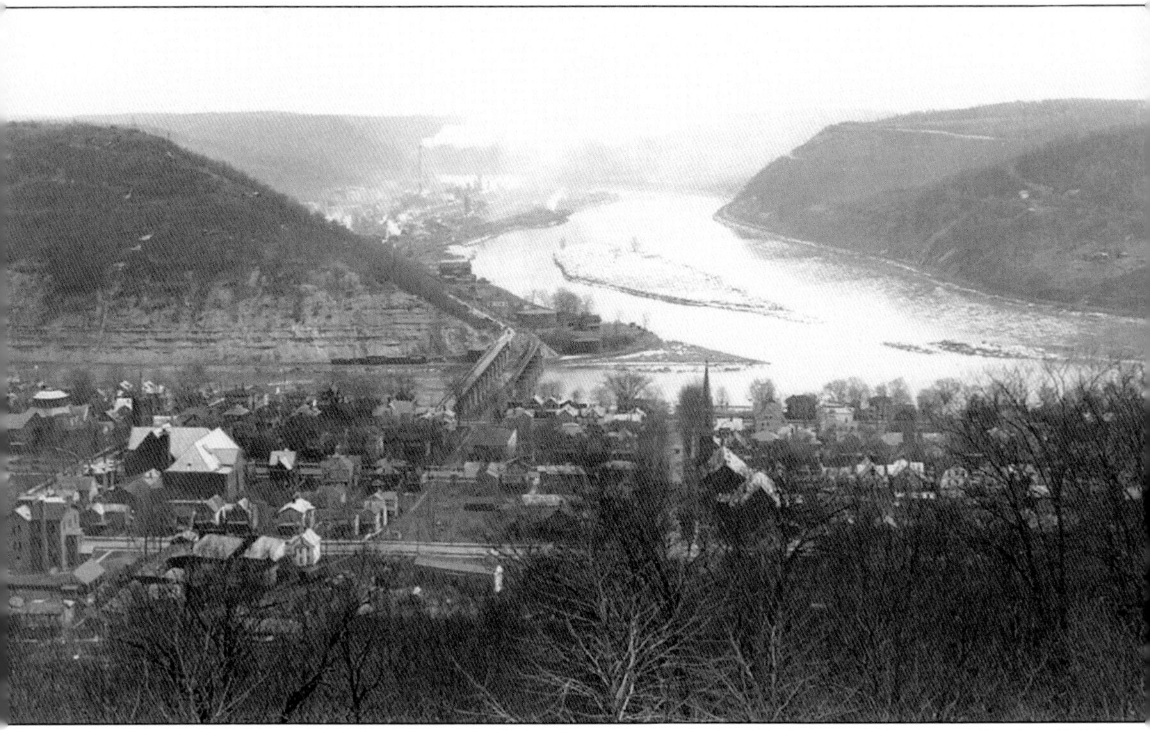

This view was taken from Gurney Hill. In the center are the Washington Crossing Bridge (left) and the railroad bridge near the confluence of French Creek and the Allegheny River. St. Patrick's Church steeple is seen just right of center, while the Eleventh Street School, First Baptist Church, and the First United Methodist Church are seen at far left. French Creek was an important connection between the Ohio River and the Great Lakes in the 1700s. The French constructed Fort Le Boeuf and Fort Presque Isle to dominate the land from French Creek's headwaters to Lake Erie. They called the waterway Cattle River due to the number of buffalo in the area, which reminded them of the cattle in France. Gen. George Washington opted to call the stream French Creek, as it originates near French Creek, New York, and ends in Franklin, a total distance of approximately 117 miles. (Courtesy of Peter Solle.)

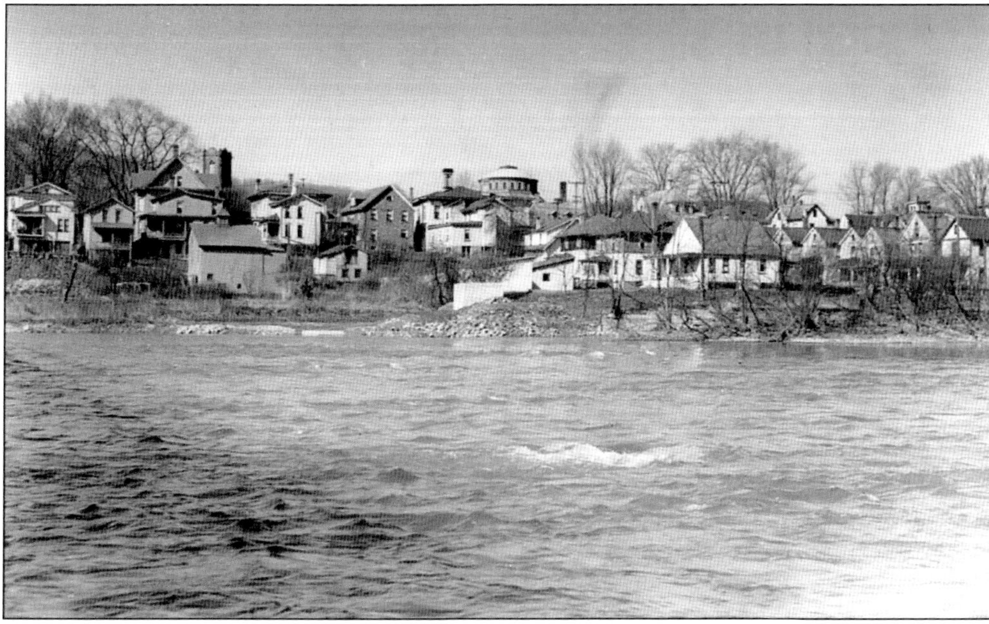

This view is looking across French Creek at Franklin. At center in this photograph is the copper dome of the First United Methodist Church. The original building was constructed in the 1100 block of Buffalo Street in 1833. Dedication for the building at its current location of 1100 Liberty Street was held on April 25, 1869. The current building's cornerstone was laid on July 7, 1914. (Courtesy of Peter Solle.)

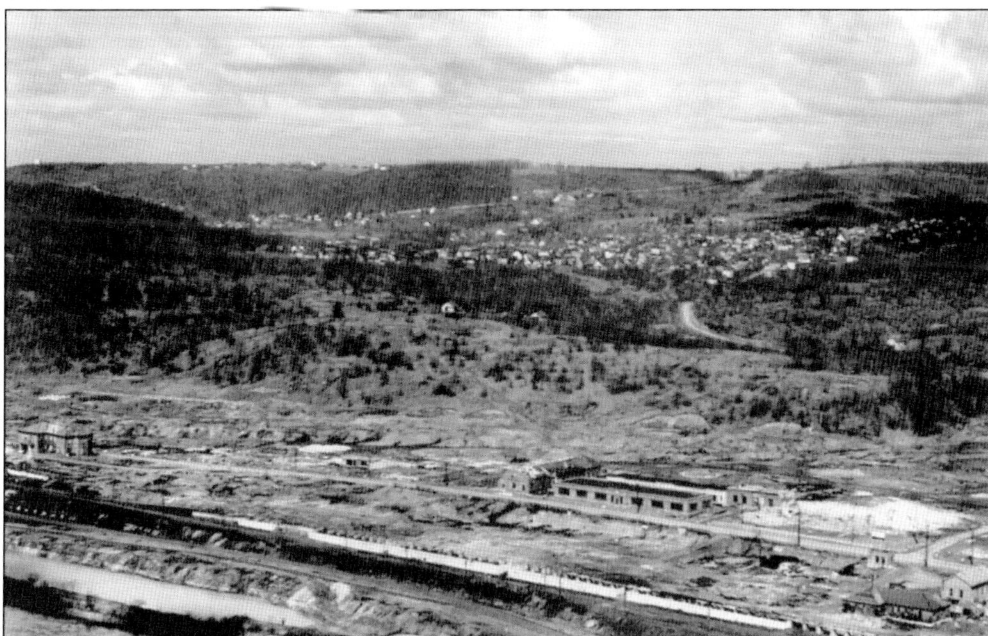

This aerial view shows the Eclipse Refinery with the village of Rocky Grove lying in the valley in the background. Established in 1872, the refinery was reportedly one of the largest refineries in the world in its time. Dr. H.W.C. Tweddle built the refinery on an eight-acre piece of land along the Allegheny River in Sugarcreek Borough. (Courtesy of Peter Solle.)

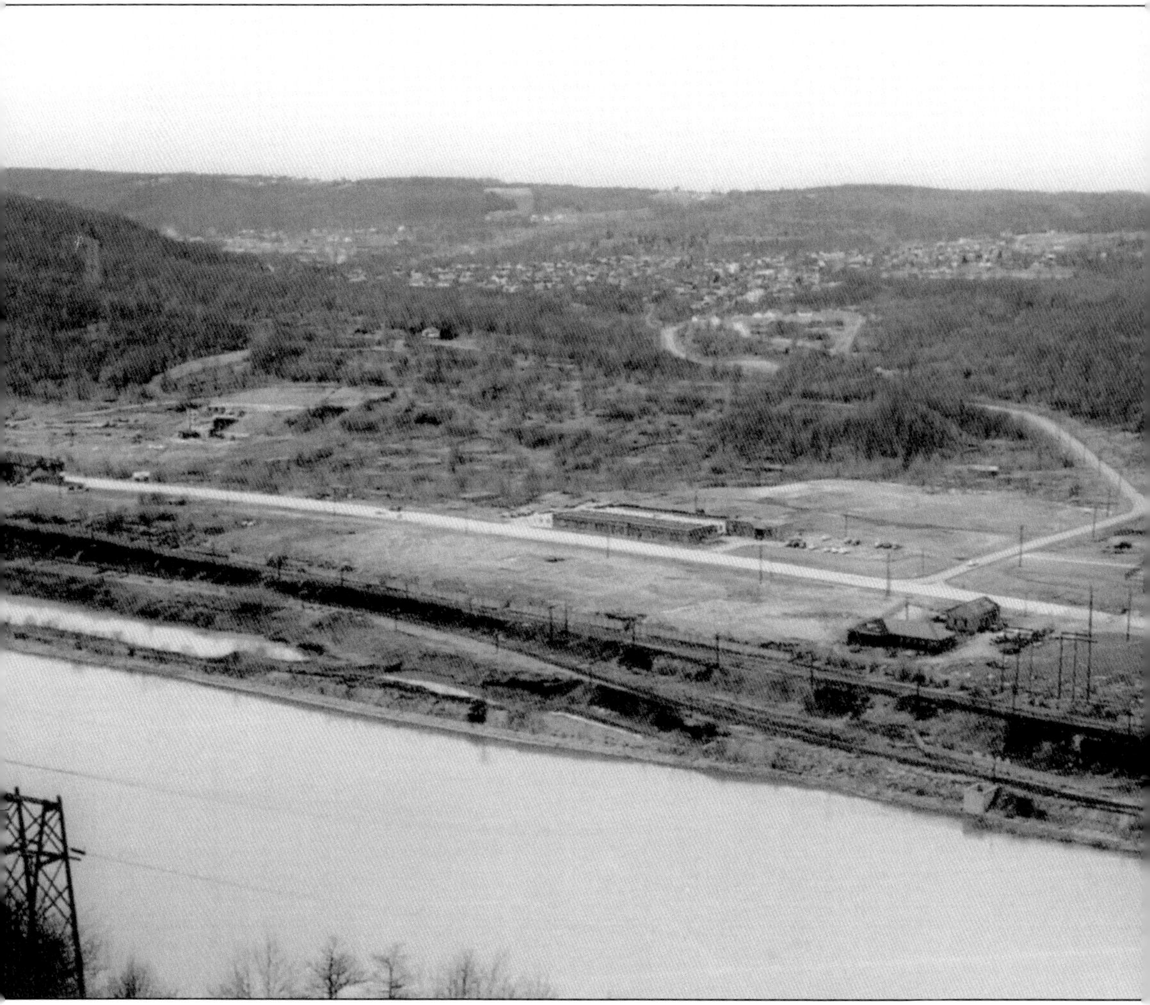

In this view of the intersection of PA Route 8 and Front Street, the village of Rocky Grove is seen in the distance. William Parker arrived in the area in 1818 and purchased land in Rocky Grove, where he built his log cabin. The first settlers of the Rocky Grove area were the Lamberton, McCalmont, and Parker families. The Franklin Hospital was built on Prospect Avenue in Rocky Grove, just across the city line in Sugarcreek Borough. The project's original plans were dated 1899, but a site could not be agreed upon, which prolonged the decision. The land in Prospect Park chosen for the site of the hospital was offered by Joseph Sibley and Gen. Charles Miller. The committee preferred this location for its higher elevation and the pure fresh air that came with it. The first hospital was built in 1902. (Courtesy of Peter Solle.)

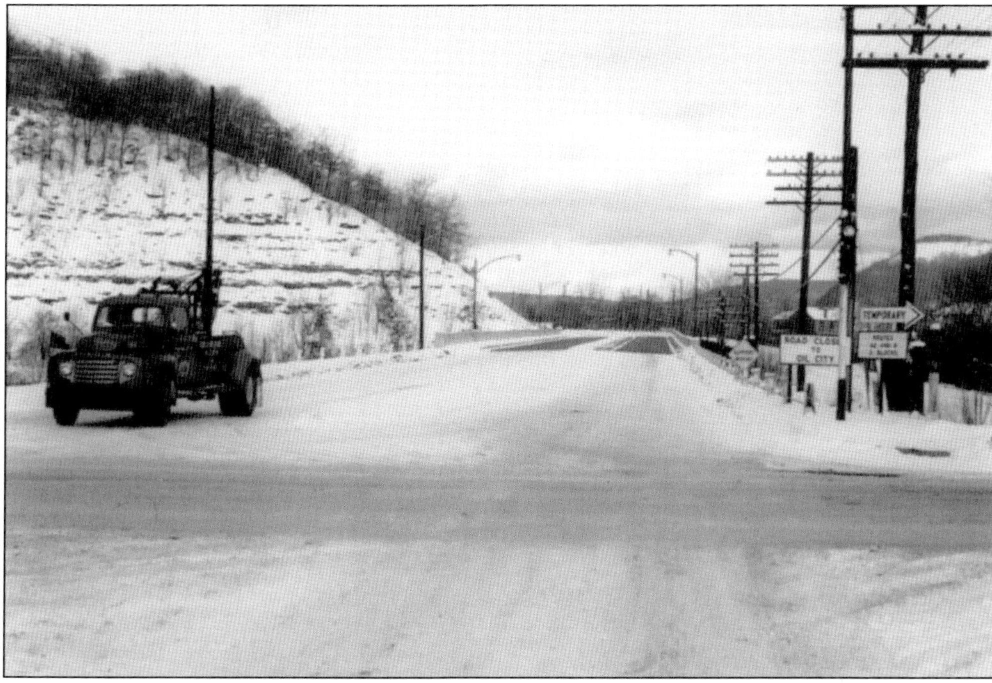

Here is an early photograph of Washington Crossing Bridge, spanning the confluence of the Allegheny River and French Creek. Its name honors the voyage of George Washington on December 4, 1753. Then known as Venango, Franklin was incorporated in 1795. This photograph is looking north toward Oil City, along PA Routes 8 and 62. Locals refer to this segment as the Four Lanes. (Courtesy of Peter Solle.)

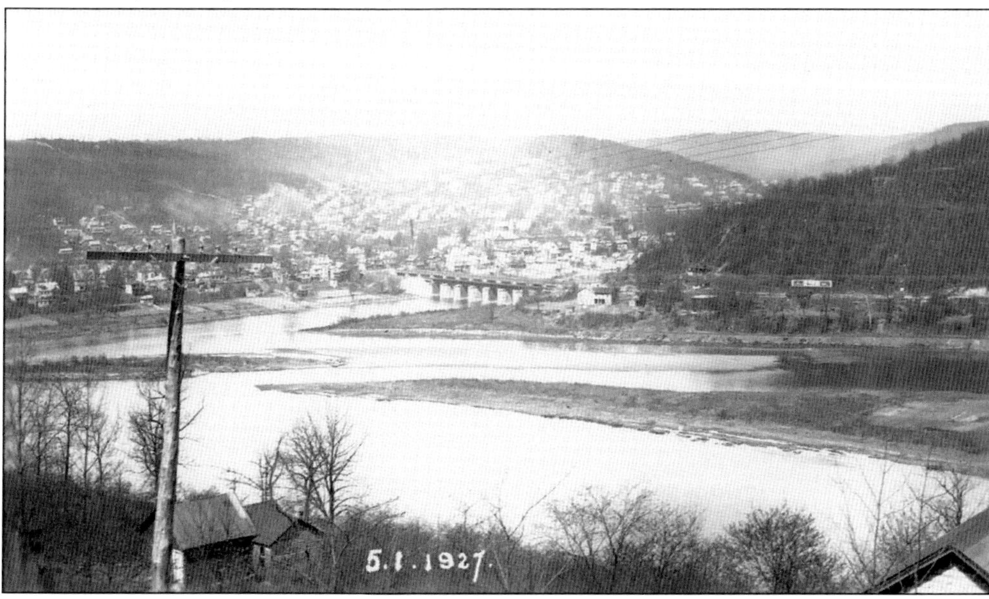

Dated May 1, 1927, this photograph shows the Washington Crossing Bridge and railroad bridge near the intersection of the Allegheny River and French Creek, with Hoge Island in the foreground and Point Hill in the background. Huge oil tanks can be seen on the far shore of the Allegheny River. The Eclipse Refinery was located just upriver from this intersection. (Courtesy of Peter Solle.)

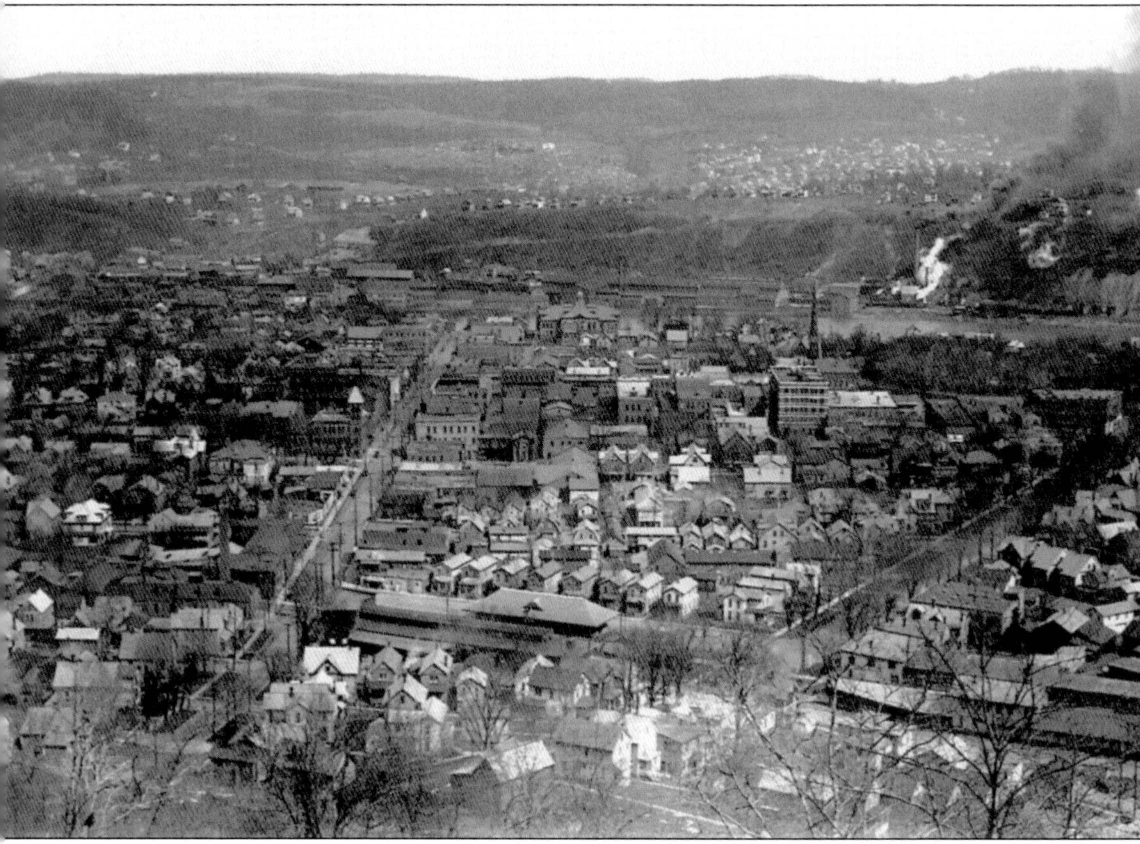

This photograph was taken from Gurney Hill in the Second Ward area of the city. The dividing streets shown are Thirteenth Street (left) and Twelfth Street. Several Franklin landmarks can be seen in this view, including, from left to right, city hall, the Exchange Hotel, the Lake Shore Railroad station, the Franklin High School, and the spire of the First Presbyterian Church. The Lake Shore & Michigan Southern Railway was a large and important part of the Water Level Route of the New York Central Railroad. From Buffalo, New York, to Chicago, Illinois, the railway mainly traveled along the southern shore of Lake Erie in the states of Ohio, Pennsylvania, and New York and across the northern part of Indiana. Now defunct, its tracks are still in use by Amtrak. In 1998, ownership of the tracks was split between Norfolk Southern (in the east) and CSX (in the west) at Cleveland, Ohio. (Courtesy of Peter Solle.)

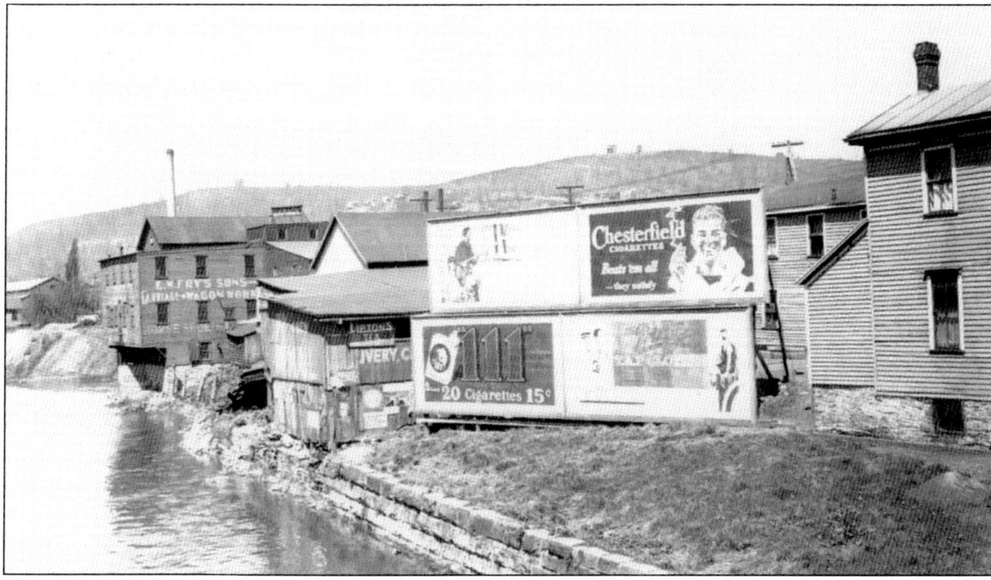

Sitting just behind the Keystone Hotel, billboards display various advertisements for cigarettes along French Creek, near the intersection of North Thirteenth and Howard Streets. E.W. Fry's Sons Carriage and Wagon Working is seen in the background. Howard Street was home to the Chicago Pneumatic Tool Company for many years. Its refinery buildings are now home to Franklin Bronze and Franklin Steel. (Courtesy of Peter Solle.)

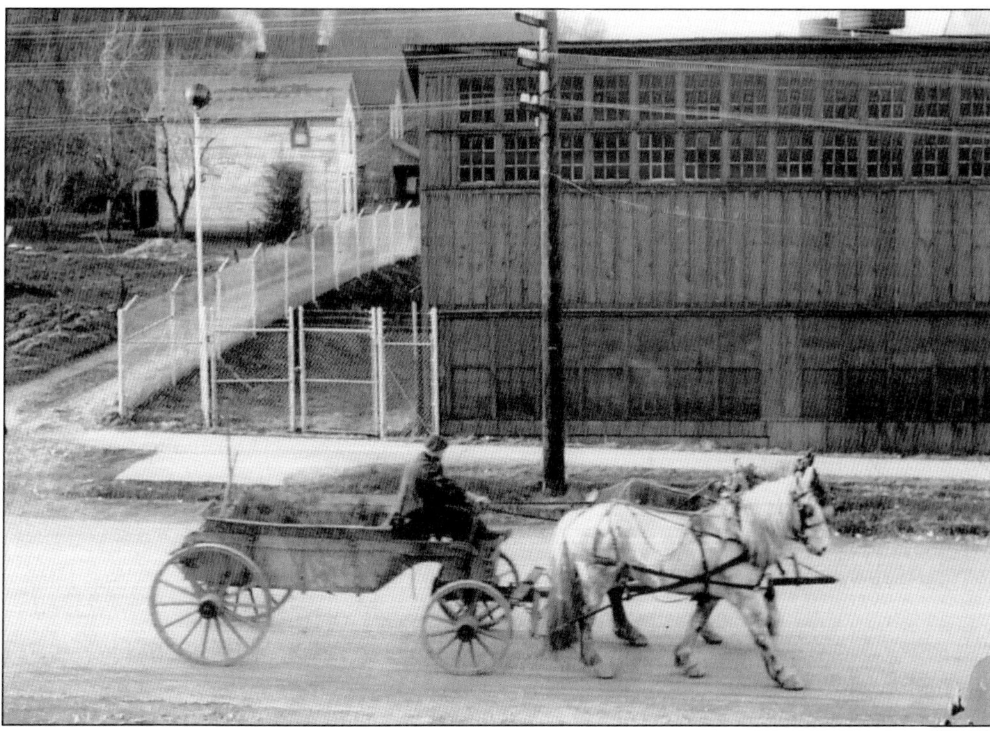

Mr. Bean drives his horses and wagon near Third Street in the lower First Ward. He and his horses (one light and one dark) were well known for many decades by those who lived in this area and by those who worked for the Joy Manufacturing Company. (Courtesy of Peter Solle.)

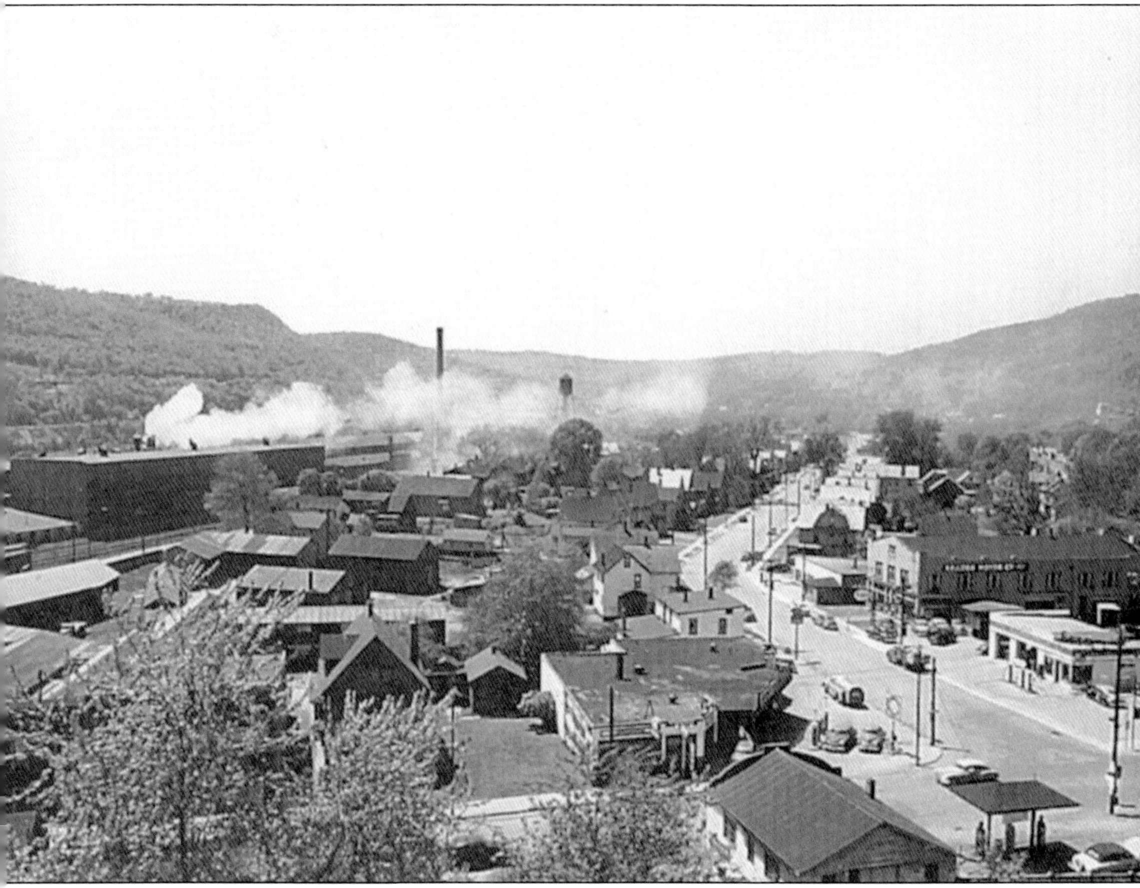

This view of Coefield's Corners from Bleakley Hill shows Grant Street heading west through the Third Ward section of the city. On the left side are the Chicago Pneumatic Tool Company and Franklin Steel; both factories employed the majority of the men of the Third Ward. In the foreground is Franklin Service and Supply, a full-service gas station and tire shop. The Third Ward was a melting pot of nationalities, including German, Italian, Irish, African, Native American, Dutch, and Polish. Everyone knew all the neighbors in their block, old and young alike. A handful of these families owned and operated neighborhood stores. Dick's Dairy was located in the 200 block of Grant Street and was the last to close in this section of town. Another was Herdzik's, located on the corner of Missouri and Grant Streets. Joe Herdzik and his elderly father owned it. Both lived in an apartment above the store. (Courtesy of Penny Haylett-Minnick.)

Four

FRANKLIN'S RAILROADS

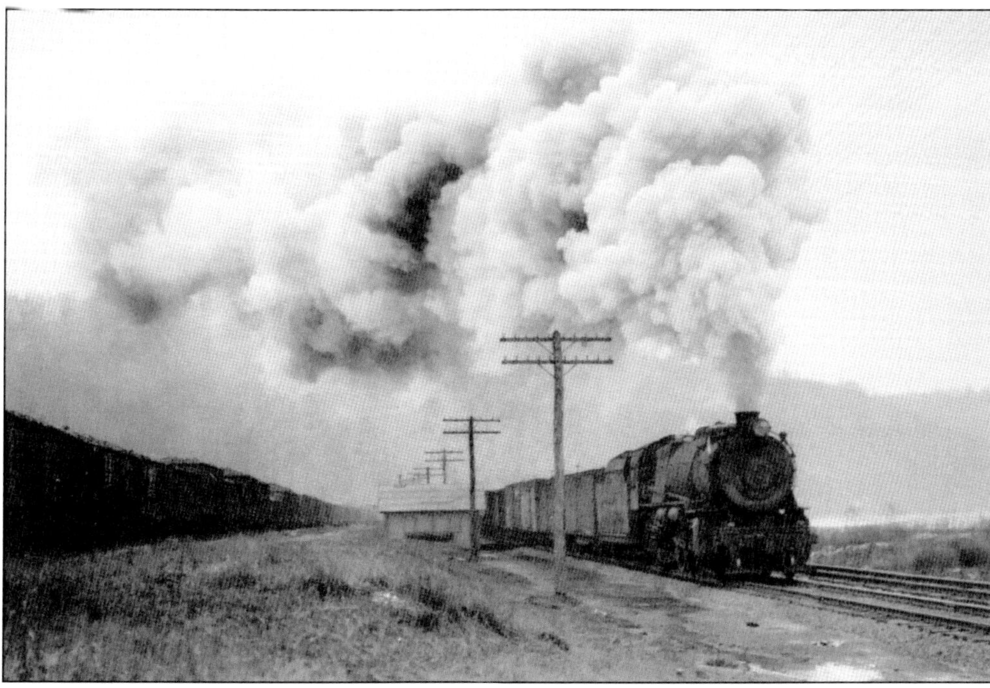

With the discovery of oil in Titusville in 1859, shippers used rivers to transport hundreds of barrels to larger cities, such as Pittsburgh and Cleveland. Because weather had a large influence on the utility of the waterways, the push for laying rail lines was constant. The first line was completed in April 1861 and connected Meadville to Utica. (Courtesy of Peter Solle.)

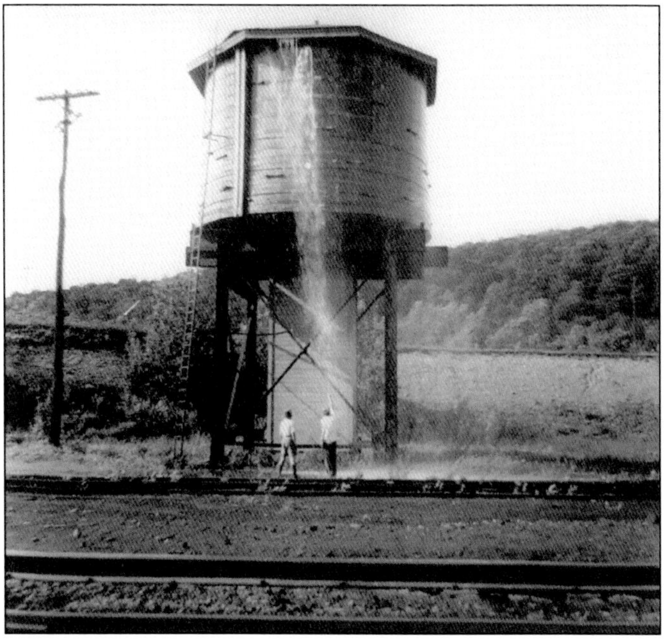

Railroad workers take a break on a hot summer day to cool off, releasing some water from a tank. Several railroads passed through the city of Franklin, including the New York Central, the Erie, the Pennsylvania, the Franklin & Clearfield, the Pennsylvania Southern, the Lake Shore, the Jamestown & Franklin, and the New York, Philadelphia & Chicago, just to name a few. (Courtesy of Peter Solle.)

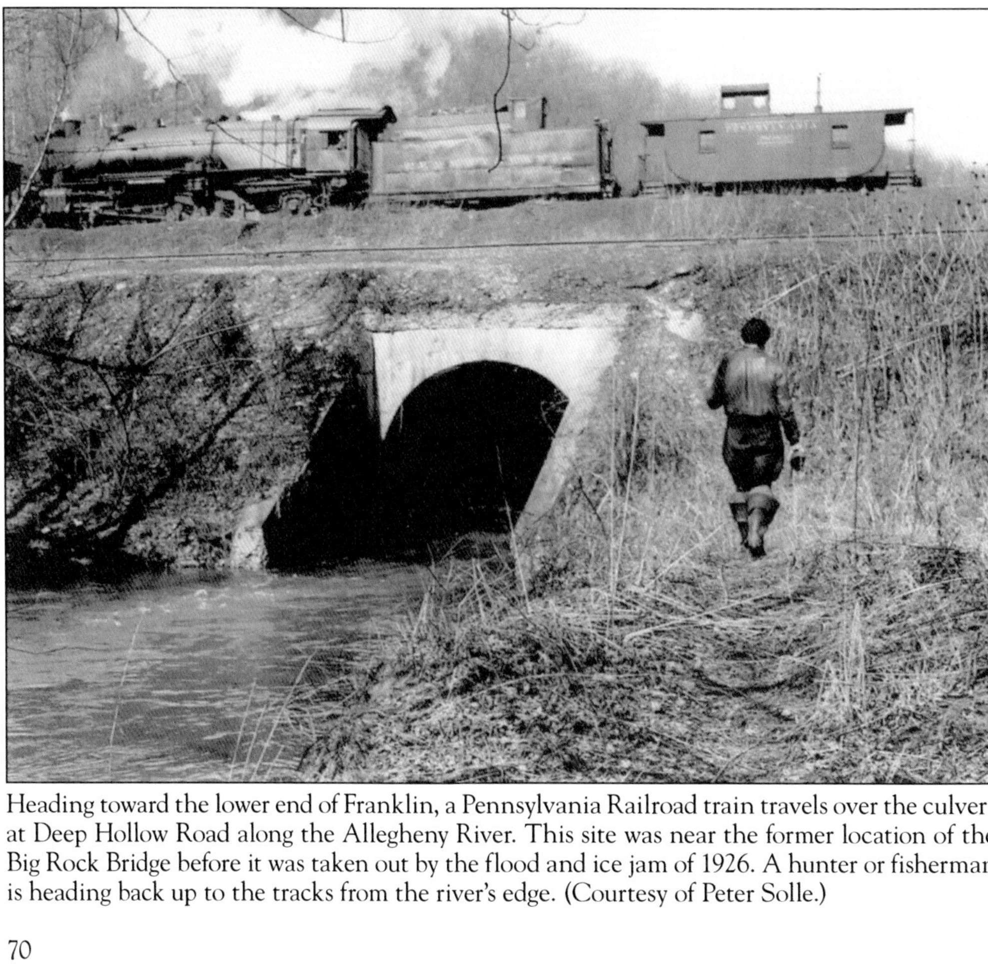

Heading toward the lower end of Franklin, a Pennsylvania Railroad train travels over the culvert at Deep Hollow Road along the Allegheny River. This site was near the former location of the Big Rock Bridge before it was taken out by the flood and ice jam of 1926. A hunter or fisherman is heading back up to the tracks from the river's edge. (Courtesy of Peter Solle.)

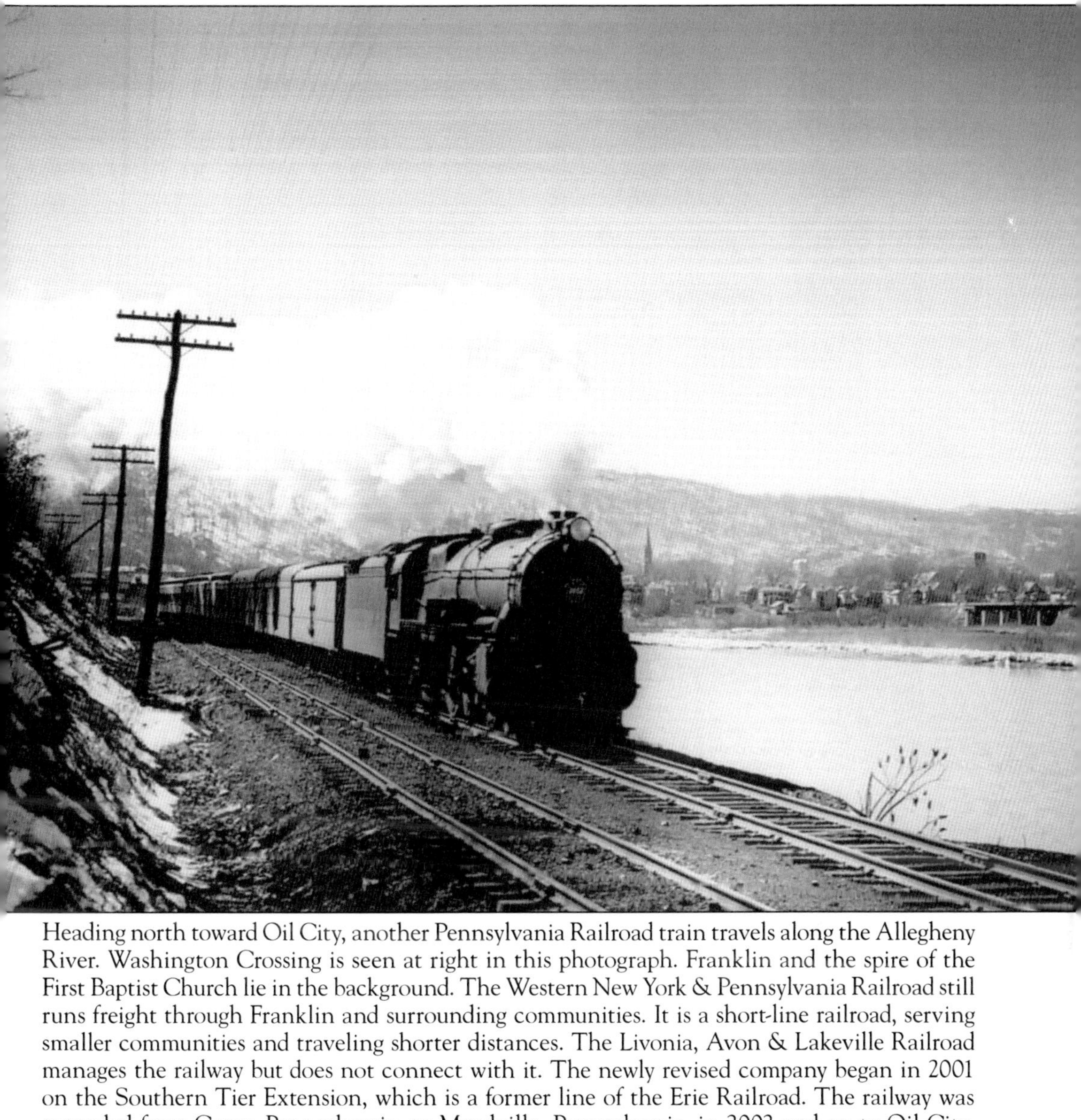

Heading north toward Oil City, another Pennsylvania Railroad train travels along the Allegheny River. Washington Crossing is seen at right in this photograph. Franklin and the spire of the First Baptist Church lie in the background. The Western New York & Pennsylvania Railroad still runs freight through Franklin and surrounding communities. It is a short-line railroad, serving smaller communities and traveling shorter distances. The Livonia, Avon & Lakeville Railroad manages the railway but does not connect with it. The newly revised company began in 2001 on the Southern Tier Extension, which is a former line of the Erie Railroad. The railway was extended from Corry, Pennsylvania, to Meadville, Pennsylvania, in 2002 and on to Oil City, Pennsylvania, in 2006. The length of its tracks is 330 miles, and its headquarters is based in Falconer, New York. (Courtesy of Peter Solle.)

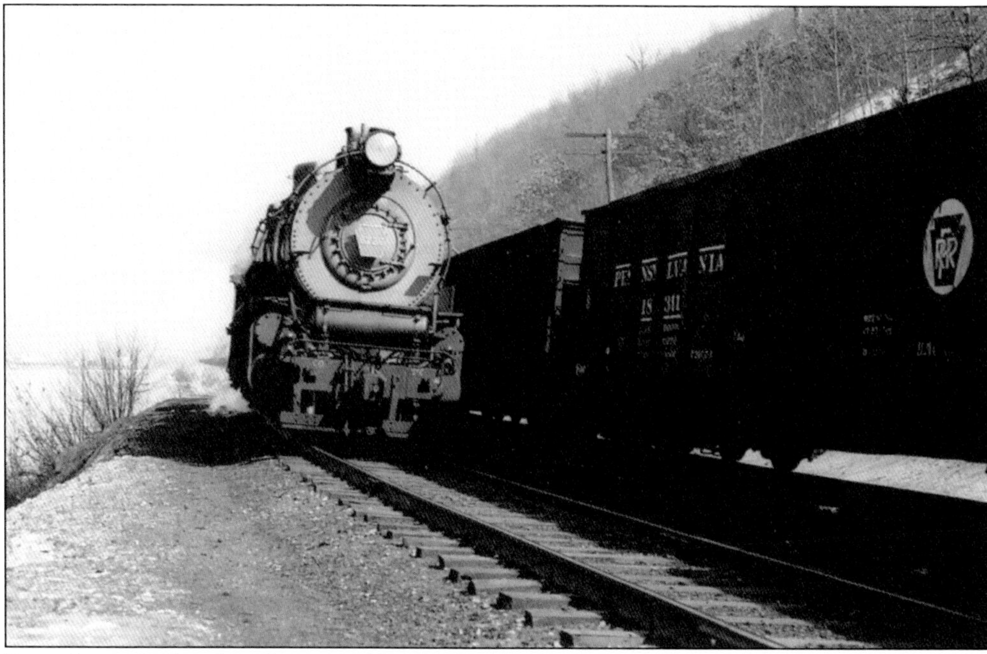

Pennsylvania Railroad freight cars and Engine No. 6726 are pictured in Franklin. On February 17, 1912, a Pennsylvania Railroad fast engine and numerous freight cars derailed near Franklin on their way to Buffalo, New York, due to a broken rail. The cars were hauling miscellaneous merchandise, including alcohol. No one was hurt. (Courtesy of Peter Solle.)

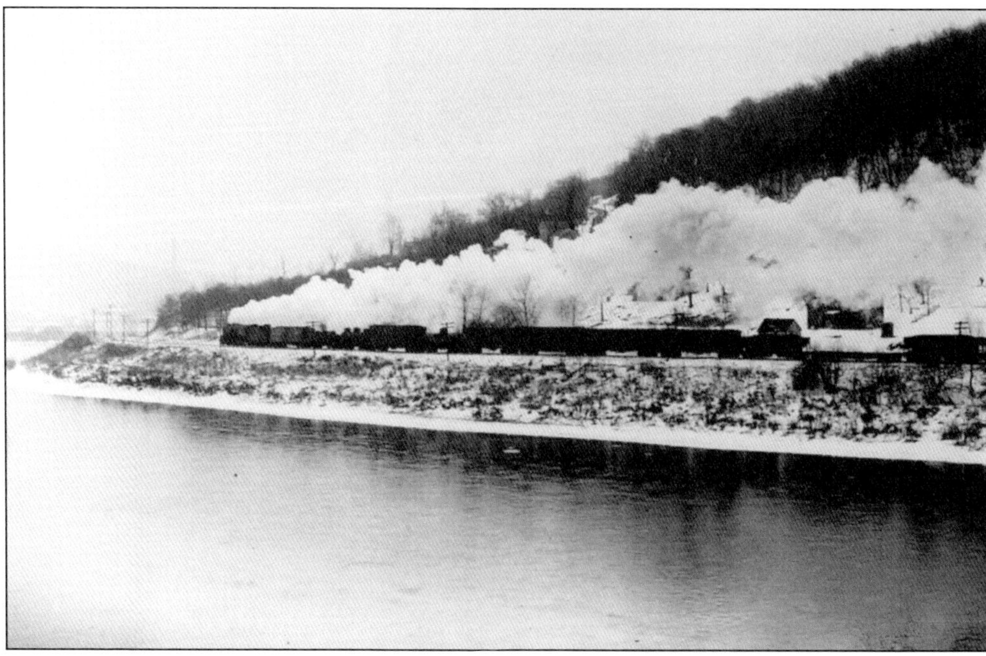

In May 1863, freight service was brought to Franklin by way of the Atlantic & Great Western Railway. The first engine crossed the county line into Venango on May 14, 1863; its name was the *Iron Horse*. The first business to benefit from this line was Martin and Epley's Drugstore, which stood at the northwest corner of Elk and South Park Streets. (Courtesy of Peter Solle.)

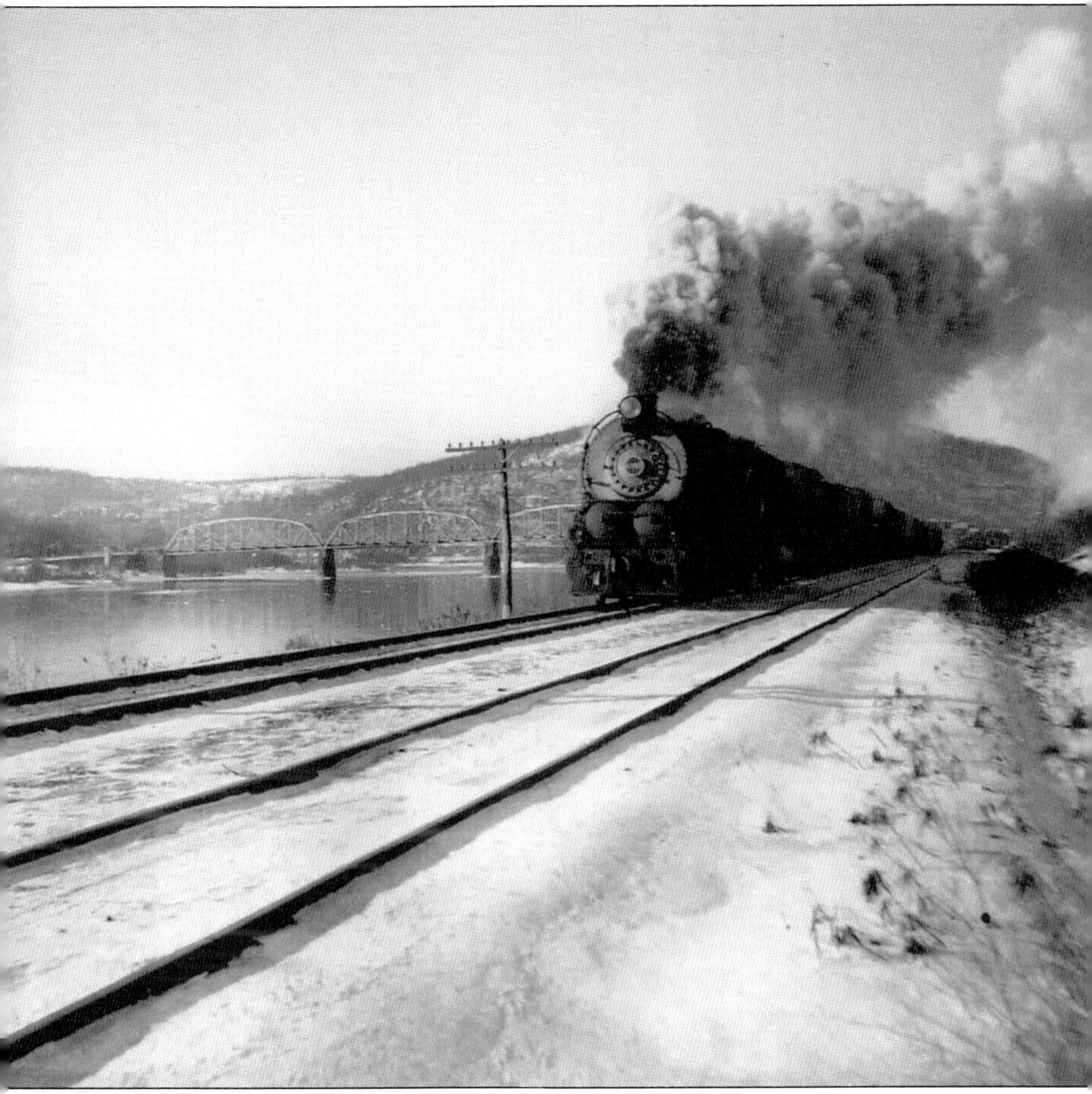

A freight train travels away from Franklin, heading toward Clarion and other points east. The Franklin & Clearfield Railroad was established in the early 1900s. The importance of the line was to conjoin the Beechcreek Railroad and the Lake Shore & Michigan Southern Railroad so that the seaboard could be accessible for shippers. The railroad company was hired on June 19, 1902, to build a 111-mile-long track from Franklin to Clearfield, Pennsylvania. On January 26, 1909, the executives of the Central Trunk Railroad, the Jackson Coal Railroad, the Franklin & Clearfield Railroad, and the Jamestown & Franklin gathered at Grand Central Station in New York City and voted to merge and create the Jamestown, Franklin & Clearfield Railroad and to appoint Gen. Charles Miller as president. In February 1909, General Miller went on an inspection ride of 60 miles with other railroad officials. (Courtesy of Peter Solle.)

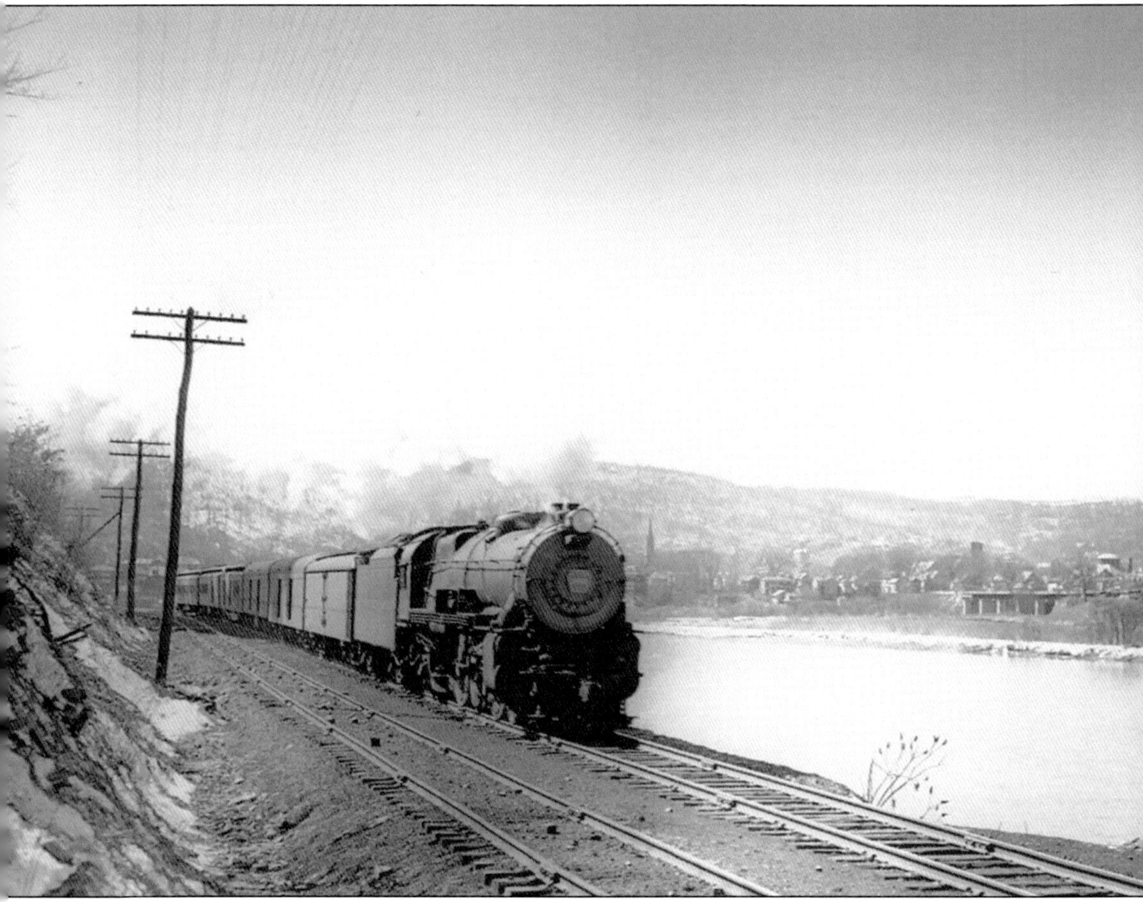

Another Pennsylvania Railroad train heads north out of Franklin. Founded in 1846, the "Pennsy" was the largest US railroad based on revenue and traffic throughout the first half of the 1900s. During its existence, the company owned part of, merged with, or acquired at least 800 other rail companies and lines. By 1926, the company maintained a total of 10,515 miles of rail. The Erie Railroad also had a depot in Franklin. The rail line originally joined New York City with Lake Erie. Merging with the defunct Atlantic & Great Western Railroad (also referred to as the New York, Pennsylvania & Ohio Railroad) in 1941, it spread west to Chicago, Illinois. The Erie Lackawanna Railroad was formed on October 17, 1960, when the Erie Railroad merged with its former contender, the Delaware, Lackawanna & Western Railroad. In 1976, Conrail took over the rail line. (Courtesy of Peter Solle.)

Five

School Days

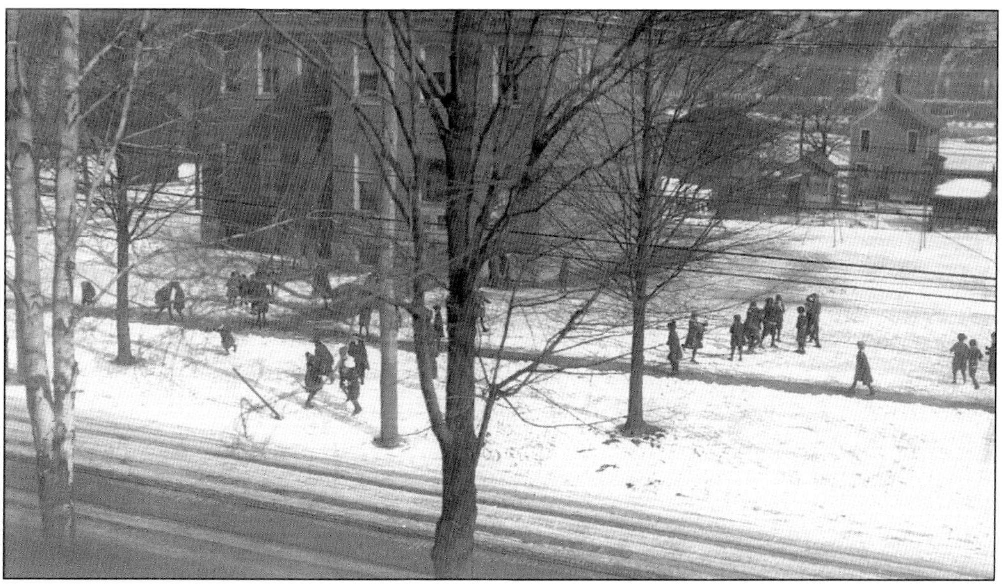

The Fourth Street School was built on the corner of Fourth and Liberty Streets in the summer of 1902. Referred to as the best school building in Franklin at the time, it had two classrooms on its first two floors and room to add up to four more without major renovations. The building still stands and is home to Studio 22 dance school. (Courtesy of Peter Solle.)

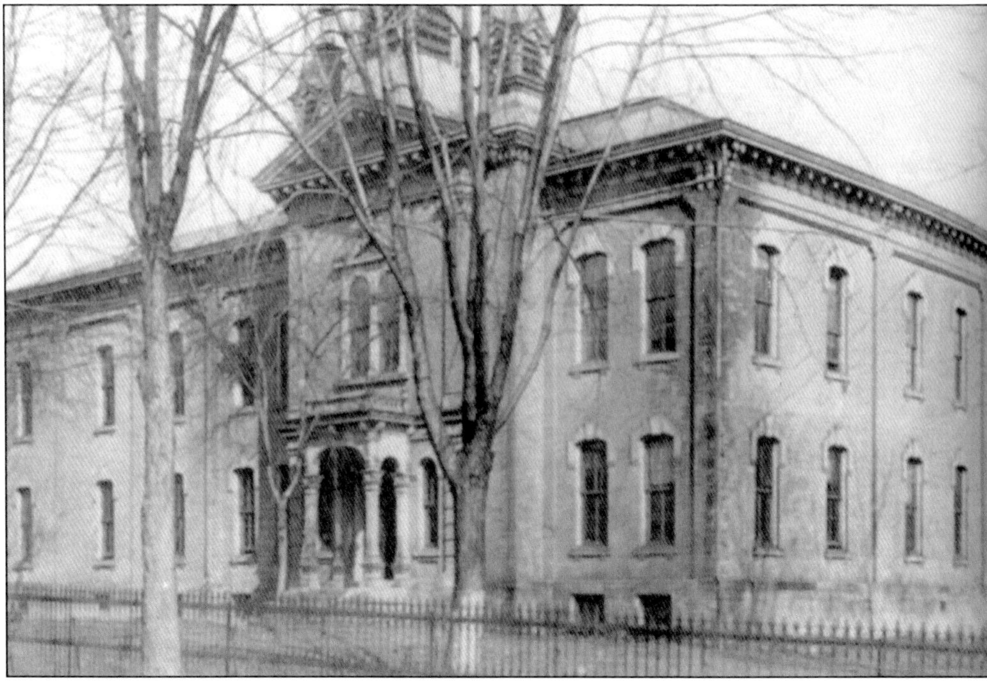

The Ninth Street School was located on the corner of Ninth and Elk Streets. It was erected in 1876 and was two stories high with four large rooms for instruction. The cost of its construction was $8,367. During renovations, graves were found on the grounds that were believed to have been affiliated with Fort Venango, which had been located on Eighth Street. (Courtesy of Penny Haylett-Minnick.)

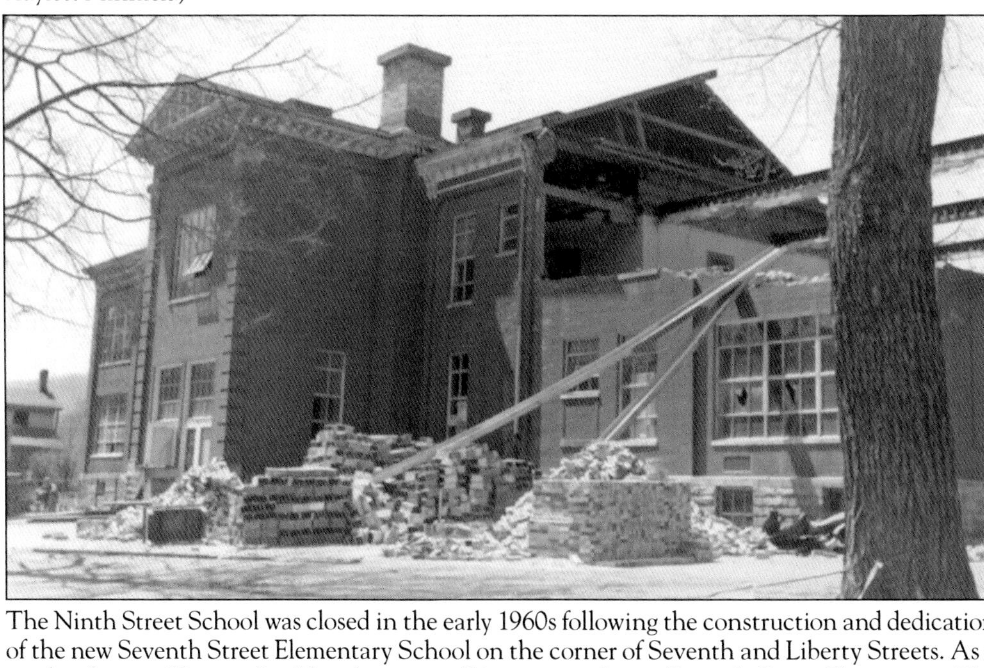

The Ninth Street School was closed in the early 1960s following the construction and dedication of the new Seventh Street Elementary School on the corner of Seventh and Liberty Streets. As a teacher for over 30 years, Jay Rhoads was a well-known teacher at Seventh Street Elementary. The author was a member of the last class he taught in 1992. (Courtesy of Penny Haylett-Minnick.)

Posing in front of his childhood home at 919 Buffalo Street, William E. Ross stands patriotically with an American flag in the early 1920s. Ross graduated from Franklin Senior High School in the spring of 1934 and gained employment with the Chicago Pneumatic Tool Company but left on good terms to enlist in the US Navy during World War II. (Courtesy of Mary Ann Benton.)

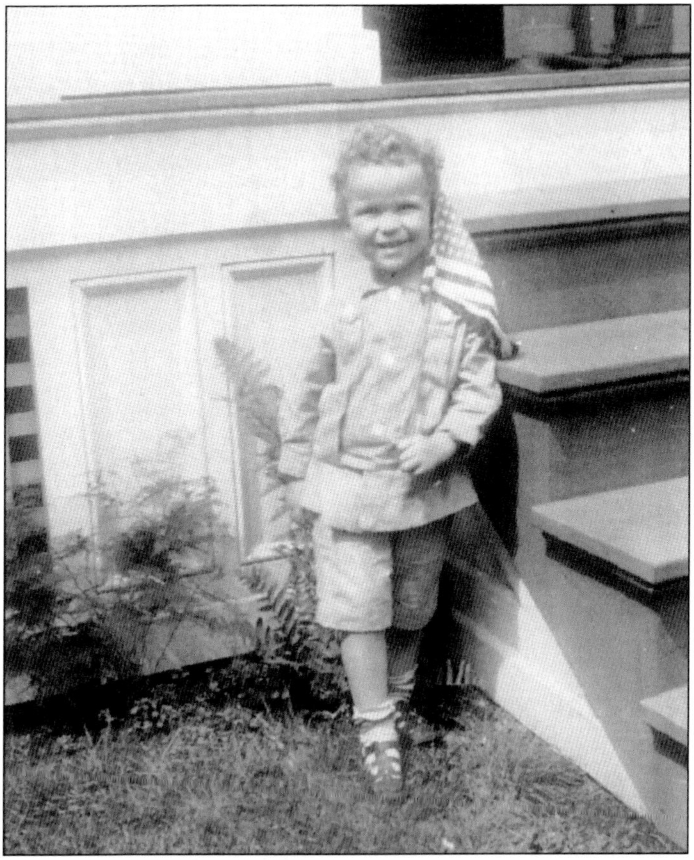

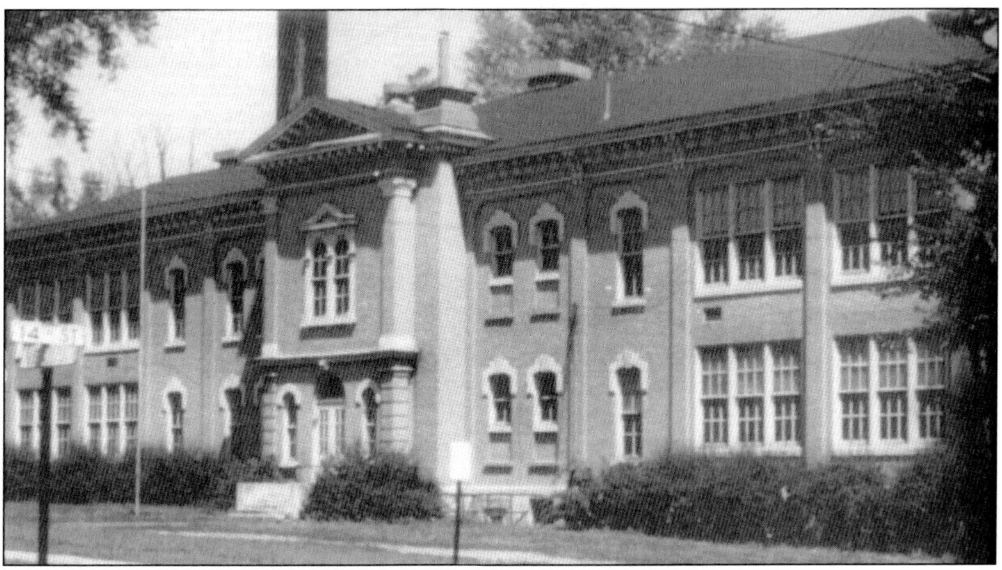

The Fourteenth Street School was located on the corner of Fourteenth and Buffalo Streets. The two-story structure was built in 1876 at a cost of $8,422. Lots purchased for the school totaled $2,400. Additions were later made to accommodate population increases. The Quality Inn now stands on this site. (Courtesy of Penny Haylett-Minnick.)

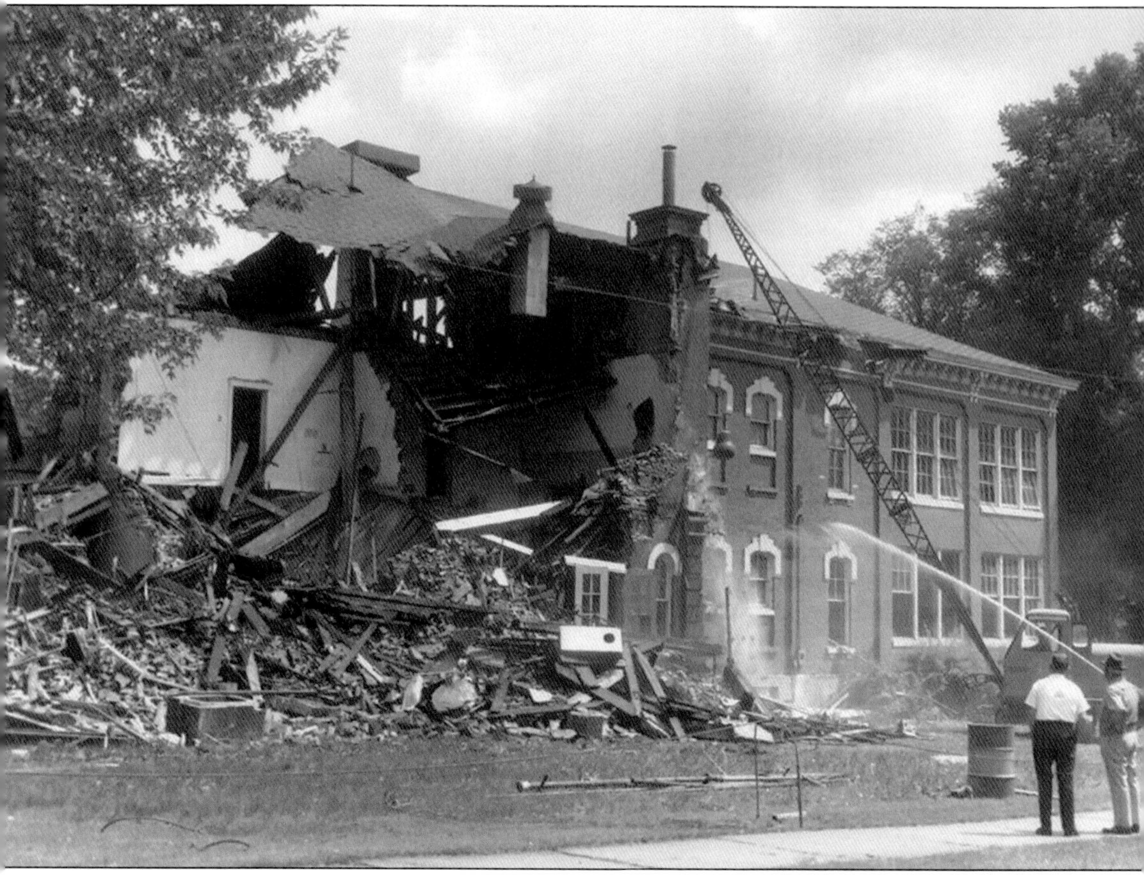

The Fourteenth Street School was closed in 1965 following the completion of renovations to the old Franklin Junior High School, converting it to Central Elementary School. In early 1964, a new high school was built at its current location on Pone Lane for a total cost of $3 million. The original high school building was razed later that same year. The Fourteenth Street School area was another city neighborhood where everyone knew each other. Many students remember looking out the windows during class and seeing Virginia Sheasley, a hometown artist, painting beautiful folk art murals on the walls and doors of her carriage house. Her artwork was saved from demolition by the Historic Franklin Preservation Association and by Rachel and James Ashbaugh. The pieces are currently on display in DeBence Alleyway off the 1200 block of Liberty Street. (Courtesy of Penny Haylett-Minnick.)

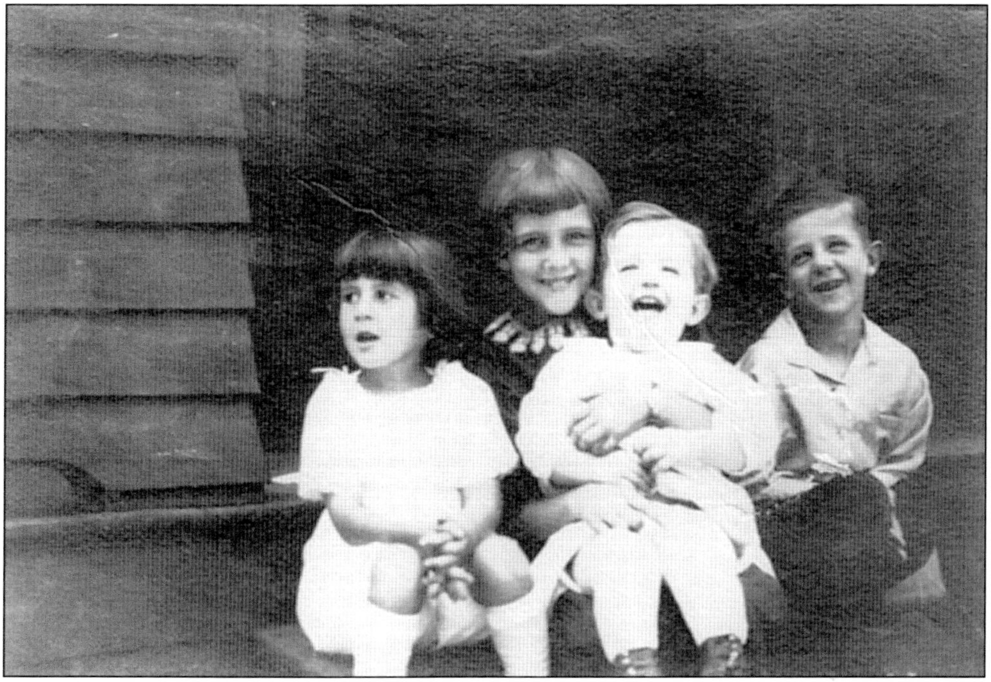

The Mosher children spend time together sitting on their front porch at 245 Pacific Street, waiting for their father, Arie Mosher, to come home from work. Mosher was a telegrapher for the Erie Railroad and worked at their station, which was located on the corner of North Thirteenth Street and Atlantic Avenue. The children are, from left to right, Dorothy, Glenna, Chuck, and Had. (Courtesy of Mary Ann Benton.)

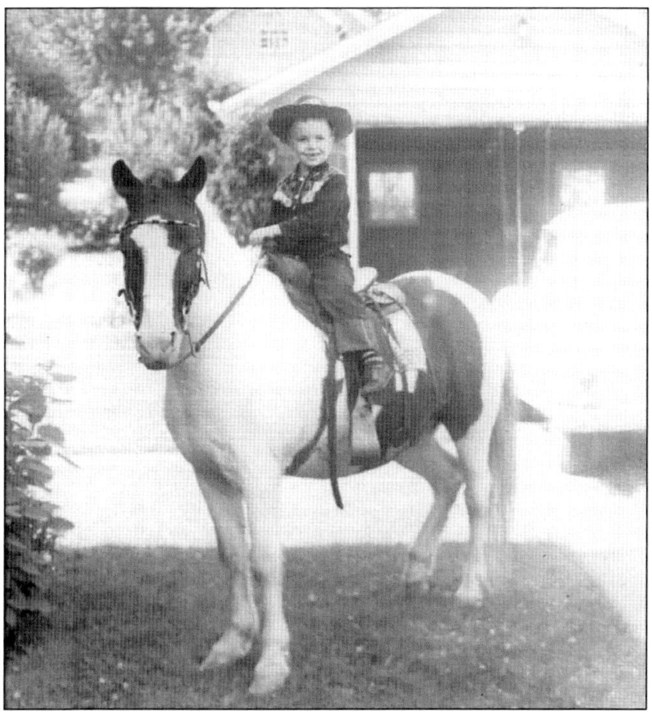

Thomas W. Ross, dressed as a cowboy, was photographed in the early 1950s. A local photographer had brought his horse into town and gone door-to-door in search of parents who would like pictures of their children posing with the animal. Positioned in the side yard of his childhood residence at 550 Grant Street, young Ross beams with happiness and delight. (Courtesy of Mary Ann Benton.)

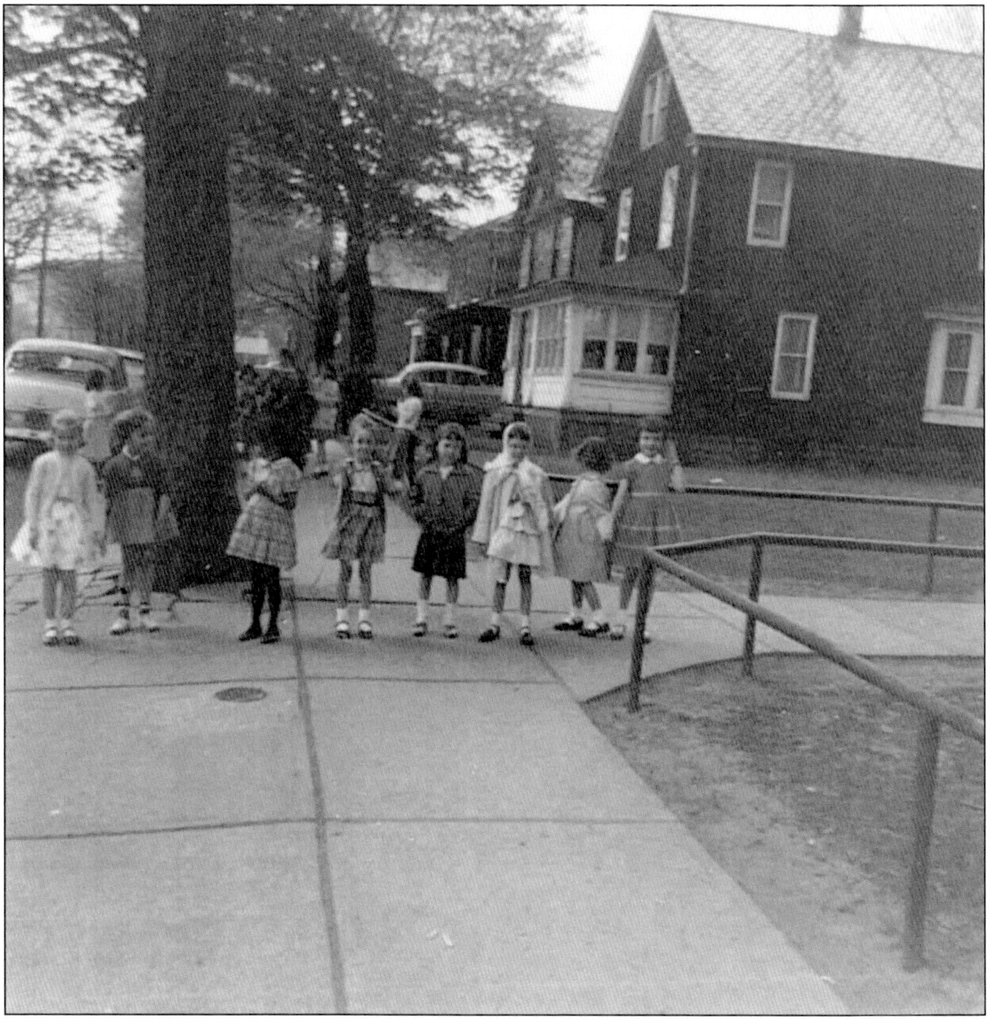

Children wait outside the Third Ward School for the bell to ring. The students walked home for a midday 30-minute lunch break. As a child, Mary Ann Benton (far right) remembered hearing the second whistle from the Chicago Pneumatic Tool Company and knew this signaled that it was time to head back to class. After school, the children of the Third Ward would stop at a neighborhood store for penny candy on their way home. Joe Felder, the school's janitor and crossing guard, always made sure to assist children in crossing the street safely, especially with the simultaneous school dismissal and shift change at the Chicago Pneumatic Tool Company. Felder would often help children cross at the corner of Center and Grant Streets, where the popular Kendzior's store was located. (Courtesy of Mary Ann Benton.)

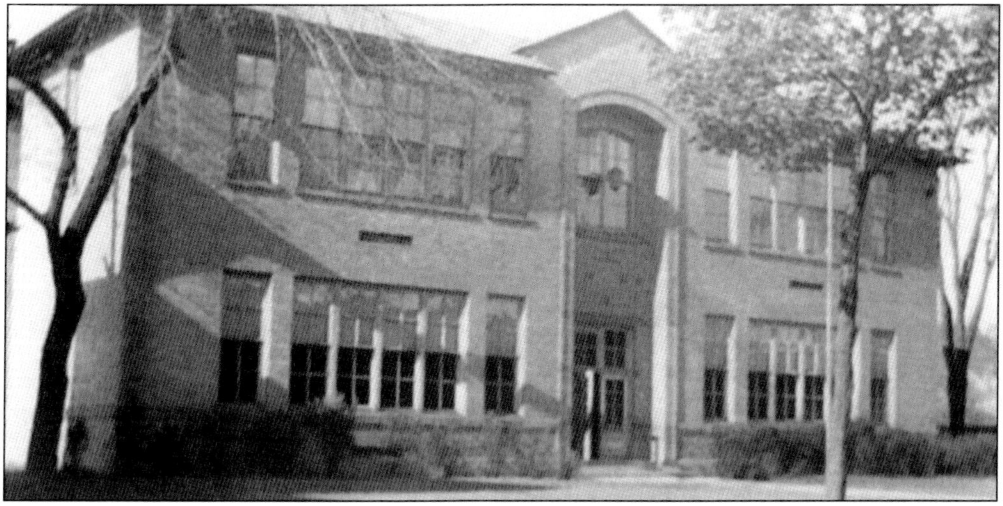

The Third Ward School was located in the 200 block of Atlantic Avenue, between Orchard and Center Streets. Constructed in the late 1870s, it was the first brick school building within the city. The total cost was $12,400. Due to the growing population of the Third Ward, many additions were made to the building. The school was discontinued in the spring of 1965. (Courtesy of Penny Haylett-Minnick.)

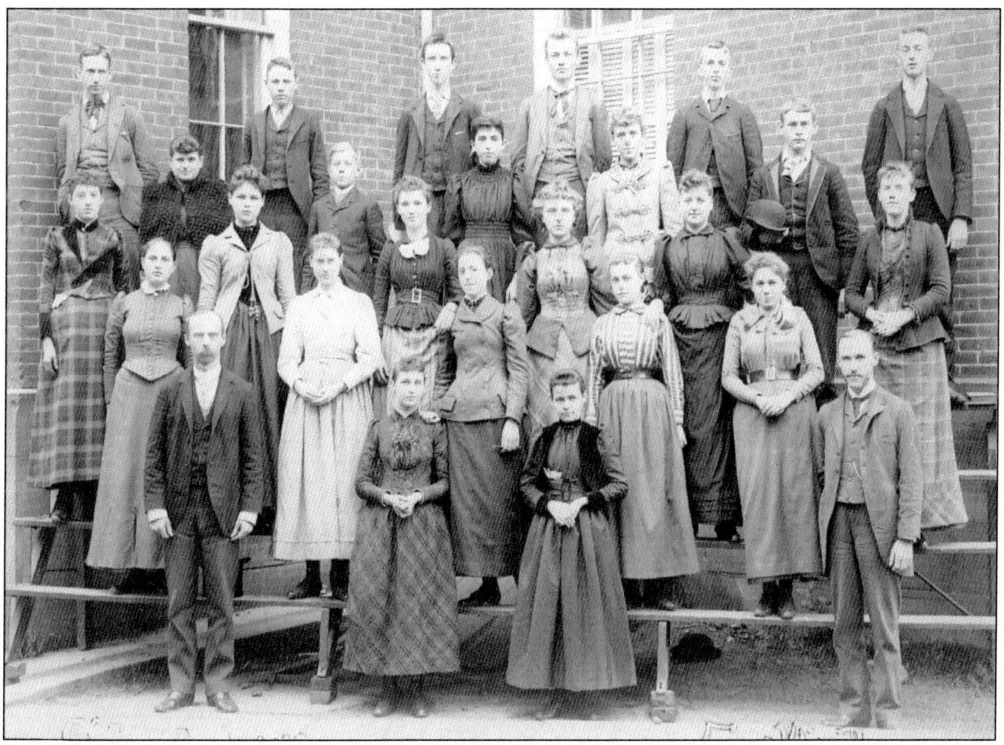

Pictured here is the Union School's graduating class of 1891. Built in the 1860s, the school originally served the elementary students of nearby neighborhoods. Beginning in the late 1870s, Room No. 11 became the home of Franklin High School, thus housing all grades in the same building. At the beginning of the 1904 school year, upperclassmen were moved to the new Franklin Junior-Senior High School complex. (Courtesy of Mary Ann Benton.)

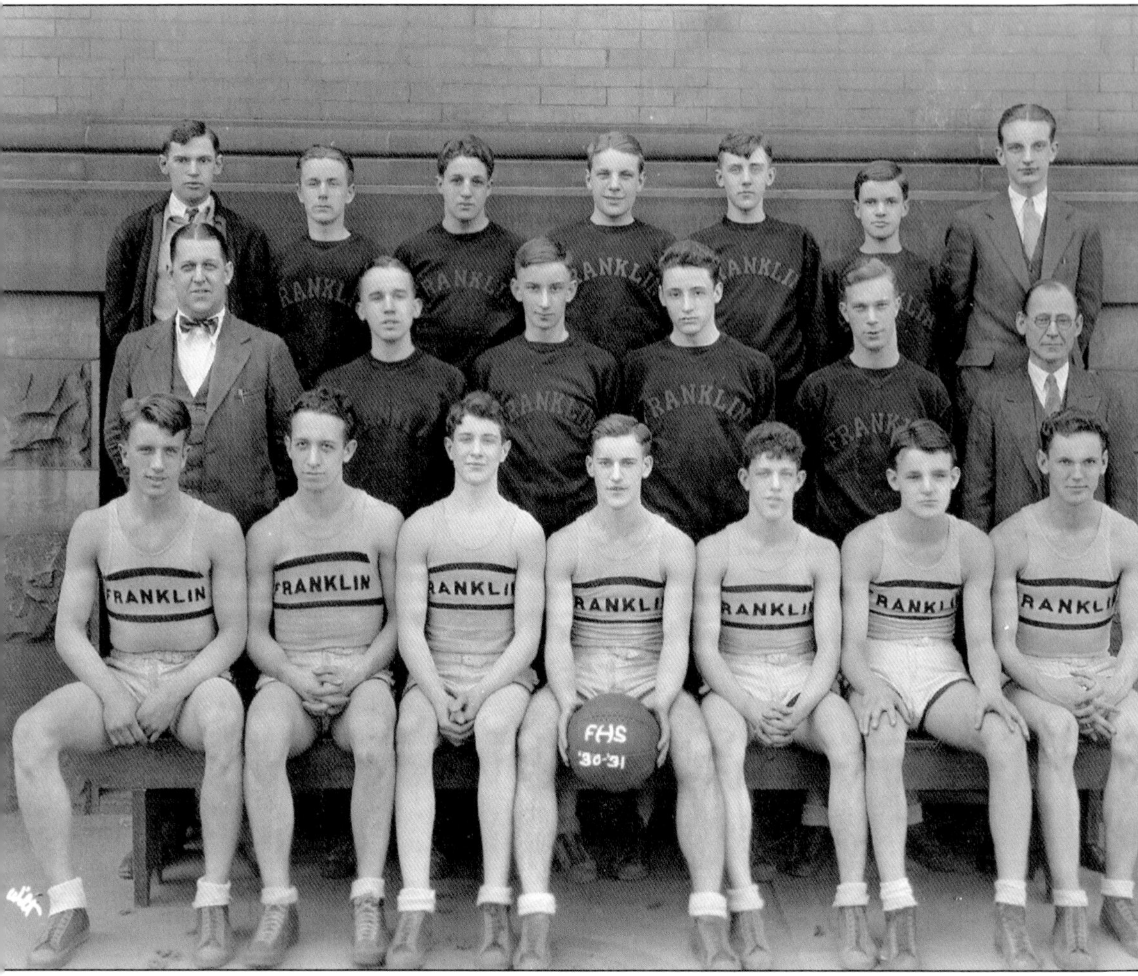

Members of the 1930–1931 Franklin High School basketball team are, from left to right, (first row) Larry Williams, Bill Sheasley, Phil Zeigler, Joe O'Polka, Bill Donahue, Pete Miller, and Jack Curtis; (second row) Ed Treadwell (coach), Andy Heath, unidentified, Joe Jordan, Dana Keely, and Fred Dean (sports director); (third row) Harry Claybaugh (manager), Ed Ellis, Fred Cardy, Leeland Rose, Bob Moyer, Bill Ross, and Walt Fenner (manager). The team went on to win the Allegheny–Kiski Valley Tournament four times, in 1927, 1928, 1929, and 1932. One athletic standout from Franklin during the late 1940s was Ted Marchibroda. Growing up in the Third Ward, he excelled on the Franklin High School football team, later playing quarterback in college. In 1953, the Pittsburgh Steelers drafted Marchibroda as pick five in the first round. He then began coaching in 1961. His first head coaching position came in 1975 with the Baltimore Colts. (Courtesy of Mary Ann Benton.)

Dorothy Mosher, seen in her cap and gown, graduated from Franklin Senior High School in the spring of 1937. After graduation, Mosher was a stock girl in the ladies' unmentionables department at McCrory's five-and-ten store. She later gained employment at the General Manifold and Printing Company, where workers assembled ration books for use during World War II, along with other items. (Courtesy of Mary Ann Benton.)

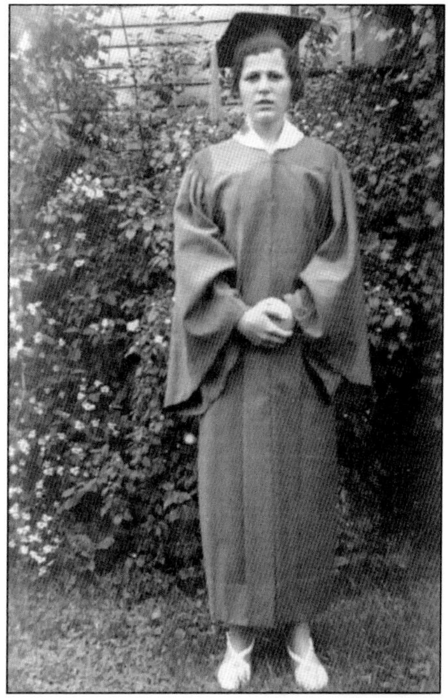

Pictured here in her band uniform, Marianne Harris, who graduated from Franklin High School in the late 1940s, was a member of the marching band. Harris played the clarinet. Currently, the band is known as the Black Knight Marching Band, which has performed in several parades in Washington, DC, as well as during both Pittsburgh Pirates and Steelers games. (Courtesy of Peter Solle.)

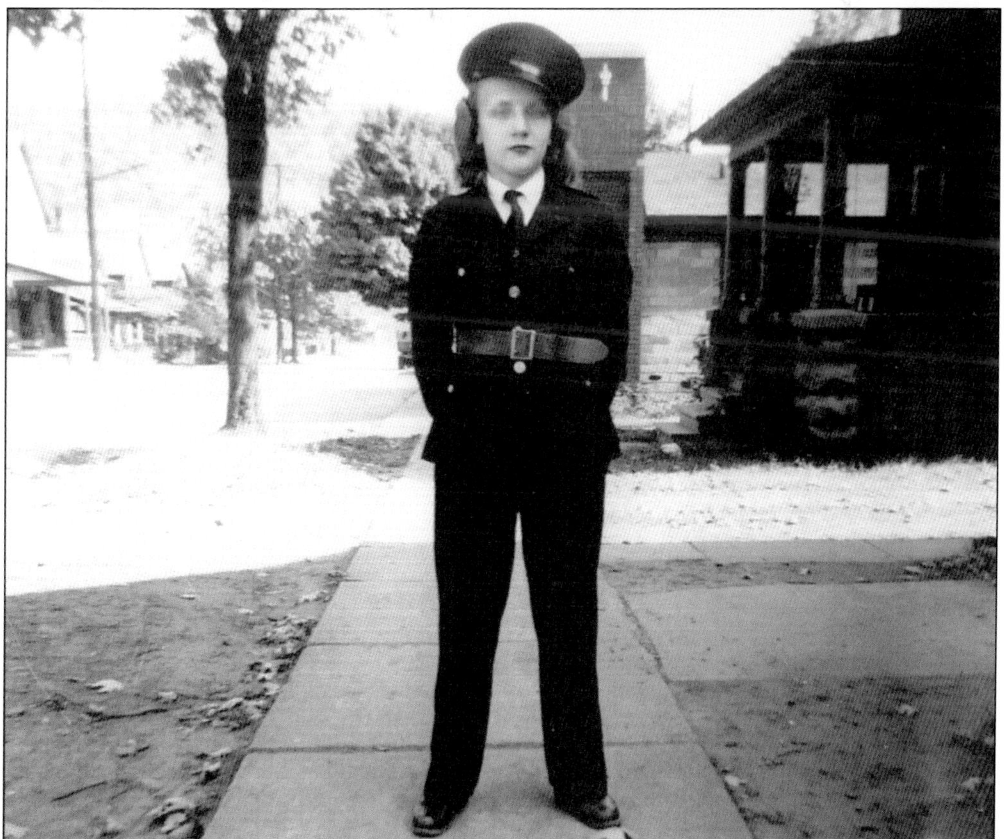

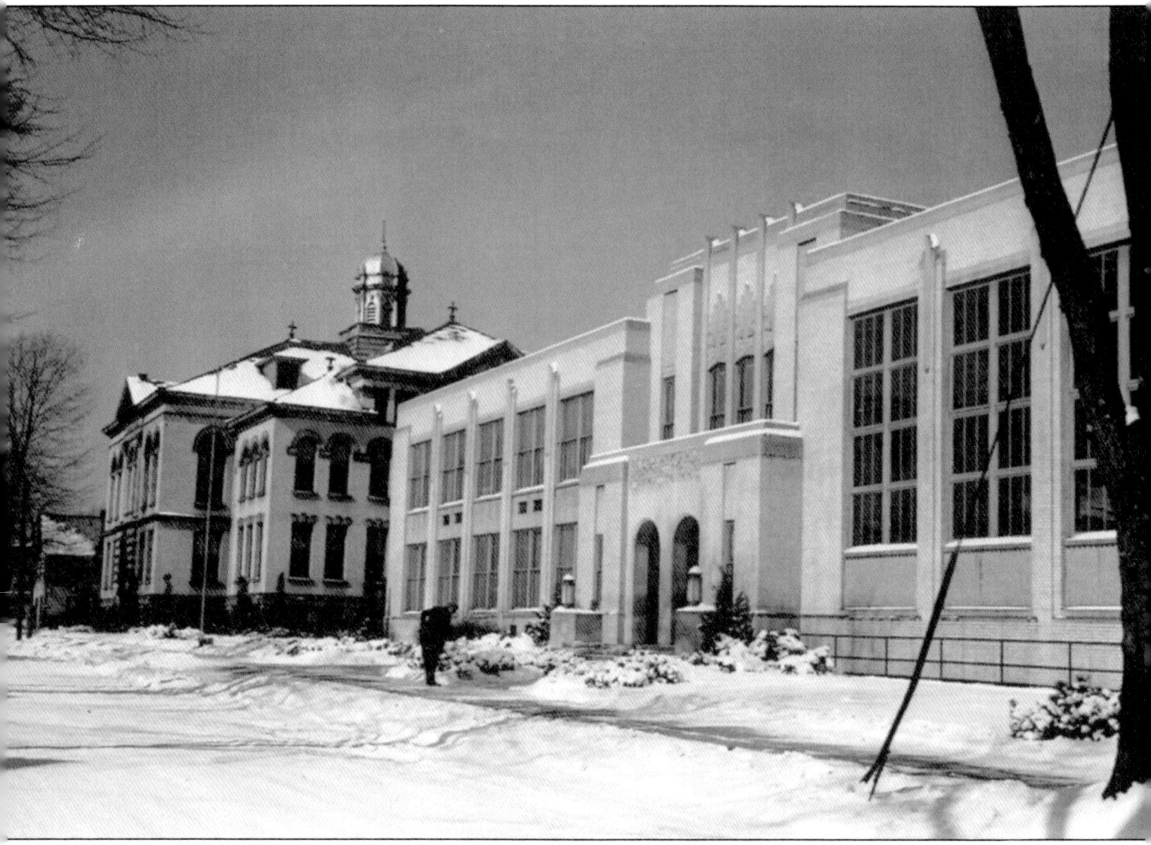

Another athletic standout from Franklin High School was Rolland "Bay" Lawrence. Born in Franklin on March 24, 1951, Lawrence played college football for the Tabor Bluejays in Hillsboro, Kansas. He was drafted into the NFL in 1973 and played cornerback for the Atlanta Falcons for his entire career, from 1973 to 1980. He participated in the 1977 Pro Bowl and continues to hold the Falcons' record for most career interceptions with a total of 39. The Franklin Junior-Senior High School complex dominated the 1200 block of Otter Street until the early 1960s. Once the Junior-Senior High School was converted into Central Elementary in 1965, the Third Ward and Fourteenth Street Schools were shut down. Seventh Street Elementary School was built in 1961, causing the discontinuation of the Ninth and Fourth Street Schools. The Franklin Fire Department now stands on the former public school site. (Courtesy of Peter Solle.)

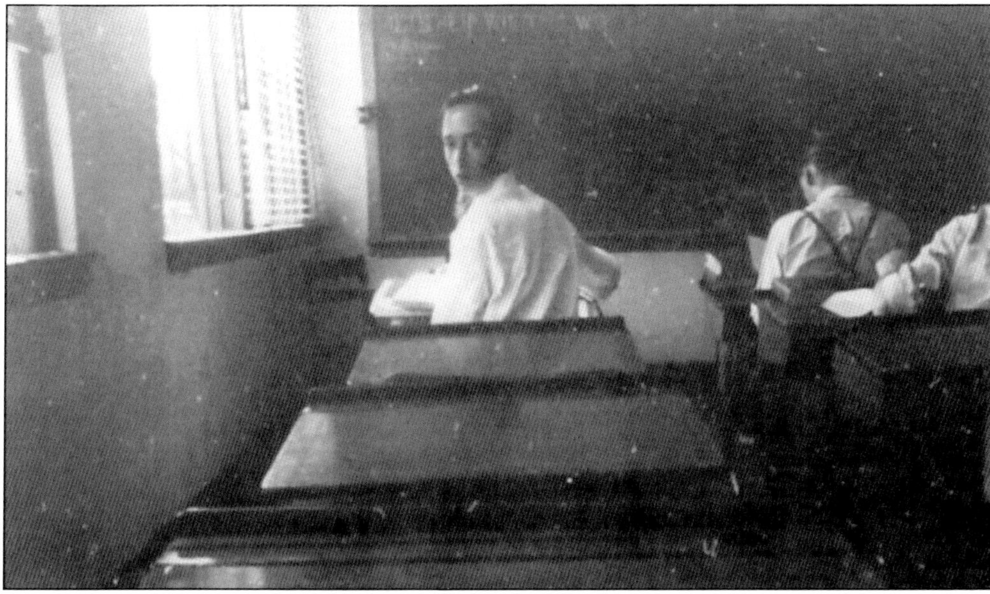

Here is a candid photograph of a student at the Franklin Junior-Senior High School complex dated April 12, 1942. Written on the blackboard just above the student's head is the following sentence: "Let's Help Win This War." During the time of World War II, many young men enlisted to aid the Allies, while women provided services as nurses or worked in factories to build bombs and machinery. (Courtesy of Frances Serge Eakin.)

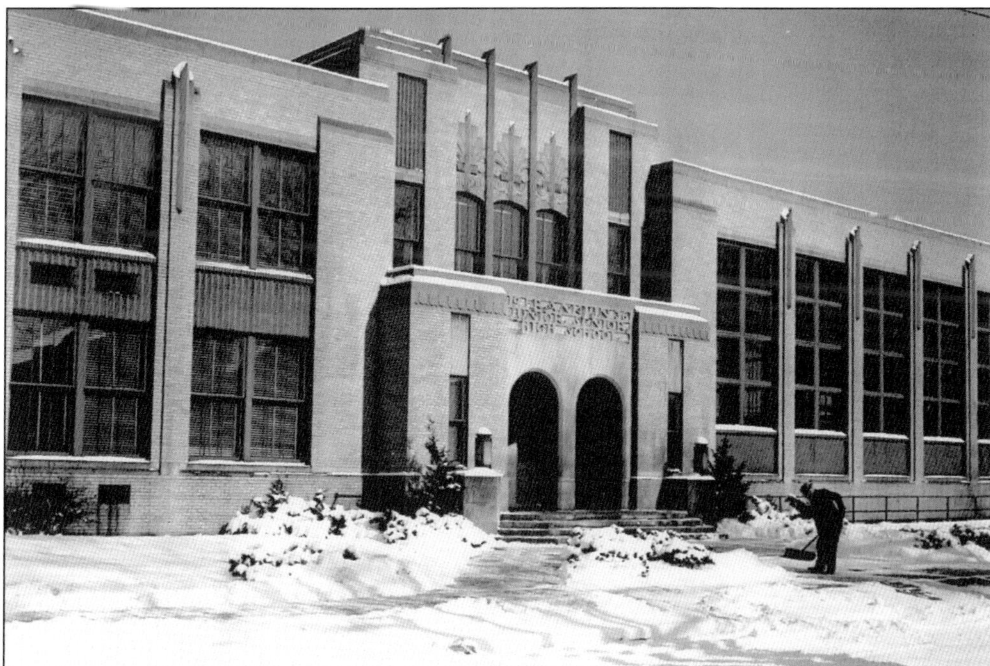

The Franklin Junior High School was part of the Franklin Junior-Senior High School complex for more than 25 years. A hallway connected the two buildings. The addition of the junior high school included a large gymnasium, while early renovations to the high school included a drinking fountain, an auditorium, and a cafeteria. (Courtesy of Peter Solle.)

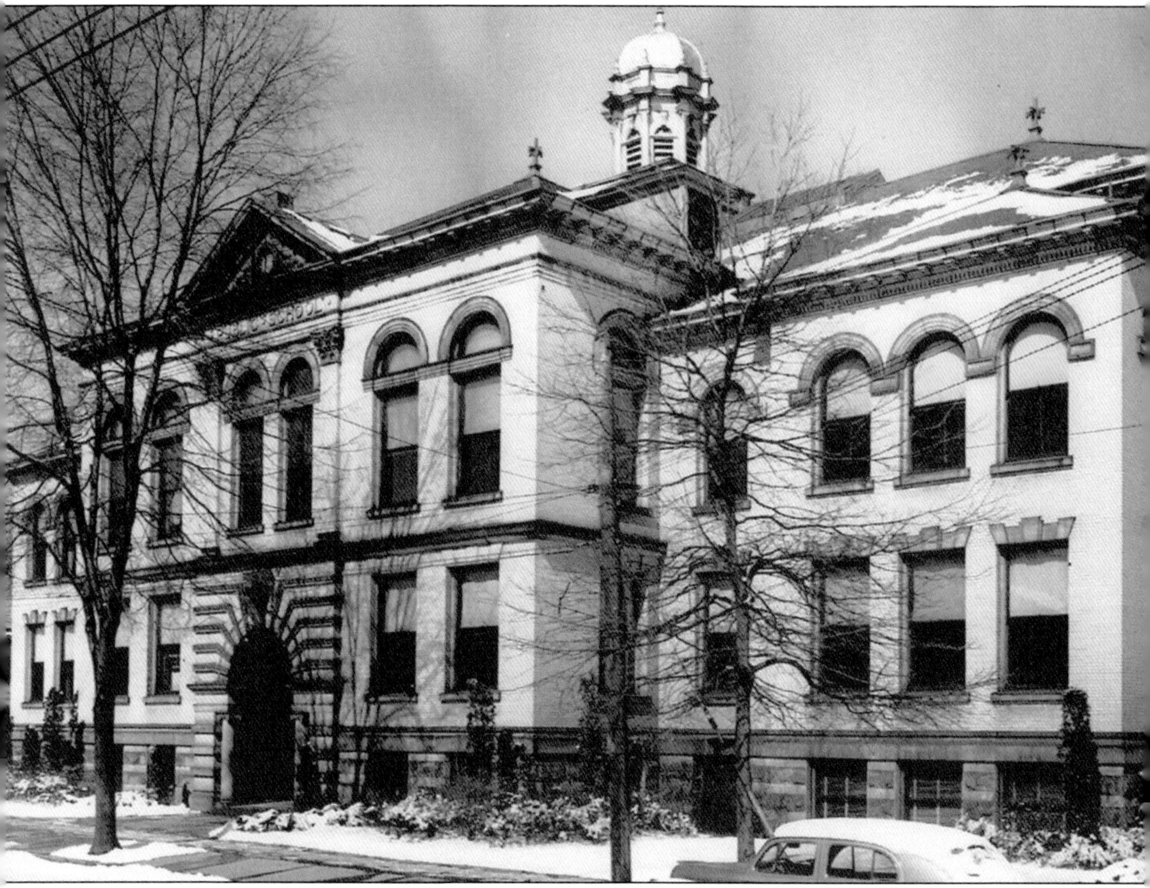

The Franklin Public School served as the city's high school from 1902 until the new facility was built on Pone Lane in 1964. Completed in 1937, the junior high school was built beside the public school with funds from a Public Works Administration grant. The public school was torn down in 1964. The junior high school was converted into Central Elementary in the 1960s. The most recent athlete to come out of Franklin High School and play professional sports is Nate Byham. Born on June 27, 1988, Byham played football for Franklin before attending college at the University of Pittsburgh, where he continued his football career as a tight end. He was recognized as one of the best blocking tight ends for the NFL Draft in 2010. The San Francisco 49ers picked him up during the sixth round. In 2012 and 2013, he played for the Tampa Bay Buccaneers, then for the New England Patriots in 2014. He is currently listed as a free agent as of 2015. (Courtesy of Peter Solle.)

Six

River Ridge

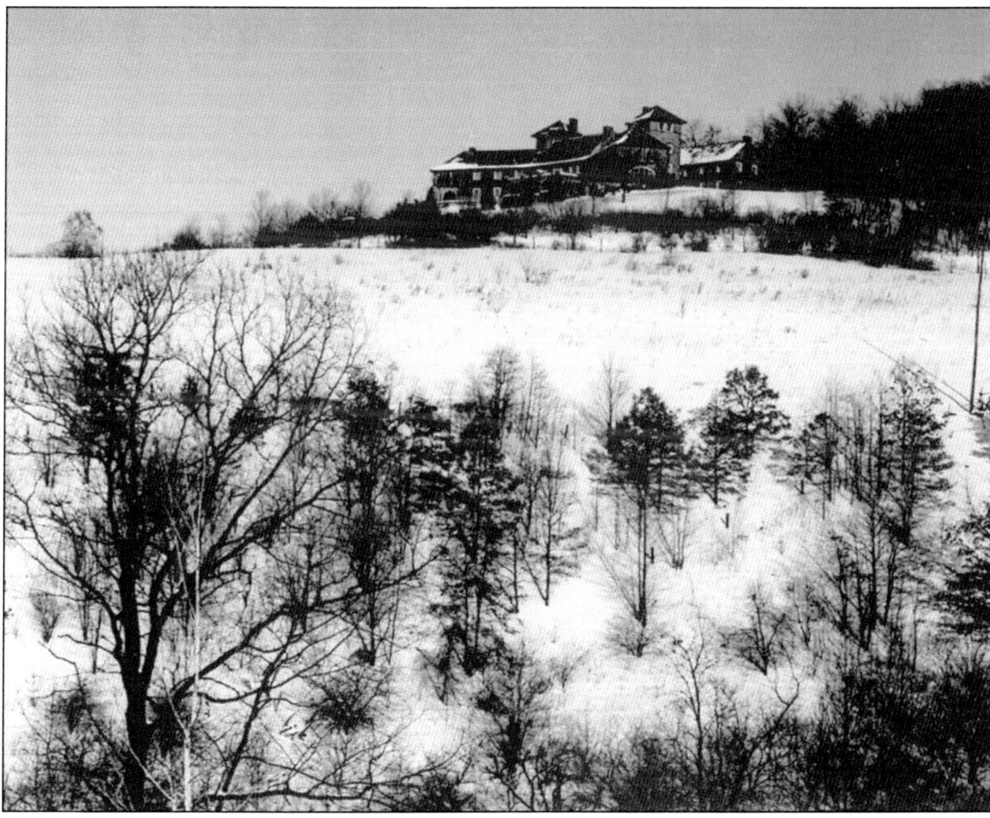

River Ridge mansion was the home of Joseph C. Sibley, cofounder of the Galena Oil Company and US representative of Pennsylvania. The construction of the entire complex was completed on November 29, 1913, and included the mansion, bell tower, farmhouse and barn, pumper's house, gardener's cottage, and several other outbuildings on 1,038 acres of land. (Courtesy of Peter Solle.)

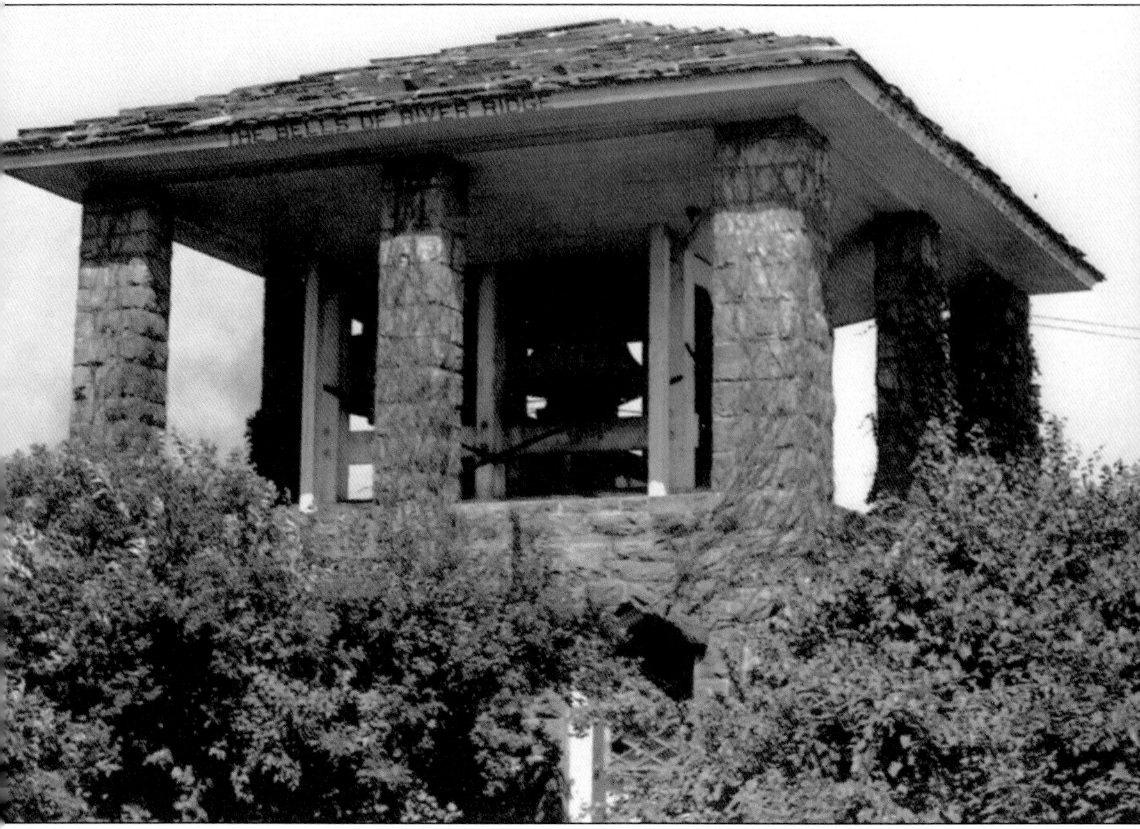

The River Ridge Bell Tower was completed in 1914 with the addition of its 11 bells, weighing a total of 12,500 pounds. (The largest bell weighed a whopping 3,780 pounds.) The bells rang each night at sunset after their introduction on Memorial Day 1914. The Eglise Notre Dame D'Anjou Church in Montreal, Canada, is now home to the bells. The farm on the grounds experimented with different methods and agricultural techniques, and the successful findings were shared with farmers of the county. Sibley often invited farmers to his estate so he could share these findings and hold demonstrations. One such demonstration was reported to have taken place on June 17, 1917, when 700 farmers, along with their families, descended on the River Ridge Farm to attend workshops on dairy farming and raising poultry. The people of the farm provided food under the direction of Supt. John L. Hanna. A box lunch of boiled eggs, salt and pepper, sandwiches, and fried cakes was given to each attendee. (Courtesy of Peter Solle.)

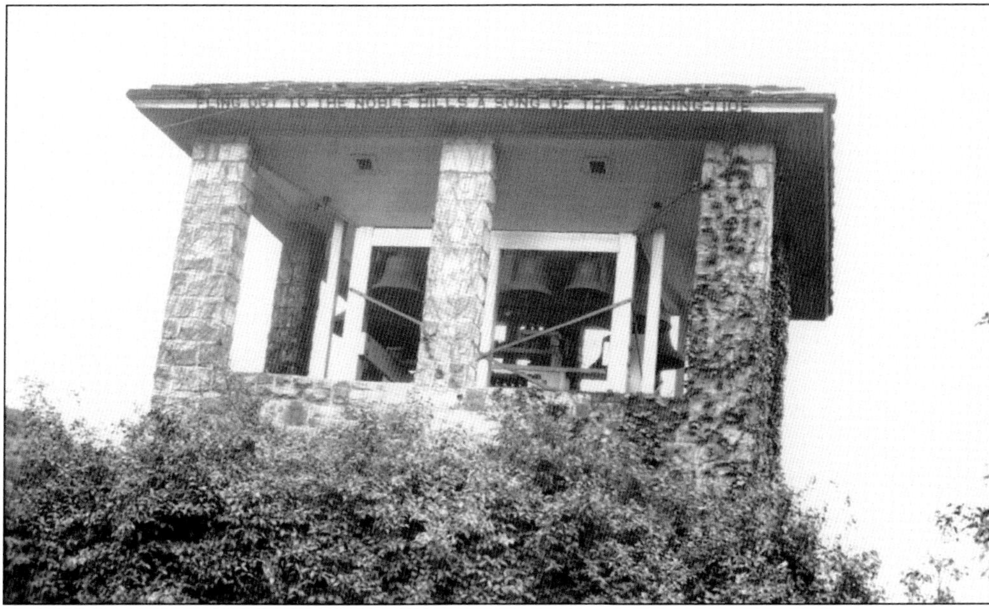

The words that adorn the roofline of the tower state, "The Bells of River Ridge Fling out to the Noble Hills a Song of the Morning-Tide." This structure is identical to the one located at West Point Military Academy. The Meneely (Troy) bell foundry of Troy, New York, made the bells for a cost of $12,500. (Courtesy of Peter Solle.)

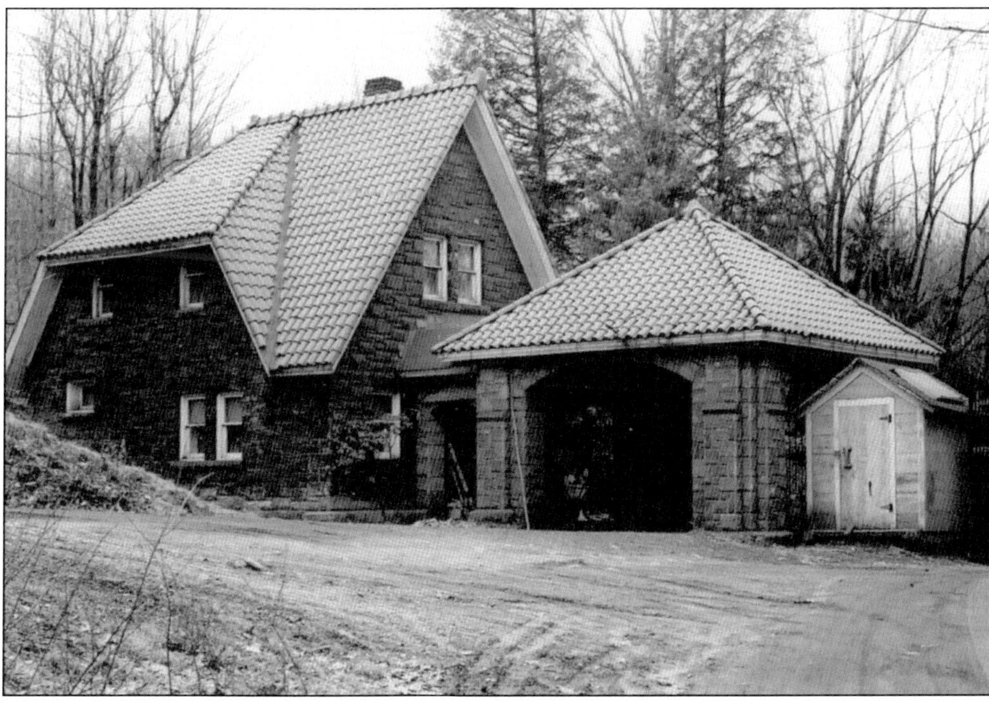

The gatehouse was three miles from the mansion. The entry road has been moved from its original path so it no longer passes through the gatehouse. Builder Ernesto Grandelis and his family originally occupied this house. Grandelis died young at the age of 40 due to dust inhalation. His wife and children were allowed to continue living at the residence. (Courtesy of Peter Solle.)

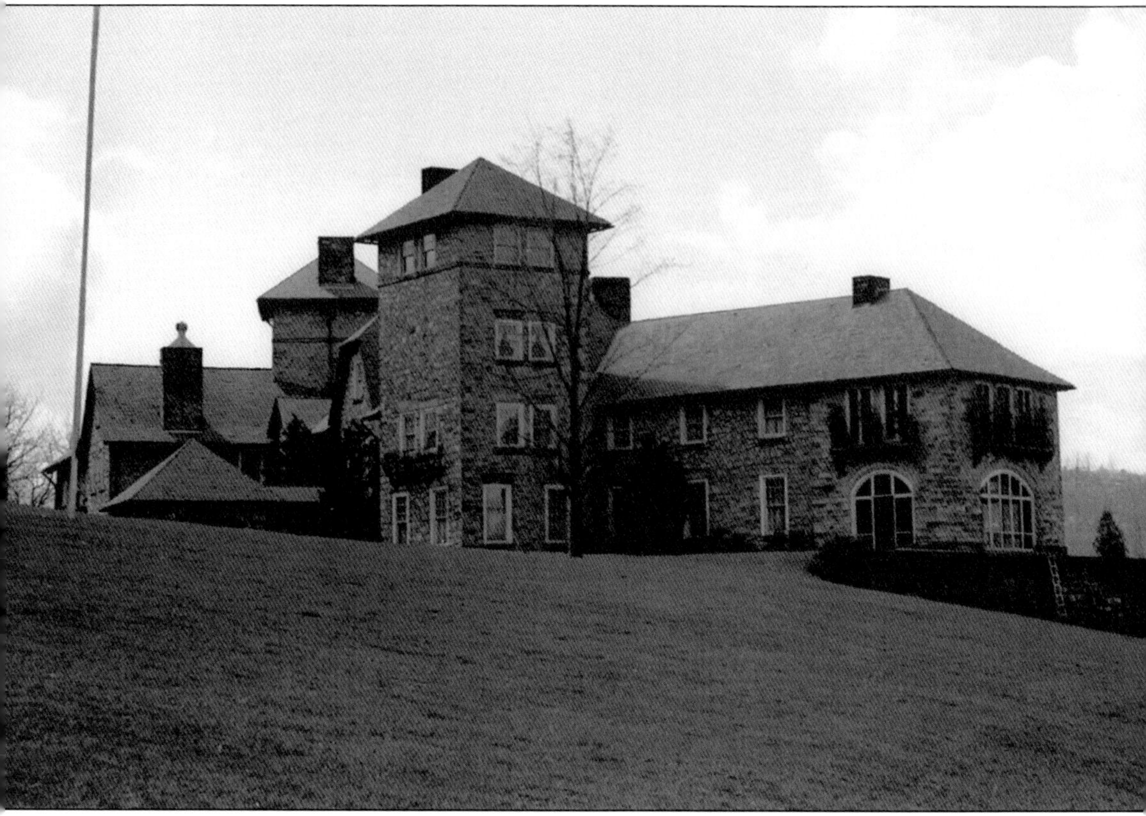

In addition to foreman Ernesto Grandelis, 75 Italian stone masons built Sibley's River Ridge in just seven months. The central part of the property originally contained the Argeon Farm, which consisted of 760 acres purchased for $1 from Robert G. Lamberton on November 15, 1911. Additions were made to the left and right of the mansion, including two porches and two solariums. The mansion was built in the French provincial style, with large, commanding chambers. The size of the living room was 25 feet by 50 feet. The kitchen included two gas stoves like those used in hotels, providing adequate room for the kitchen staff to prepare lavish meals for Sibley and the many guests he often entertained. Sibley also set aside land on his estate for teaching the proper techniques of gardening to interested boys ages 10 to 15. (Courtesy of Peter Solle.)

Seven

Religious Franklin

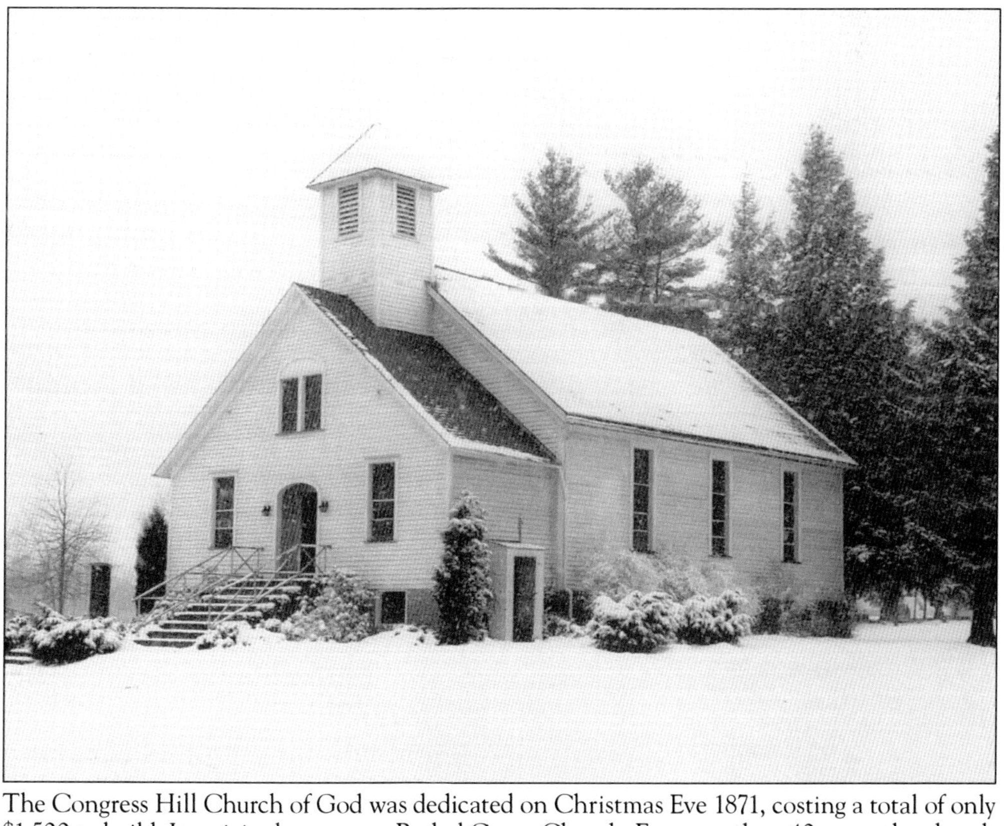

The Congress Hill Church of God was dedicated on Christmas Eve 1871, costing a total of only $1,500 to build. Its original name was Bethel Grove Church. For more than 40 years, the church had a twin, a Methodist church called the Pleasant Grove Church, located 150 feet away. Both were often referred to as "the Twin Churches." (Courtesy of Peter Solle.)

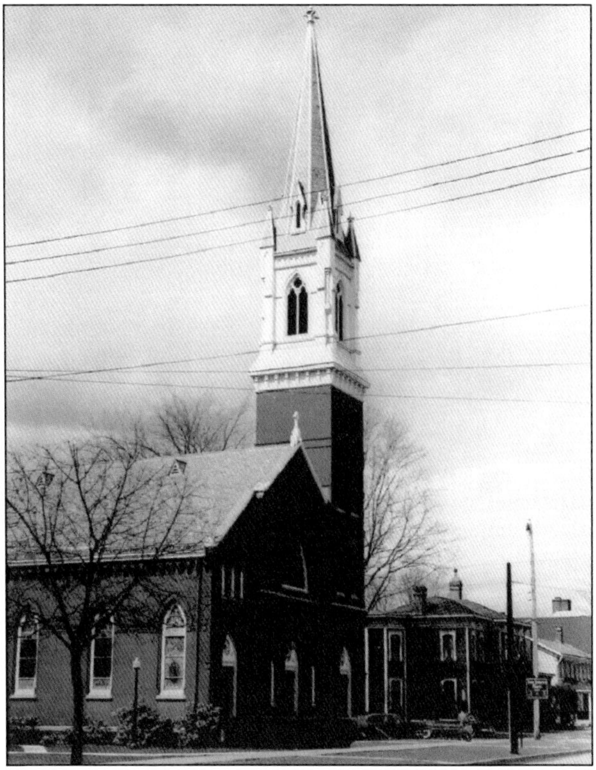

St. Patrick's Church is a Roman Catholic church that has been serving the parishioners of Franklin for more than 100 years. St. Patrick's School opened in September 1894. Dion Auditorium was added in October 1956. The school included high school grades for some years, but now students must attend Venango Catholic High School in Oil City or transfer to a public high school to graduate. (Courtesy of Peter Solle.)

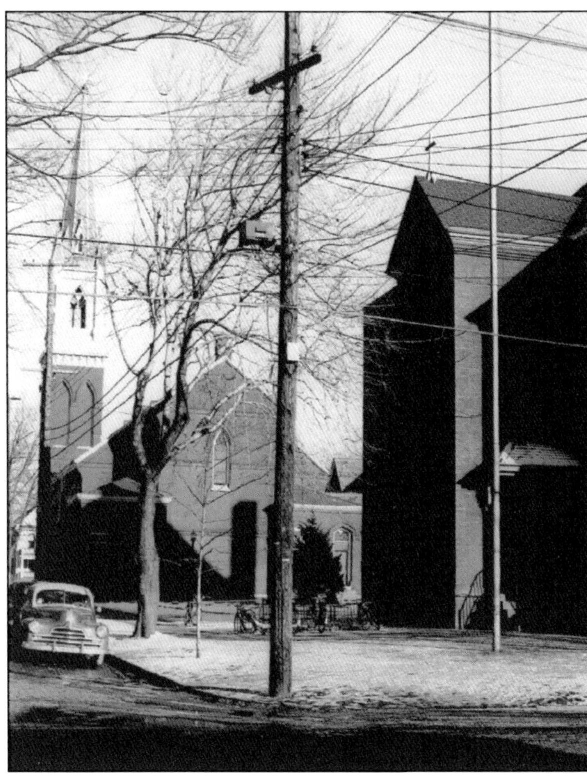

Here is a view of the 400 block of Tenth Street in the 1940s. In the background stands St. Patrick's Church, which fronts on Liberty Street; St. Patrick's School fronts on Buffalo Street. Dion Auditorium was built in the empty space between these buildings in 1956. An addition was also made to the school in the early 2000s. (Courtesy of Peter Solle.)

Farther Grode is pictured with several students outside St. Patrick's Church and School in the late 1940s. In June 1952, the school graduated its first class of students who had completed their primary and secondary education in the church's facility. Due to inadequate space for classes, the remaining high schoolers had to finish their studies at public schools. (Courtesy of Peter Solle.)

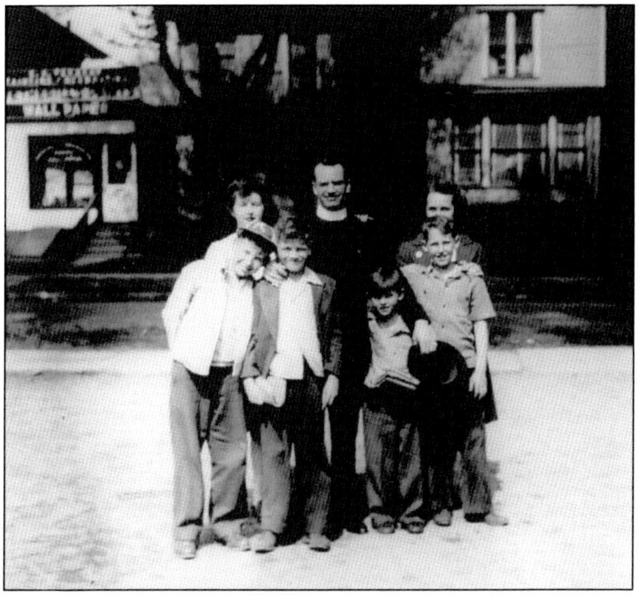

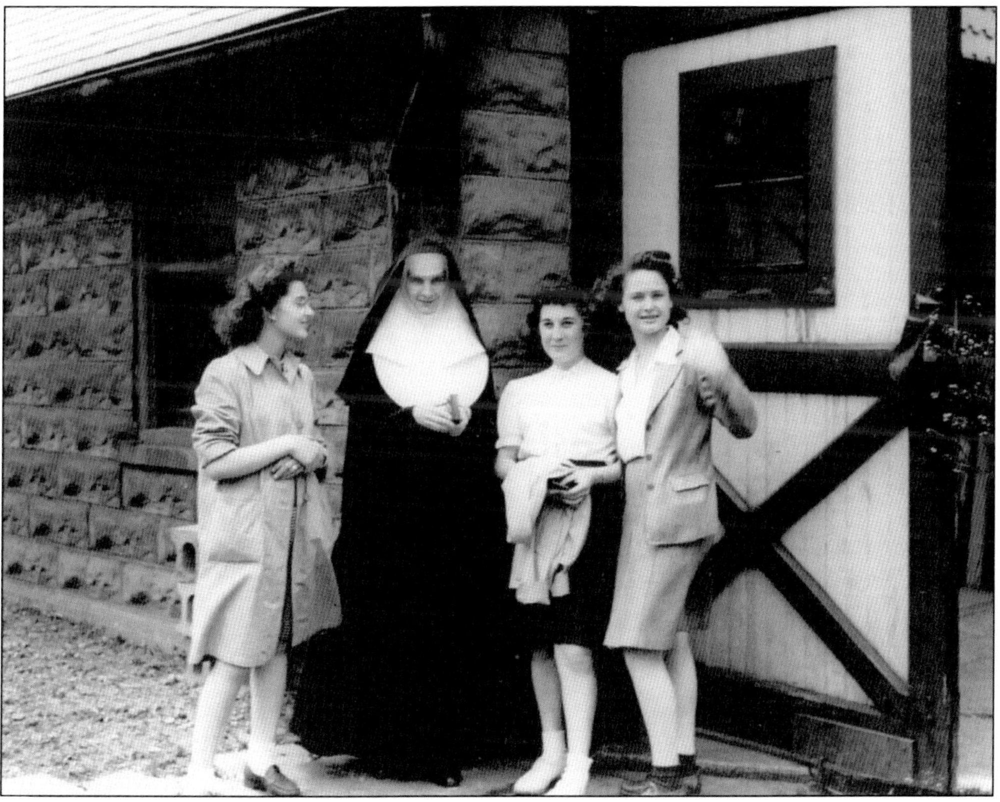

Sister Berthe poses with students outside St. Patrick's Church and School. The present church was dedicated in 1882, prior to which services were held in a wooden church building. The organization first began in the 1860s. St. Patrick Church sold the wooden building to the Free Methodist Church as an interim location until its permanent building was finished. (Courtesy of Peter Solle.)

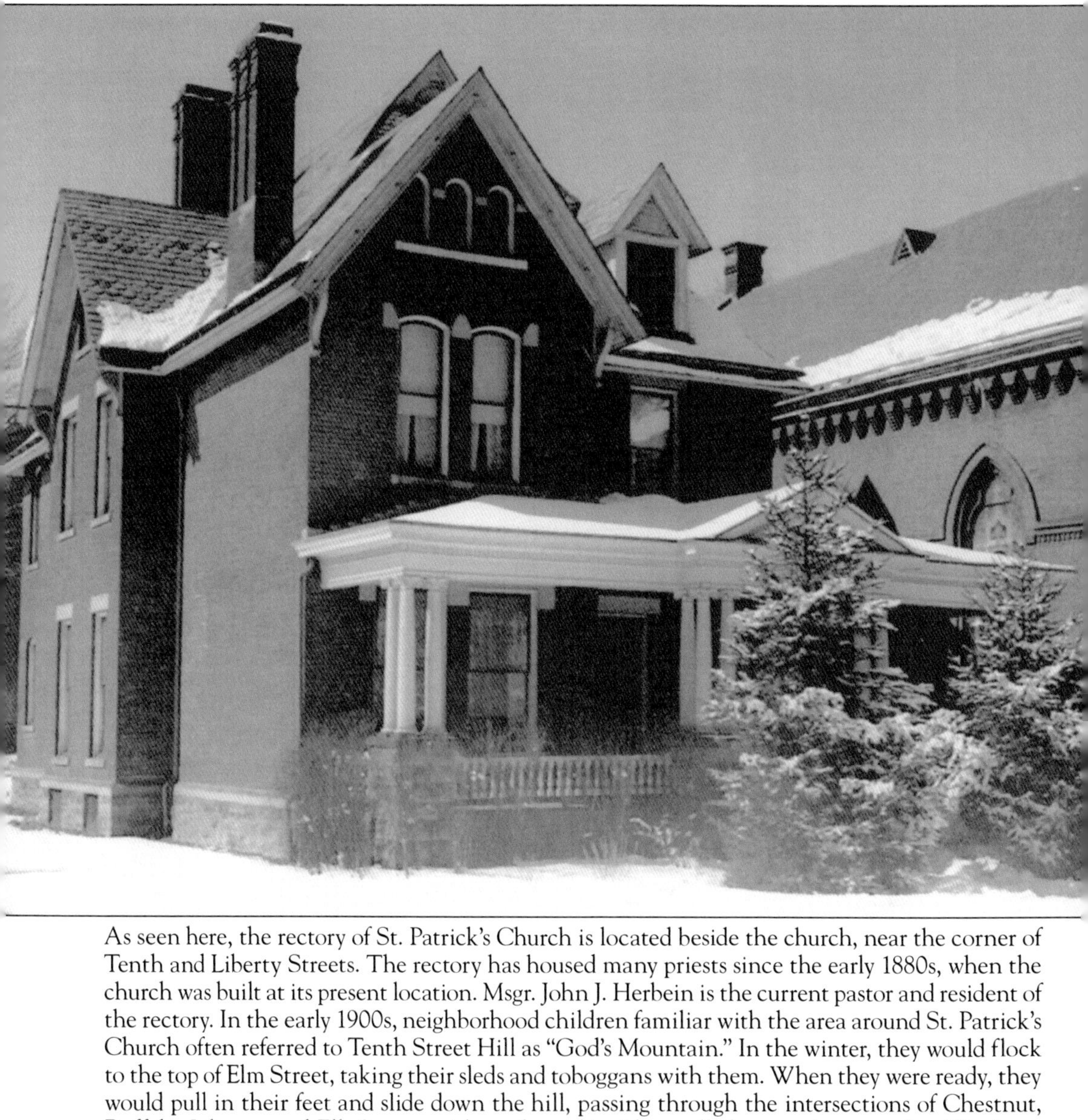

As seen here, the rectory of St. Patrick's Church is located beside the church, near the corner of Tenth and Liberty Streets. The rectory has housed many priests since the early 1880s, when the church was built at its present location. Msgr. John J. Herbein is the current pastor and resident of the rectory. In the early 1900s, neighborhood children familiar with the area around St. Patrick's Church often referred to Tenth Street Hill as "God's Mountain." In the winter, they would flock to the top of Elm Street, taking their sleds and toboggans with them. When they were ready, they would pull in their feet and slide down the hill, passing through the intersections of Chestnut, Buffalo, Liberty, and Elk Streets without fear of incident, all the way down to the Allegheny River. (Courtesy of Peter Solle.)

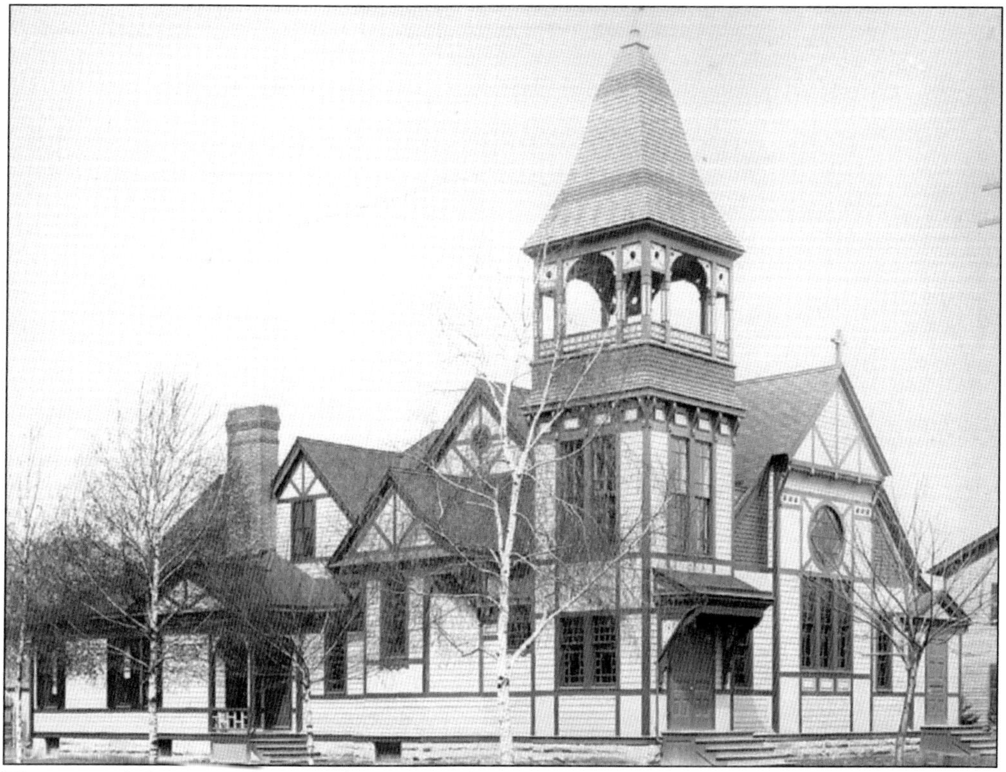

The second Grace Lutheran Church stood on the corner of Eleventh and Buffalo Streets. Rev. J.H. Kunkleman was the church's officiant. The cornerstone was laid in 1886, and the church was dedicated in 1887. The total cost of the building was $7,000. The congregation voted to build a new church in 1956, with construction beginning in 1957. (Courtesy of Penny Haylett-Minnick.)

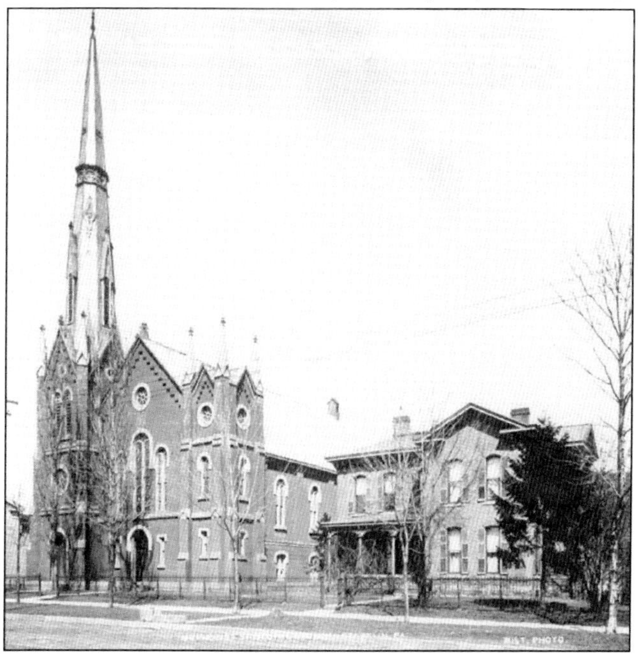

The plans for building the First Methodist Church, located on the corner of Eleventh and Liberty Streets, were initiated in 1863. The parsonage (right) was constructed approximately 10 years later. In September 1913, the last service was held in this building. This church and parsonage were demolished, making way for the current building. (Courtesy of Penny Haylett-Minnick.)

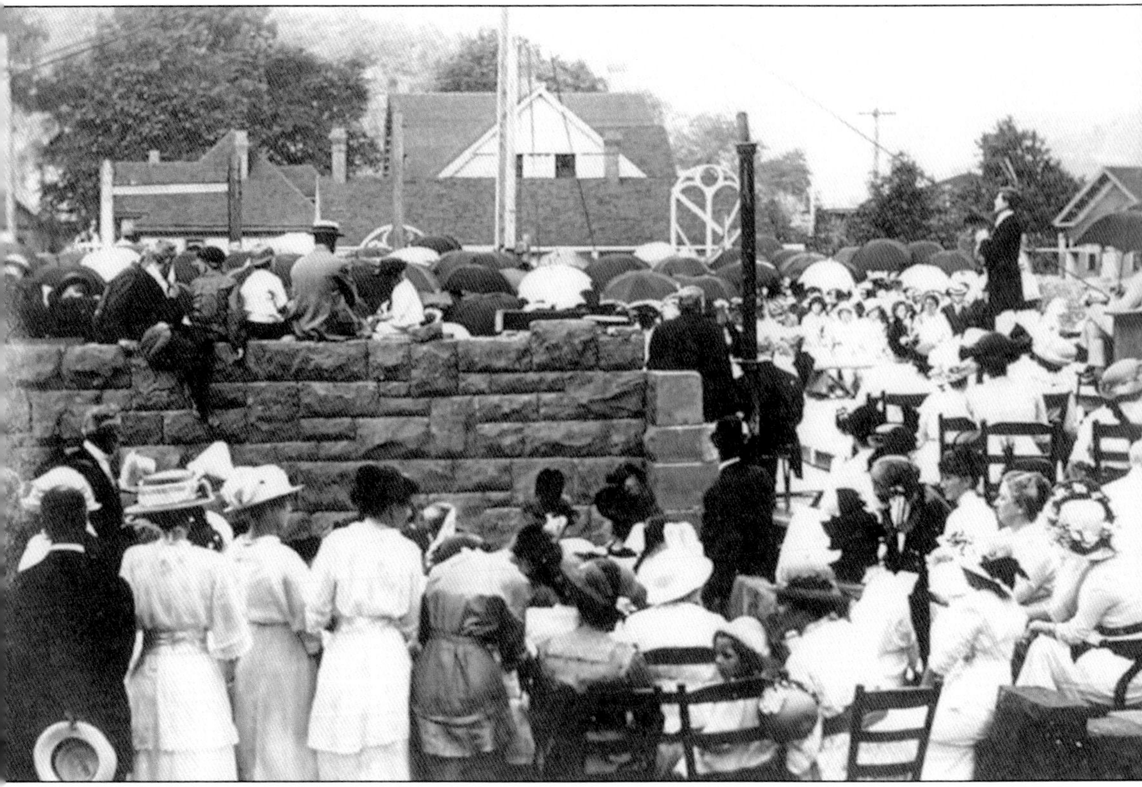

Several large groups of Franklin citizens watch as William Burt, the resident bishop of Buffalo, New York, lays the cornerstone for the current First Methodist Church in the 1100 block of Liberty Street on July 7, 1914. The total cost of the building was $135,000. After arriving from Baltimore, Maryland, in 1804, Andrew Hemphill held the first Methodist services in the city, reportedly in the public square. In 1810, Joshua Monroe created the first Methodist class. The members of the First Methodist Church decided to update the facade of their church from brick to brownstone in the 1860s due to the recent success of the oil boom, not to mention the large number of new citizens coming into the area. (Courtesy of Penny Haylett-Minnick.)

Pictured here is Christ United Methodist Church's original building, located at 1135 Buffalo Street. This building was destroyed by fire. The remnants of the church and the home seen at right were torn down, and the church was rebuilt, without the tower, across both lots. Additions have been made to the church several times over the past few decades. (Courtesy of Penny Haylett-Minnick.)

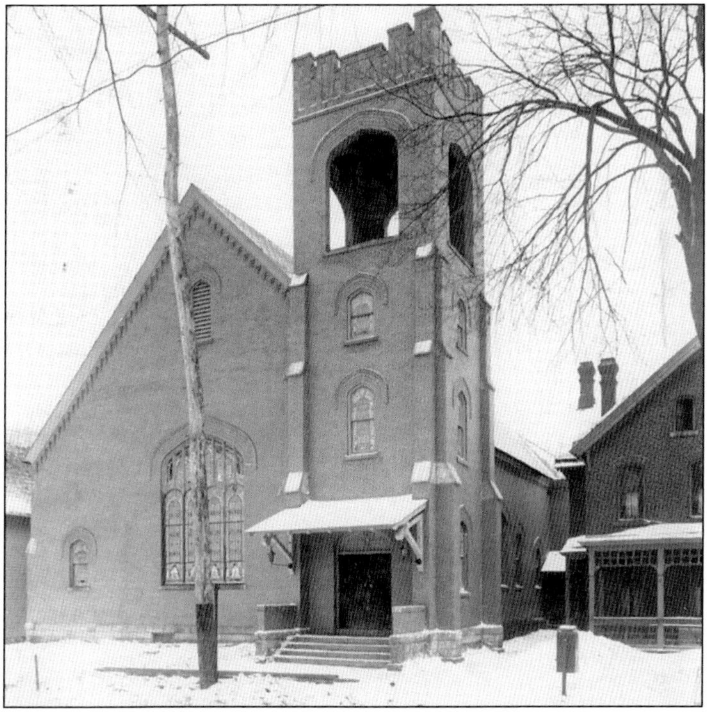

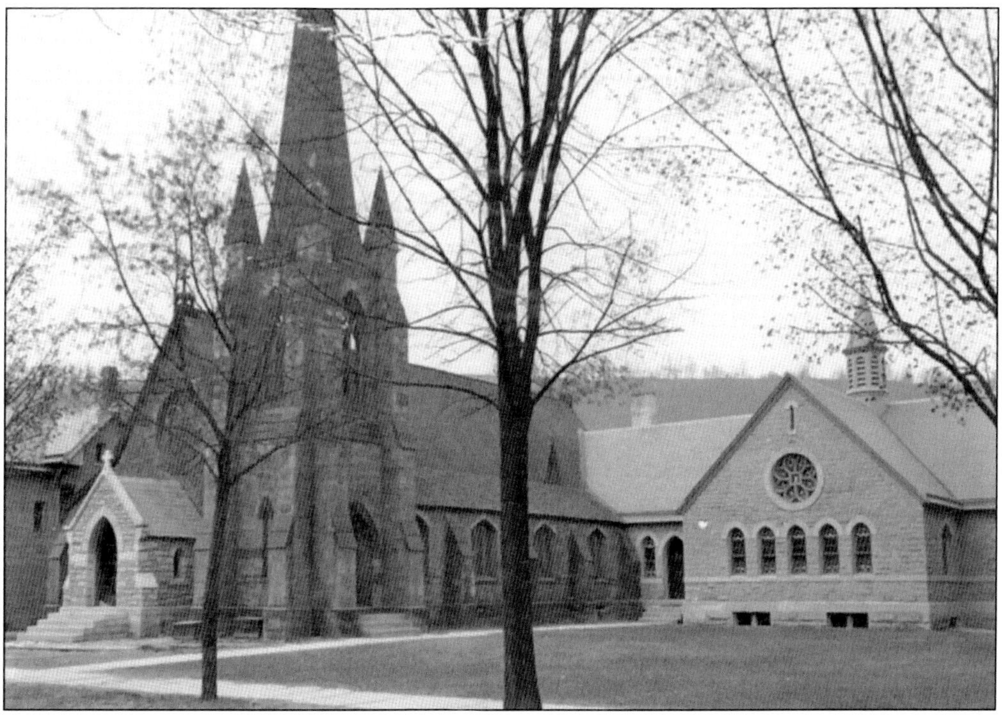

St. John's Episcopal Church is located at 1145 Buffalo Street. Its original brick structure was started in 1826, but funding fell through, leaving only the walls and roof completed. The partial building was razed in 1865, and the first stone building was erected in 1866. On February 24, 1900, a fire destroyed everything but the outer walls and bell tower. (Courtesy of Penny Haylett-Minnick.)

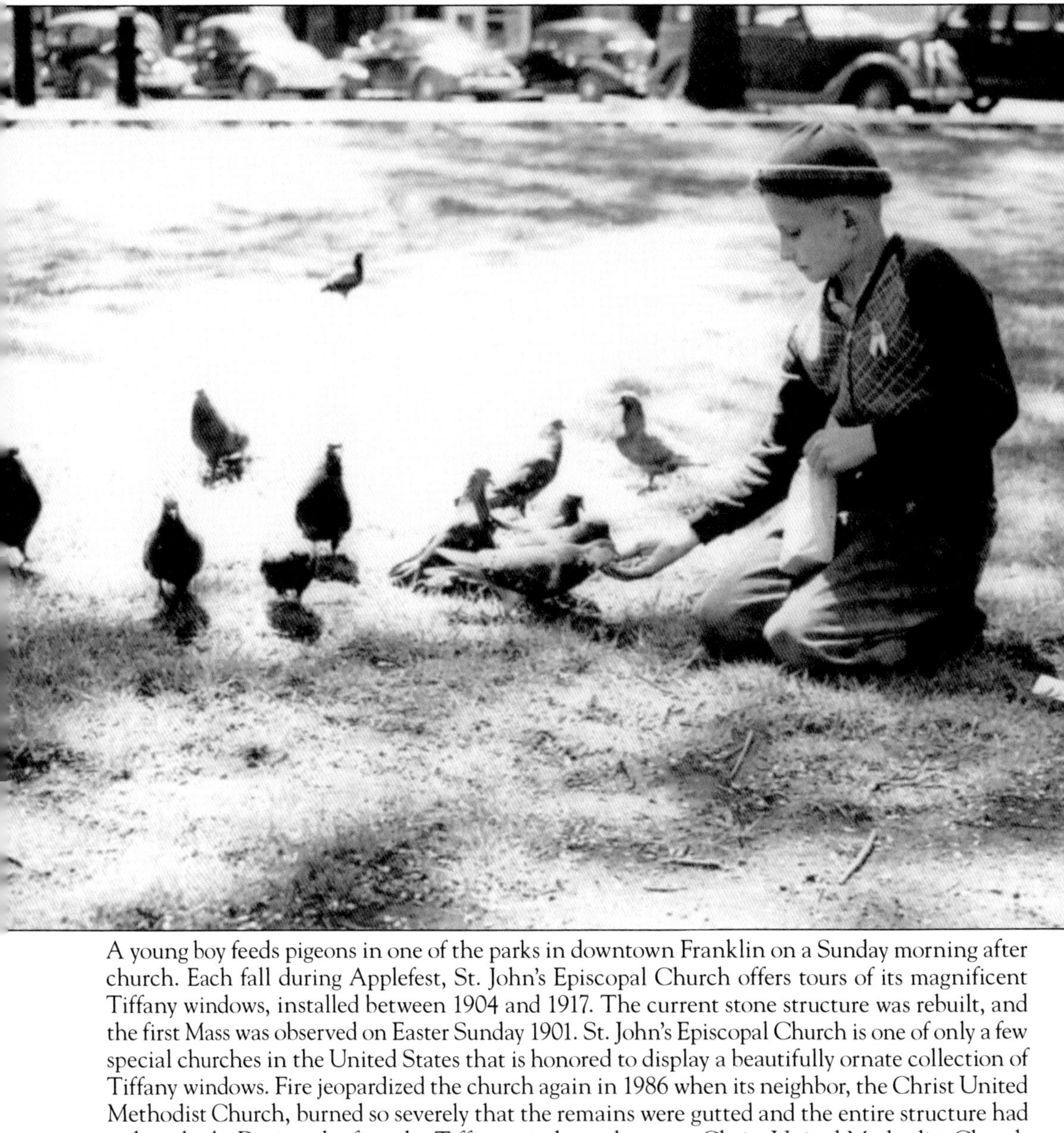

A young boy feeds pigeons in one of the parks in downtown Franklin on a Sunday morning after church. Each fall during Applefest, St. John's Episcopal Church offers tours of its magnificent Tiffany windows, installed between 1904 and 1917. The current stone structure was rebuilt, and the first Mass was observed on Easter Sunday 1901. St. John's Episcopal Church is one of only a few special churches in the United States that is honored to display a beautifully ornate collection of Tiffany windows. Fire jeopardized the church again in 1986 when its neighbor, the Christ United Methodist Church, burned so severely that the remains were gutted and the entire structure had to be rebuilt. During the fire, the Tiffany windows closest to Christ United Methodist Church were said to have been moving due to the intensity of the heat. (Courtesy of Peter Solle.)

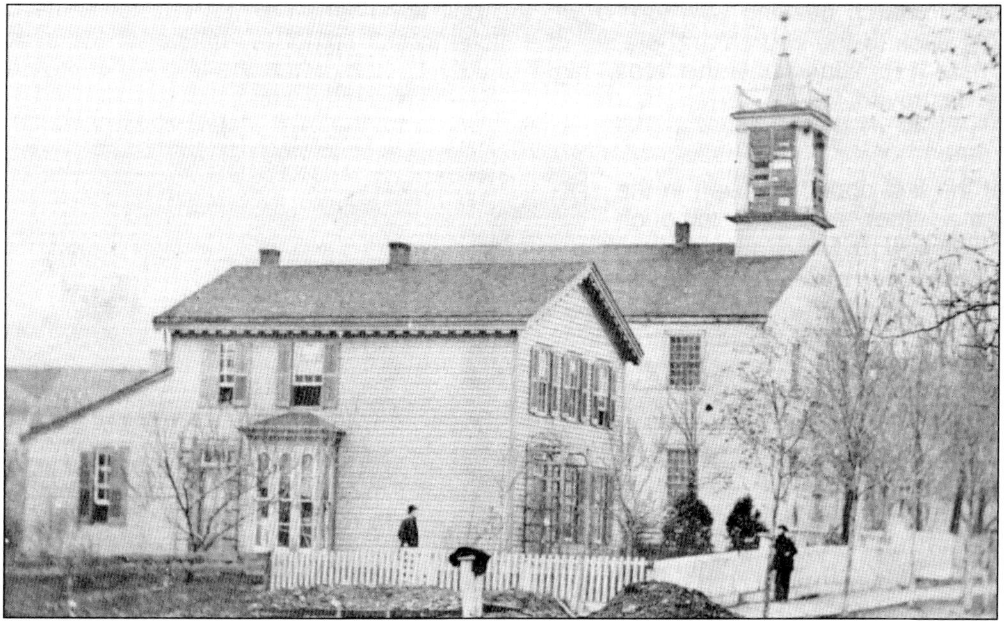

This view from West Park Street shows the original First Presbyterian Church and its manse. Currently, the church offers nursery school, a youth group, an after-school program, bell and sanctuary choirs, fellowship meals, various clubs, a Bible reading group, and monthly fellowship events. (Courtesy of Penny Haylett-Minnick.)

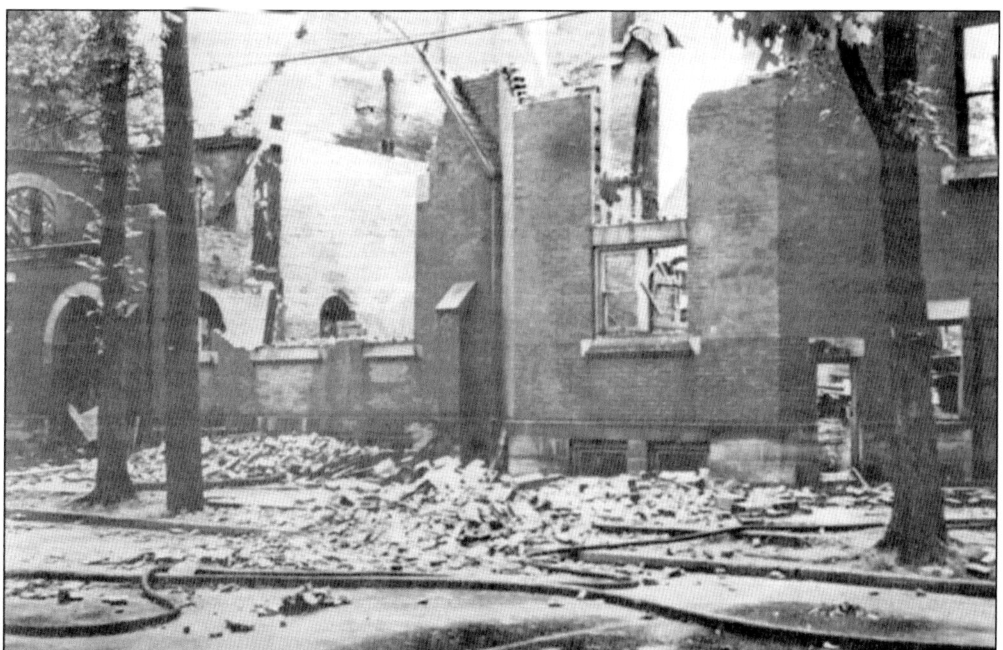

The First Presbyterian Church is located on the corner of West Park and Elk Streets. This photograph shows the fire that destroyed the second church building and its parsonage. The church was rebuilt, and the new parsonage was relocated farther down West Park Street, near the corner of Otter Street. (Courtesy of Penny Haylett-Minnick.)

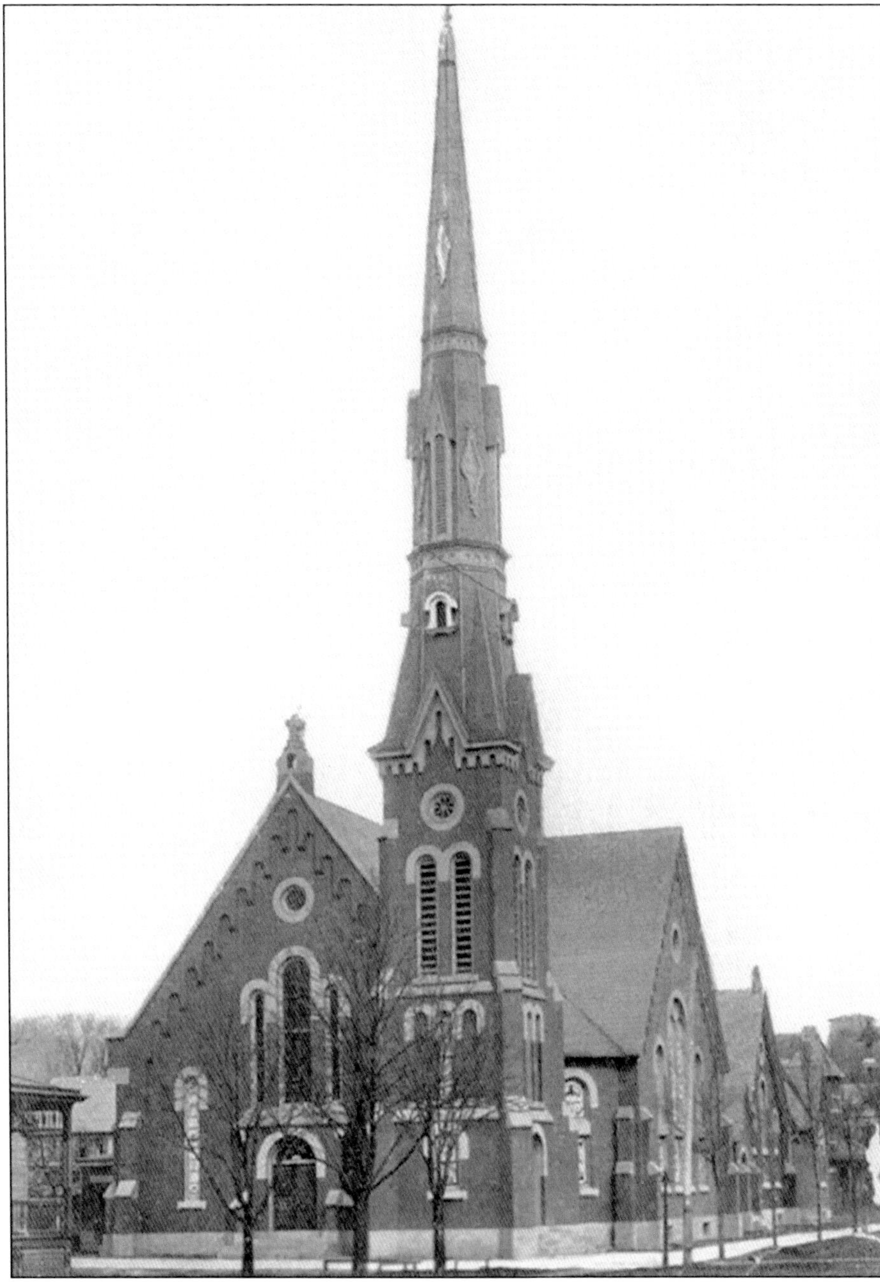

The second building of the First Presbyterian Church is pictured here before it was destroyed by fire. The steeple was located right at the corner of West Park and Elk Streets. When the third and final building was erected, no steeple was added. Each year, the church performs a live nativity at Christmas. The first Presbyterian Communion in Franklin was noted to have been held along the banks of French Creek in 1817. After the fire on July 1, 1946, destroyed the majority of the building (with the exception its walls), the First Baptist Church allowed the Presbyterian parishioners to hold services in their Sunday school rooms until the church's reconstruction was completed in October 1950. In 1953, the church added an education branch and a Sunday school branch to the facility. (Courtesy of Penny Haylett-Minnick.)

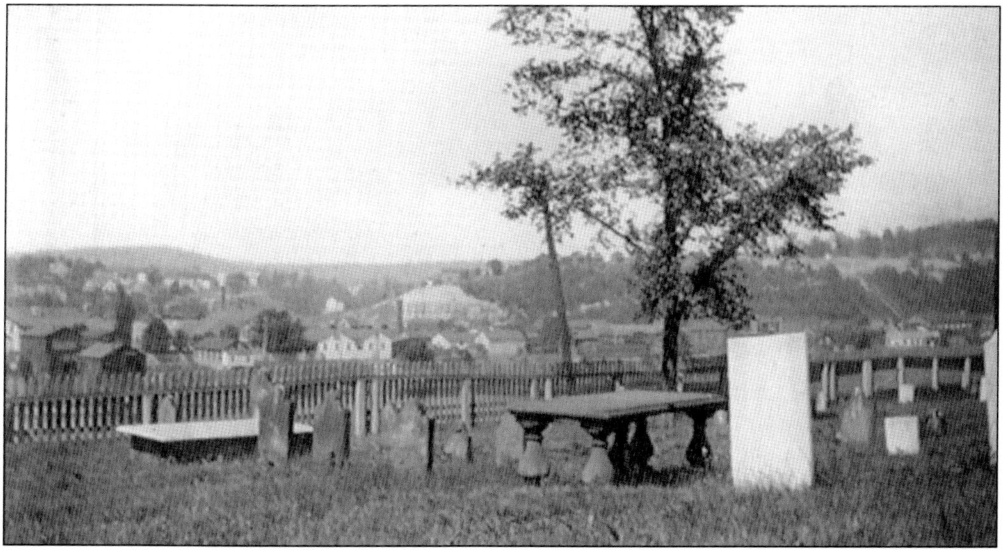

Pioneer Cemetery is the oldest in Franklin, dating back to the city's year of incorporation in 1795. George Power, one of the city's first settlers, is buried here. He helped build Fort Franklin in 1787 and also owned an inn. The Daughters of the American Revolution, Venango County Chapter, restored the cemetery in 1952. A soldier of Napoleon's army is also buried here. (Courtesy of Penny Haylett-Minnick.)

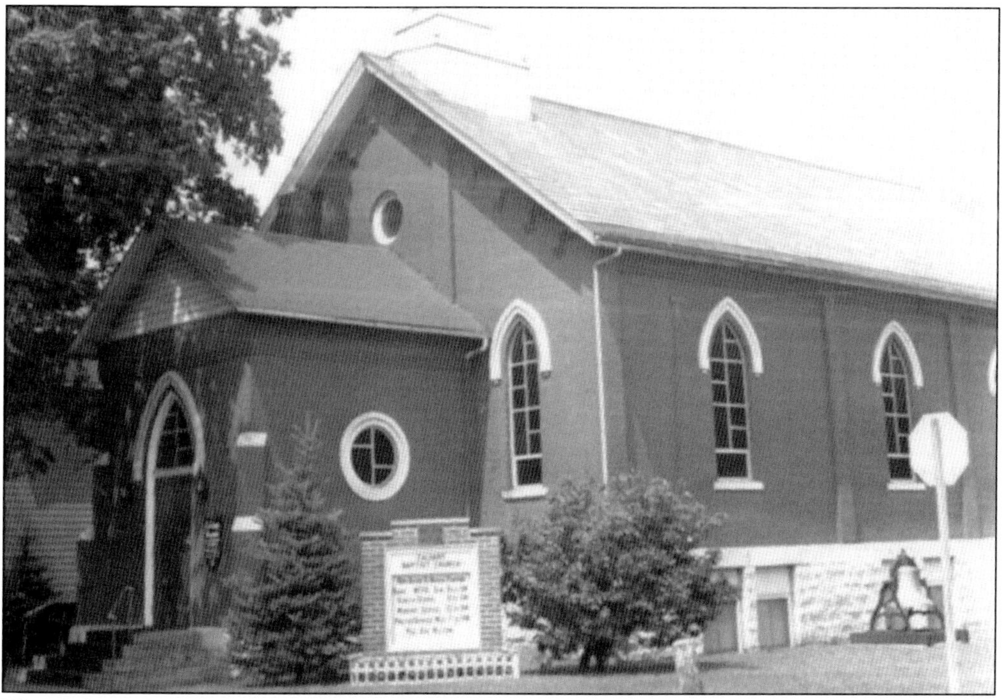

The Calvary Baptist Church was formed under this name on May 3, 1920. The original little Wynebannarain Church passed through a few hands until Gen. Charles Miller purchased it and turned it into a mission church. General Miller also taught the men's Bible class. The author's great-grandfather Arie E. Mosher served as church treasurer starting in 1927. (Courtesy of Penny Haylett-Minnick.)

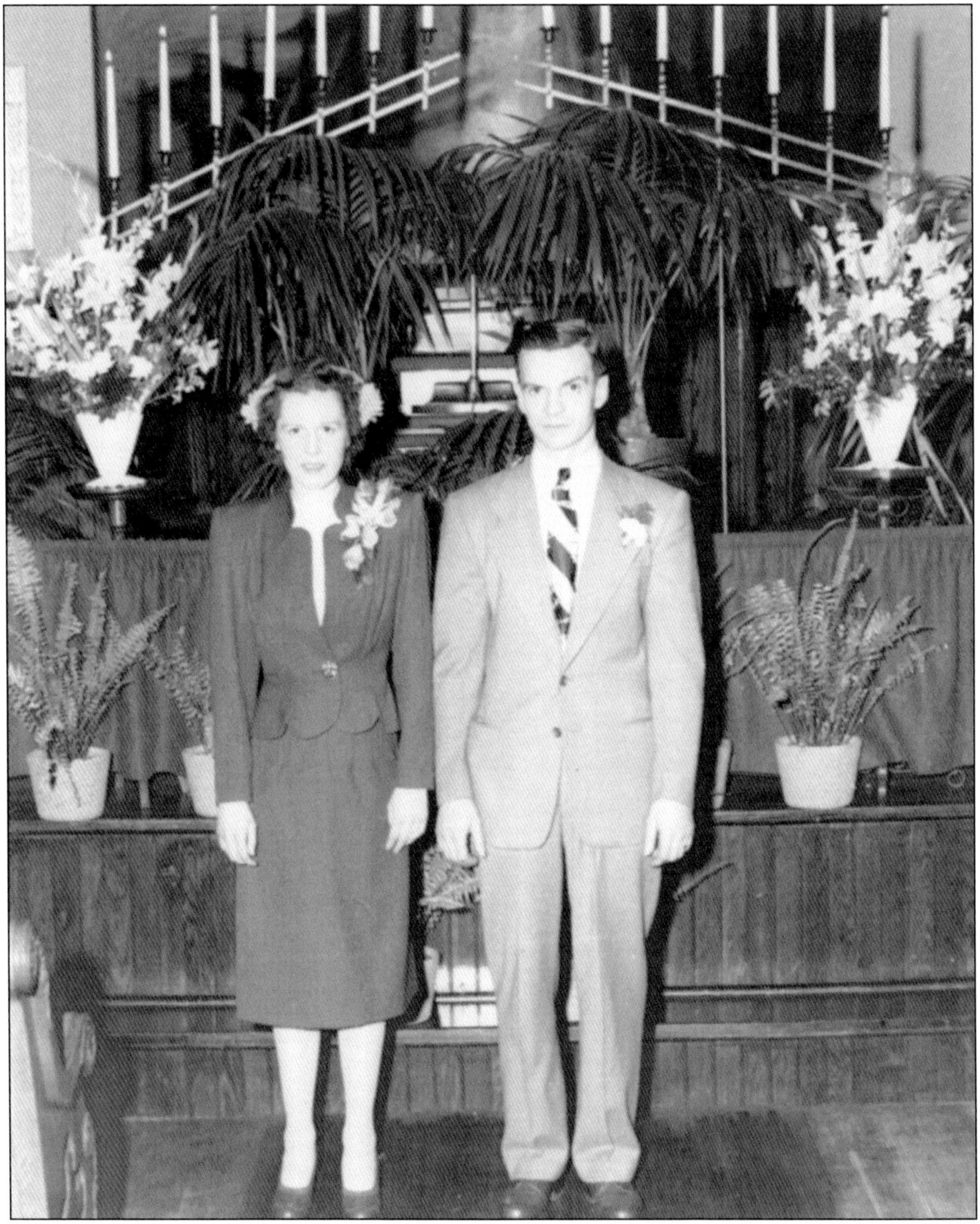

Shown on their wedding day, William E. Ross Jr. and Dorothy (Mosher) Ross pose in the sanctuary of Calvary Baptist Church on February 25, 1947. The former Mosher had been an employee of the General Manifold and Printing Company since her early 20s, while Ross had been employed by the Chicago Pneumatic Tool Company since his discharge from the US Navy. Having attended different elementary schools and there being a three-year difference in age, Mosher and Ross were not acquainted with each other through their school years. Mosher recalled noticing Ross about town in his Navy uniform while home on leave. Upon their marriage, they purchased a home on Buffalo Street and resided there for a little over six years prior to purchasing her dream home on Grant Street and returning to her beloved Third Ward, where they remained until their deaths. (Courtesy of Mary Ann Benton.)

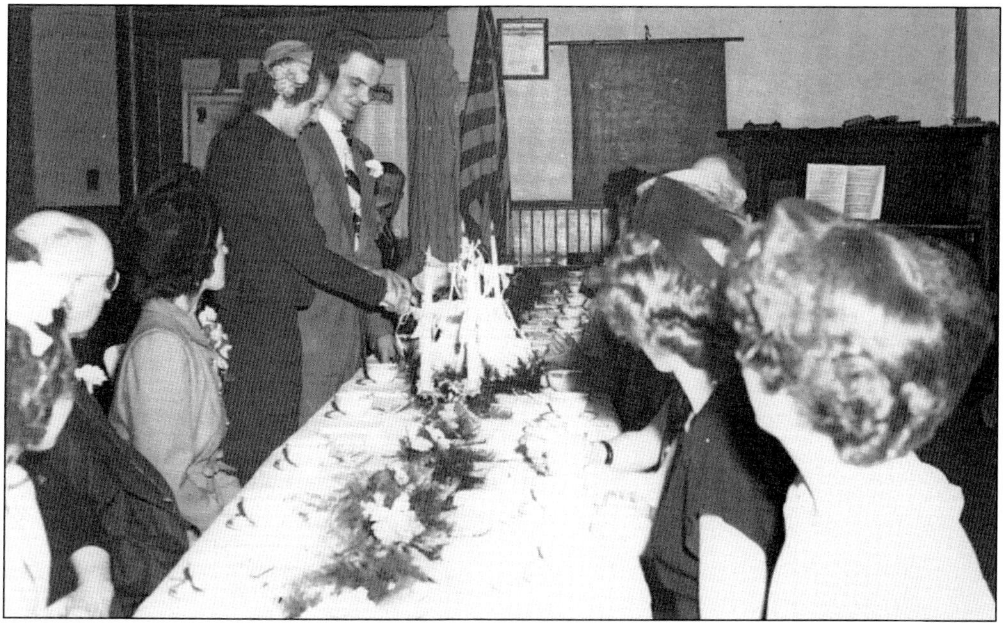

Pictured in the multipurpose room of Calvary Baptist Church after their wedding ceremony, William E. and Dorothy (Mosher) Ross cut their wedding cake. The building was originally erected in 1884 and had several different names and denominations throughout the first 50 years of its existence. Rev. Dr. G. Morgan Davis was the first to lead the Calvary Baptist Church. (Courtesy of Mary Ann Benton.)

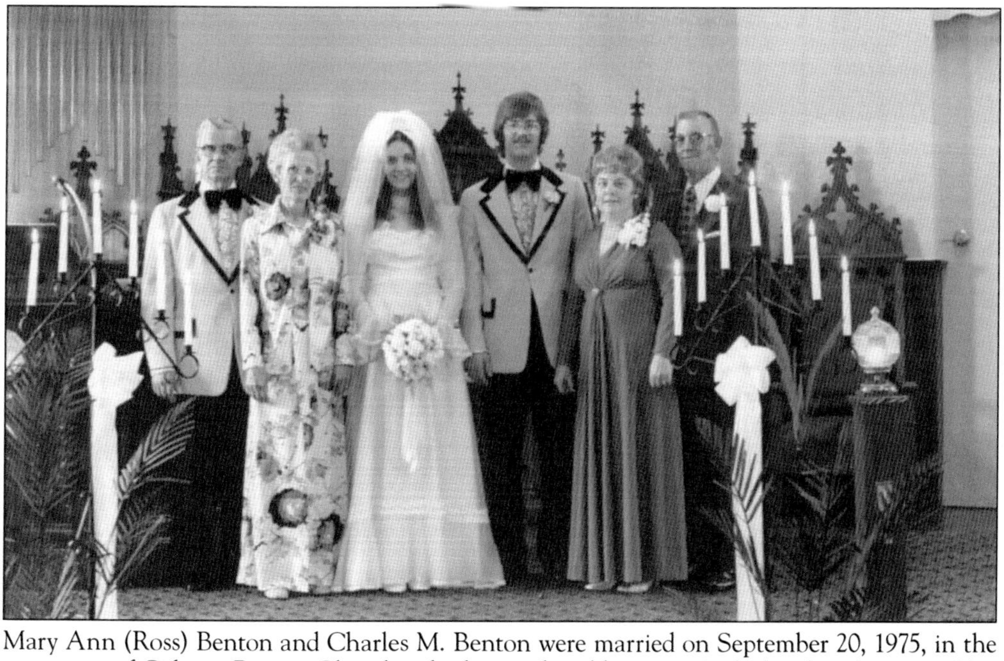

Mary Ann (Ross) Benton and Charles M. Benton were married on September 20, 1975, in the sanctuary of Calvary Baptist Church, which was the oldest non-Catholic church in Franklin before a suspicious fire destroyed it on Christmas Eve 1995. Also pictured are the parents of the happy couple, William E. and Dorothy Ross (left) and Jesse V. and Pauline Benton (right). (Courtesy of Thomas W. Ross.)

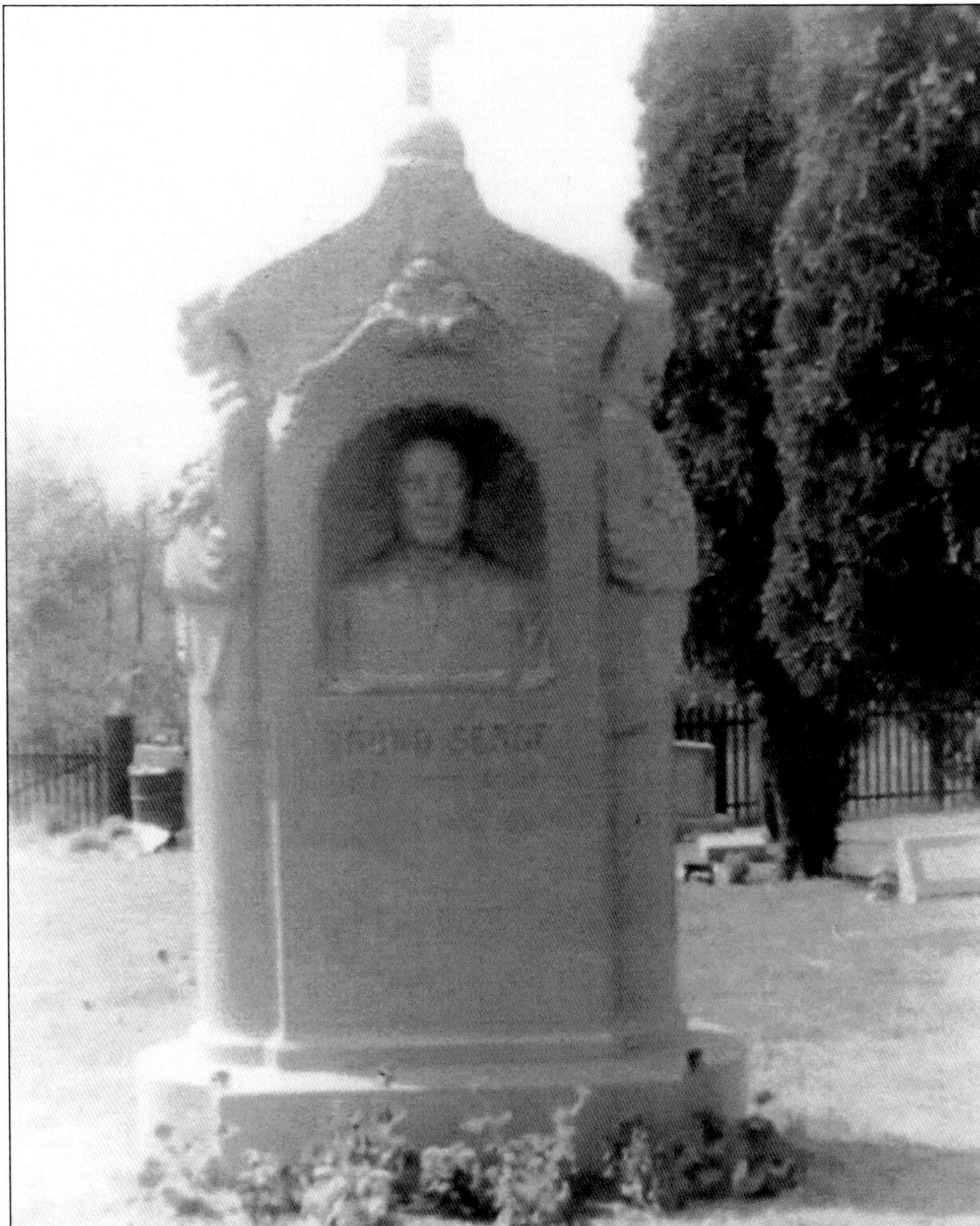

The headstone of Bruno Serge, located in St. Patrick's Cemetery, was created by his stepson Domenic Zappia, who was born in Italy but grew up in Franklin. He later attended the Cleveland Art Institute while spending summers working in Franklin. Zappia created a life-size carving of *The Last Supper* that was displayed at the 1964 World's Fair in New York City. St. Patrick's Cemetery is located on the corner of Meadville Pike and Washington Street in the Oak Hill neighborhood of the city. The Oak Hill softball field once occupied the lot behind the cemetery. The Oak Hill Apartments are now located there. The Oak Hill Methodist Church serves the parishioners of the area. Located at 10 Adams Street, the church also provides a camp area for religious activities. The streets in this neighborhood are named after past presidents of the United States. (Courtesy of Frances Serge Eakin.)

Eight

FLOODWATERS

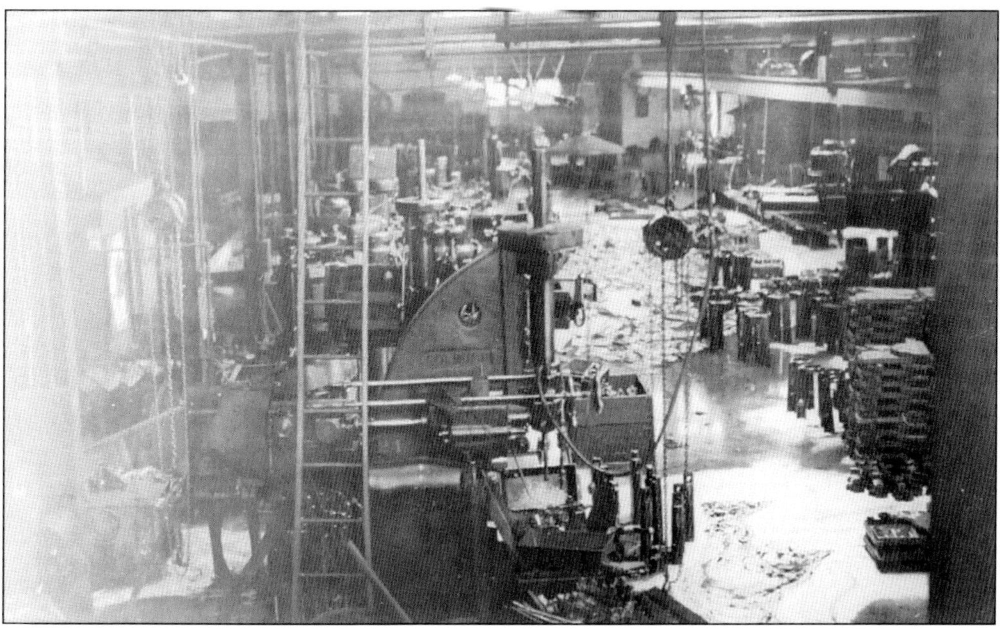

Damaging floodwaters infiltrate Plant No. 1 of the Chicago Pneumatic Tool Company in the 1910s. Formerly located on the northeastern side of the present-day Thirteenth Street Bridge, the plant then changed hands and was purchased by the Joy Manufacturing Company, under which it became Plant No. 3, locally known as "the chain plant." The plant burned on June 2, 1961. (Courtesy of Peter Solle.)

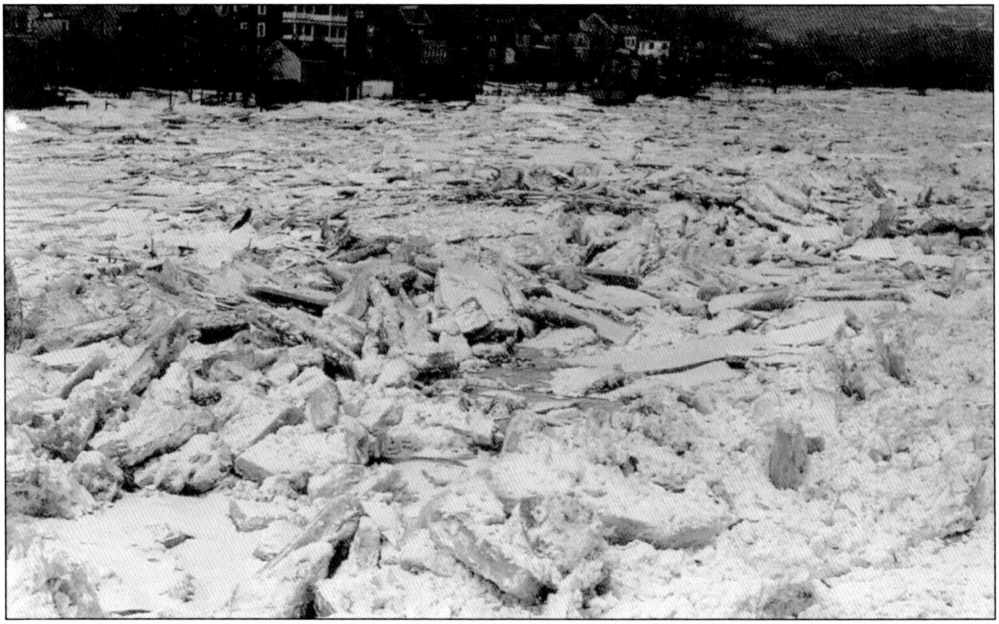

During the flood and ice jam of 1926, the process of melting combined with the downstream current of the Allegheny River caused the ice to break apart and collect in the area of Riverfront Park behind the 800 block of Elk Street. The ice is so thick that it has completely covered the park and is encroaching on the backyards of the residences up the hill on Elk Street. (Courtesy of Peter Solle.)

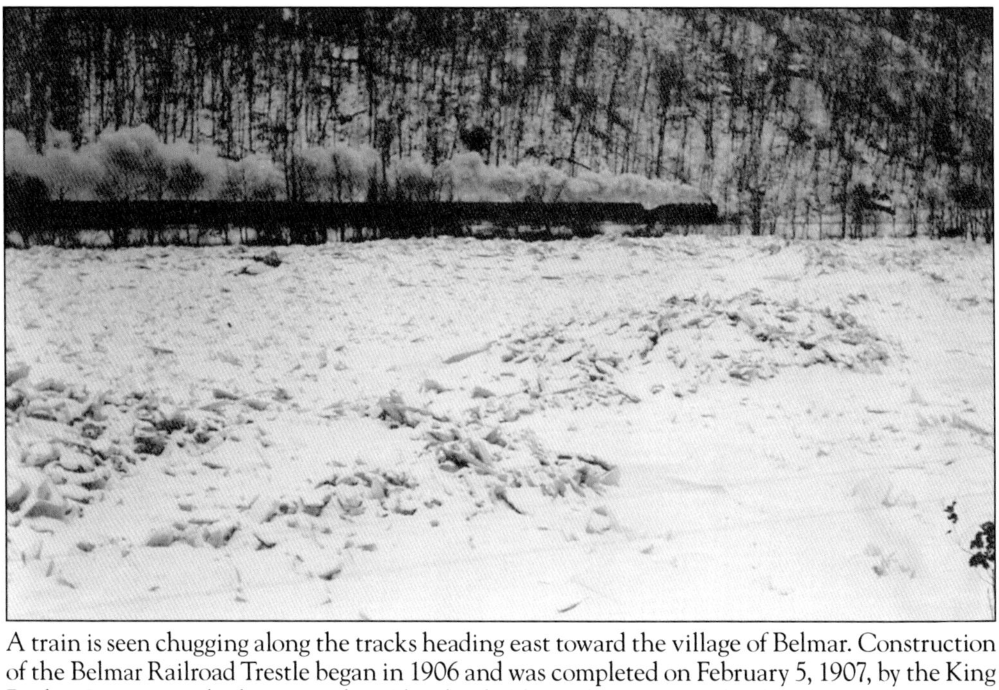

A train is seen chugging along the tracks heading east toward the village of Belmar. Construction of the Belmar Railroad Trestle began in 1906 and was completed on February 5, 1907, by the King Bridge Company, which operated in Cleveland, Ohio. This section of railroad ceased operation in the 1980s, and the Rails to Trails project has since converted the bridge for pedestrian and bicycle use. (Courtesy of Peter Solle.)

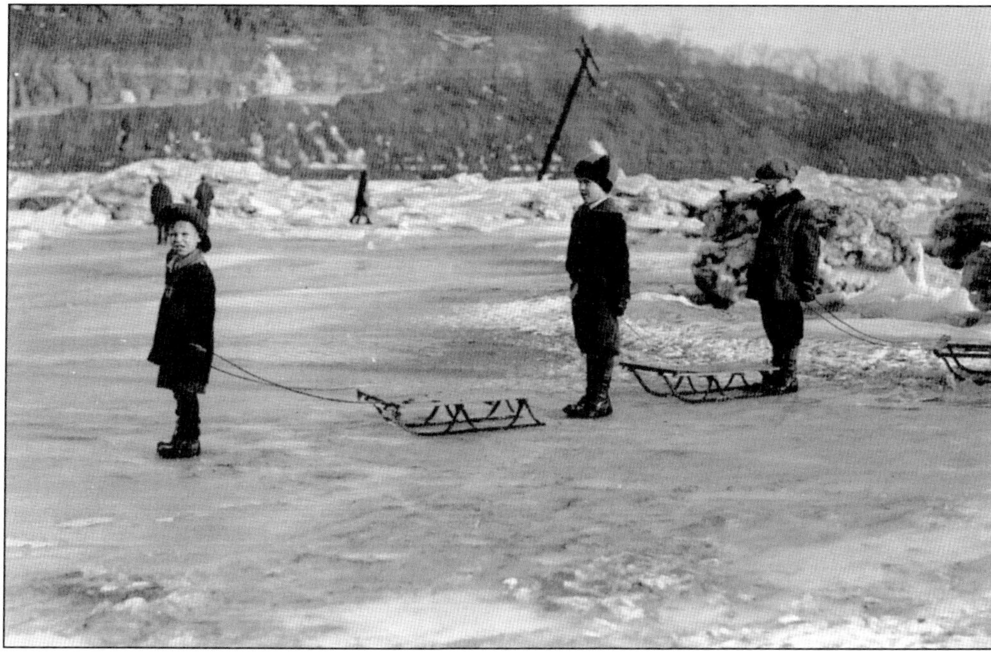

Children pause for a photograph while sledding on the frozen Allegheny River at the lower end of town. Before the creation of the Kinzua Dam in Warren County in the early 1960s, Franklin experienced many ice jams and floods. The Big Rock Bridge, once located near Deep Hollow Road, was taken out by ice jams in the early 1900s. (Courtesy of Peter Solle.)

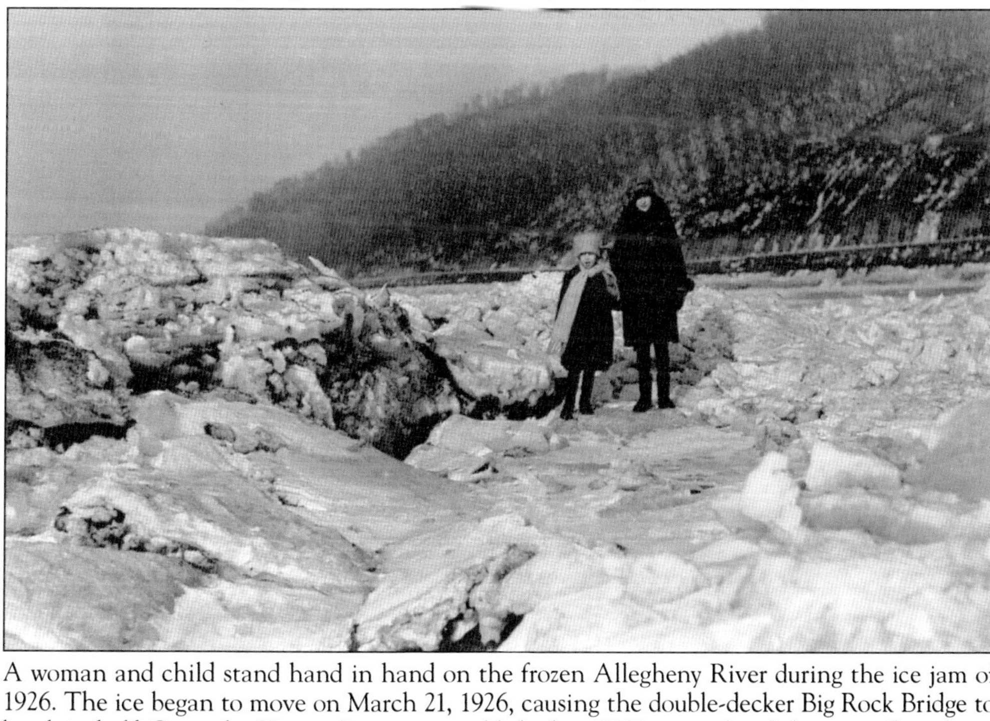

A woman and child stand hand in hand on the frozen Allegheny River during the ice jam of 1926. The ice began to move on March 21, 1926, causing the double-decker Big Rock Bridge to break in half. Once the Kinzua Dam was established in 1965, it regulated the water flow down river, which eliminated ice flows and major floods in the city. (Courtesy of Peter Solle.)

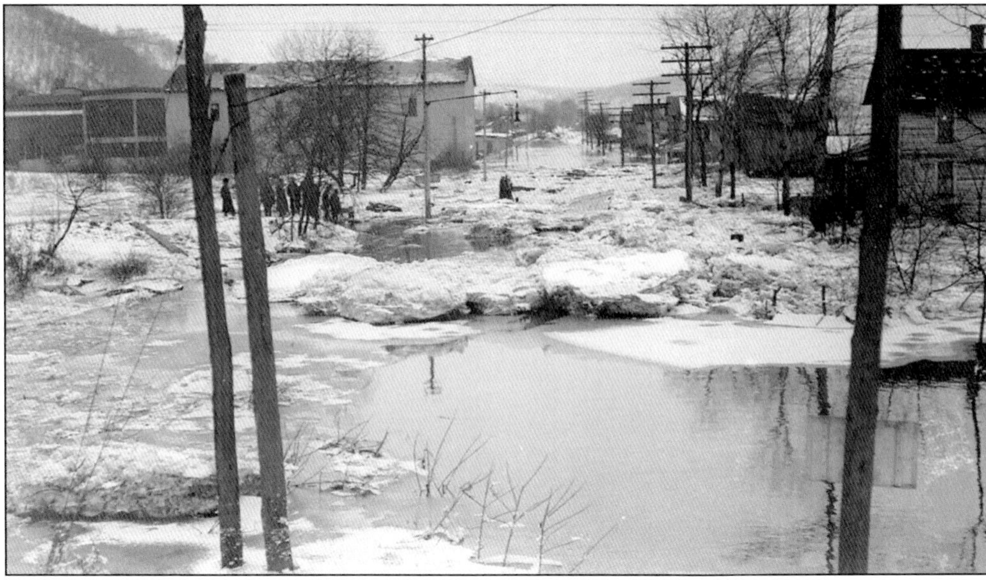

More flood damage is seen in this photograph taken near the Joy Manufacturing Company in the lower part of the city's First Ward area. As the spring thaw began, the water of melting ice from north of the city brought large ice chunks into the streets, parking lots, and backyards of businesses and homes. (Courtesy of Peter Solle.)

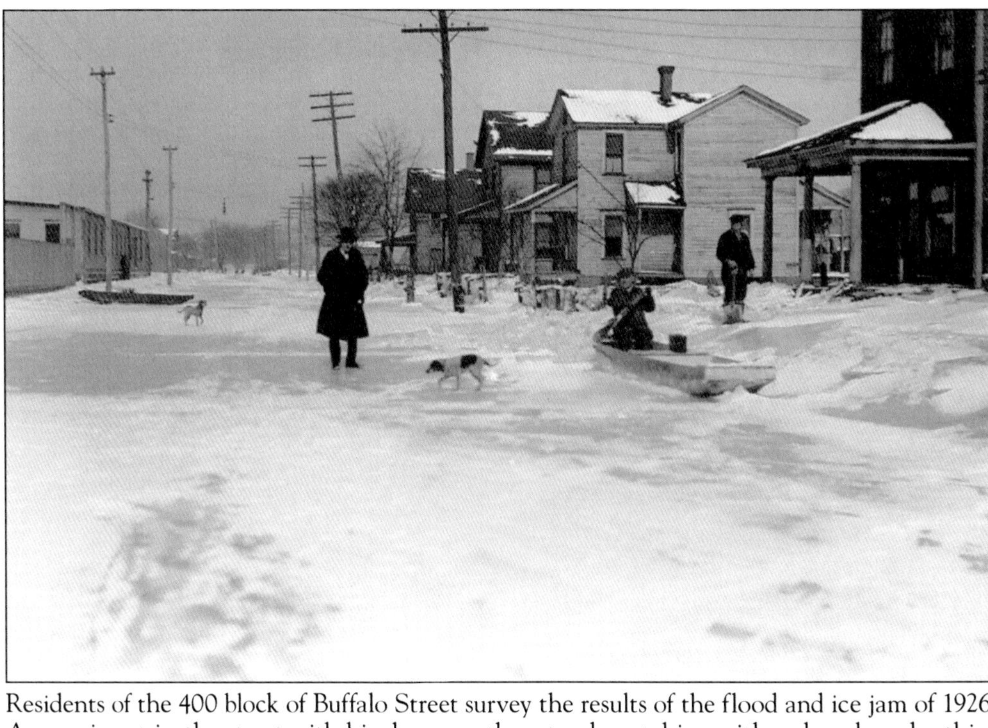

Residents of the 400 block of Buffalo Street survey the results of the flood and ice jam of 1926. A man is out in the street with his dogs, another stands watching with a shovel, and a third is rowing his boat down the street. Two other floods occurred in 1913 and 1916. (Courtesy of Peter Solle.)

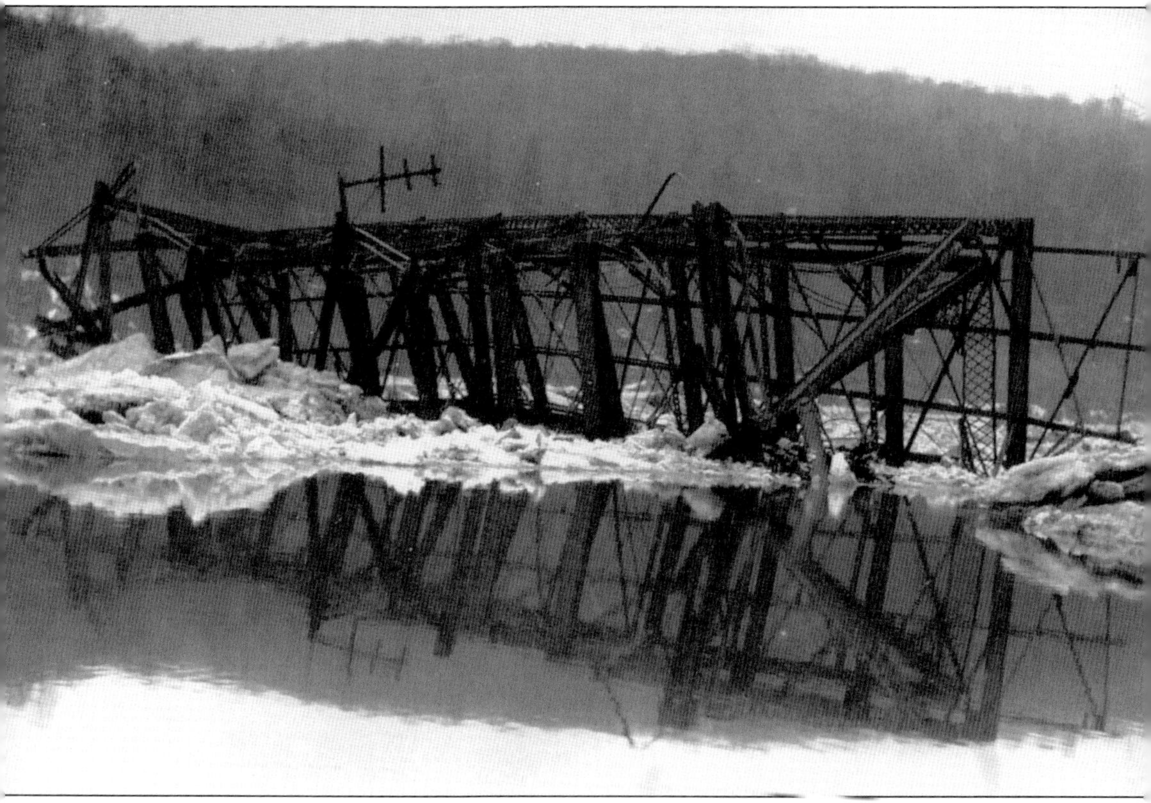

The twisted remnants of the Big Rock Bridge are seen here after it was taken out by ice jams during the early 1900s. The bridge crossed the Allegheny River at the eastern end of Franklin, near the intersection of US Route 322 and Deep Hollow Road. It was a double-decker bridge, with one level for cars and the other for a trolley. John Smithman founded the Oil City Railway Company in 1886, bringing electric streetcars to the Oil Region. The rail line was extended down Deep Hollow Road to Smithman Park (later renamed Monarch Park) in 1896. The line was then extended to Franklin in January 1901. The Citizens Traction Company purchased the railways of Oil City, Franklin, and the Big Rock Bridge, which was equipped with the upper deck trolley tracks in 1904, connecting Franklin to Monarch Park and Oil City. (Courtesy of Peter Solle.)

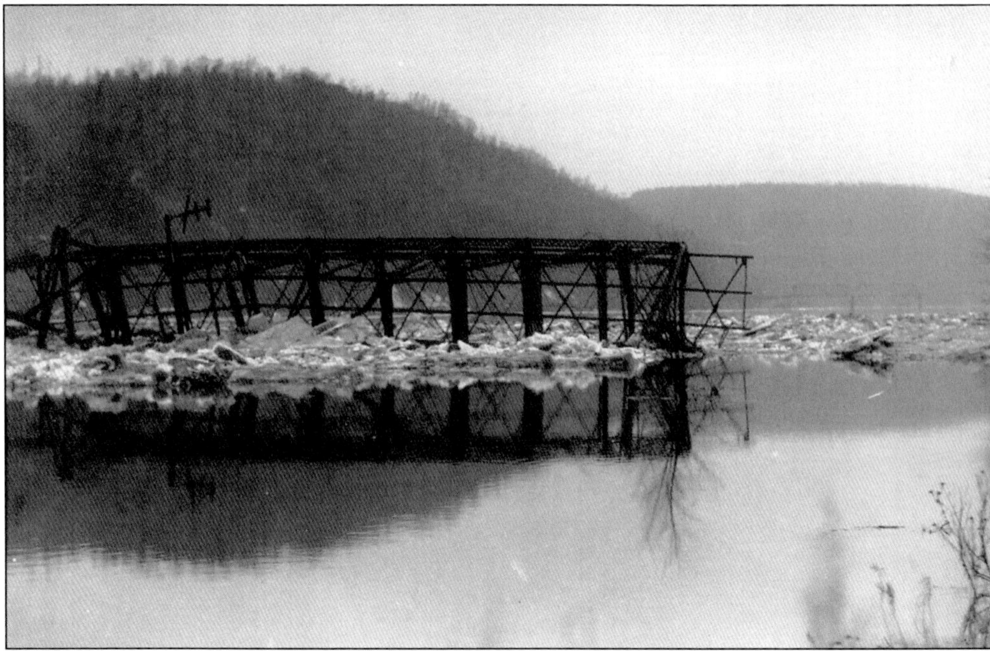

Here is another view of the Big Rock Bridge broken and dislodged from its placement spanning the Allegheny River. The bridge's trolley tracks carried patrons to Monarch Park, which boasted flower gardens and a theme park in the woods off Deep Hollow Road between Franklin and nearby Oil City. Monarch Park was the first home of the Blue Streak roller coaster of Conneaut Lake Park. (Courtesy of Peter Solle.)

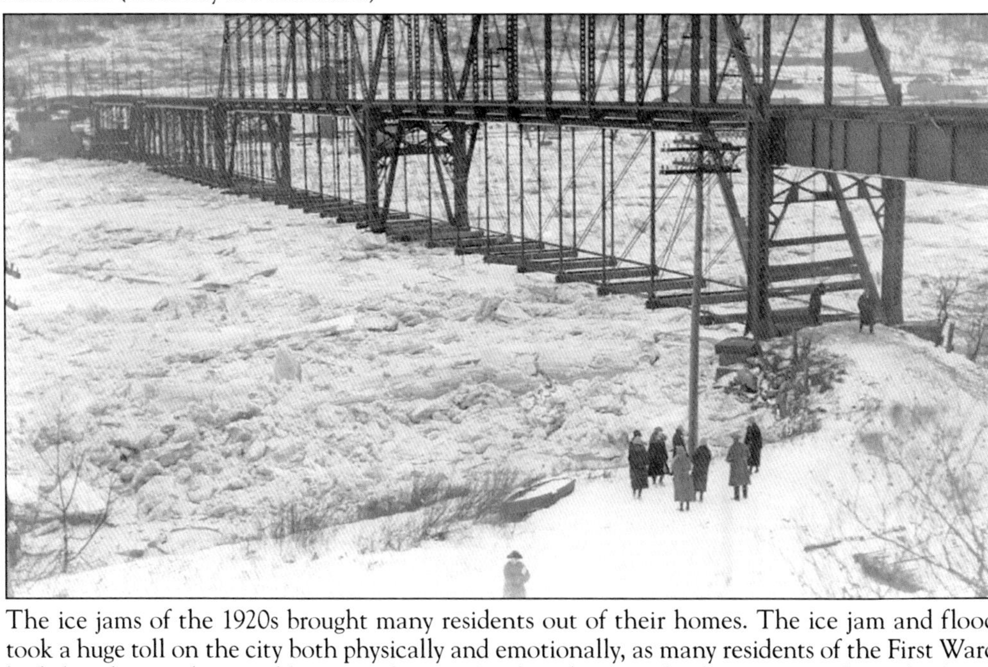

The ice jams of the 1920s brought many residents out of their homes. The ice jam and flood took a huge toll on the city both physically and emotionally, as many residents of the First Ward had their homes destroyed by water damage. In this photograph, the ice is touching the lower level of the Big Rock Bridge. Once the ice took out the bridge, it was never rebuilt. (Courtesy of Peter Solle.)

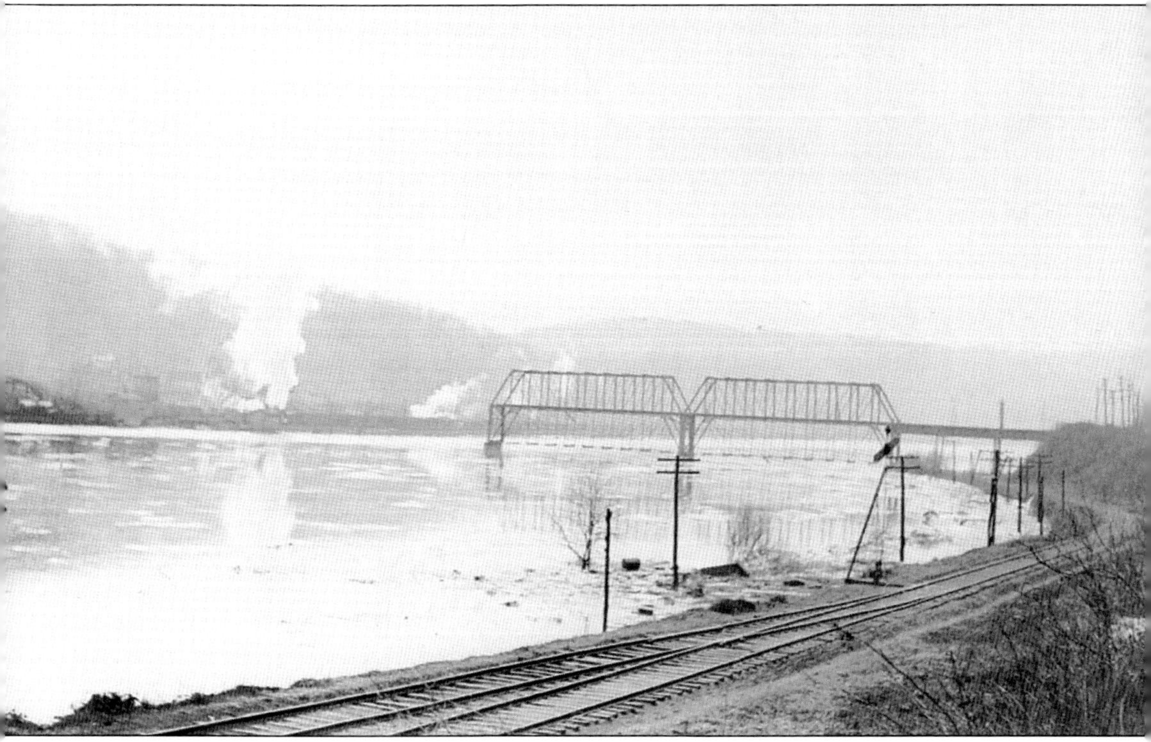

In this photograph, the remaining spans of the Big Rock Bridge are seen after the ice jam and flood took out the missing section. As seen here, railroad tracks flanked both banks of the Allegheny River, with a factory and its smoke billowing at left. The railroad bed across the river has since been converted into a recreational bicycle trail. During the ice jam and flood of 1926, the Pennsylvania Railroad chartered special train cars to bring curious spectators north to see the ice. A 15-to-20-foot-high ice jam formed near Brandon, approximately 10 miles down the Allegheny River from Franklin. The jam expanded when the current carried ice from Oil Creek, which was farther north. Some of the ice broke free and drifted down to Franklin, where it was halted and trapped by the Big Rock Bridge. As seen here, the eastern portion of the bridge fell on March 21, 1926, a mere eight minutes after a trolley full of passengers had crossed en route to Franklin. (Courtesy of Peter Solle.)

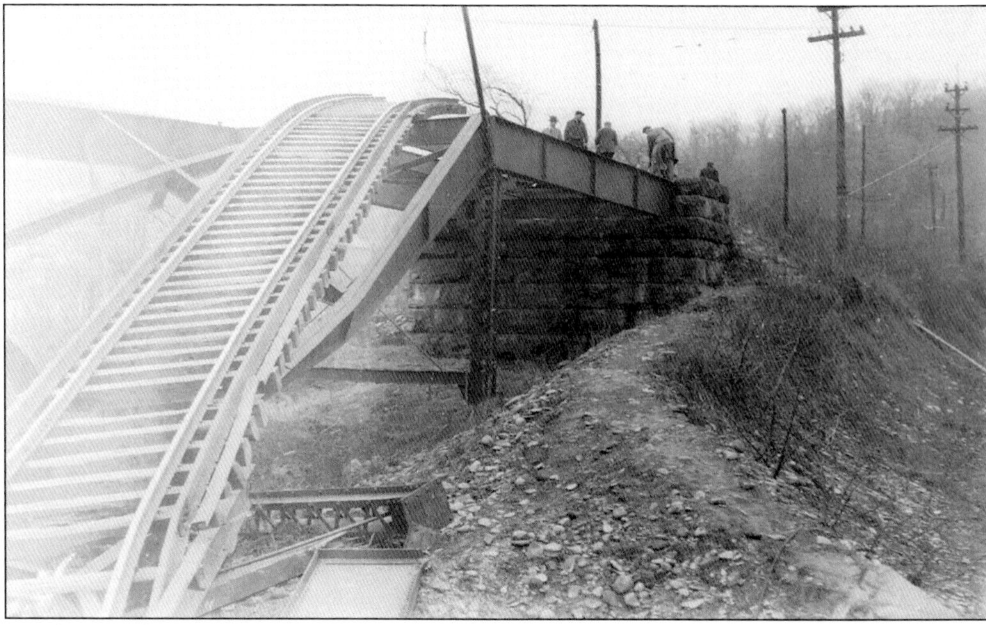

Locals view the damage to the trolley line portion of the Big Rock Bridge from the ice jam and flood of 1926. The bridge, originally a single-deck structure, had three pylons. The upper deck was added after years of use to accommodate trolley service to the local amusement park and points north. (Courtesy of Peter Solle.)

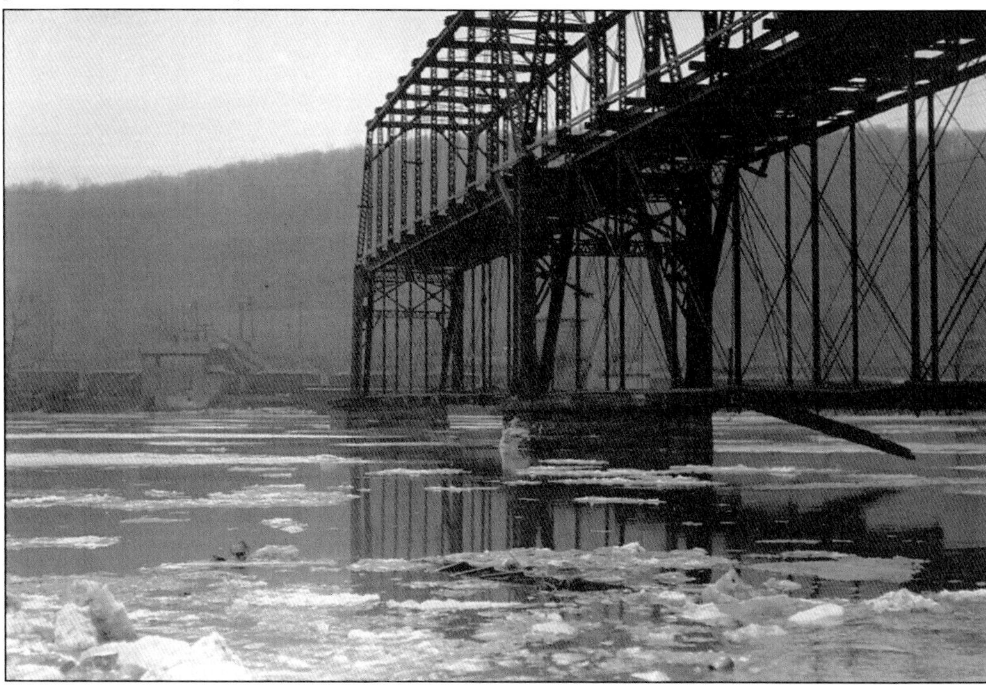

Along with the collapse of the Big Rock Bridge, lower sections of Franklin were flooded with five feet of water, the Reno Bridge and several Oil City bridges were threatened by ice, low-lying highways between Franklin and Reno were closed, and all factories were closed in Oil City, which was also under up to 15 feet of water depending on elevation. (Courtesy of Peter Solle.)

Nine

Petroleum Influence

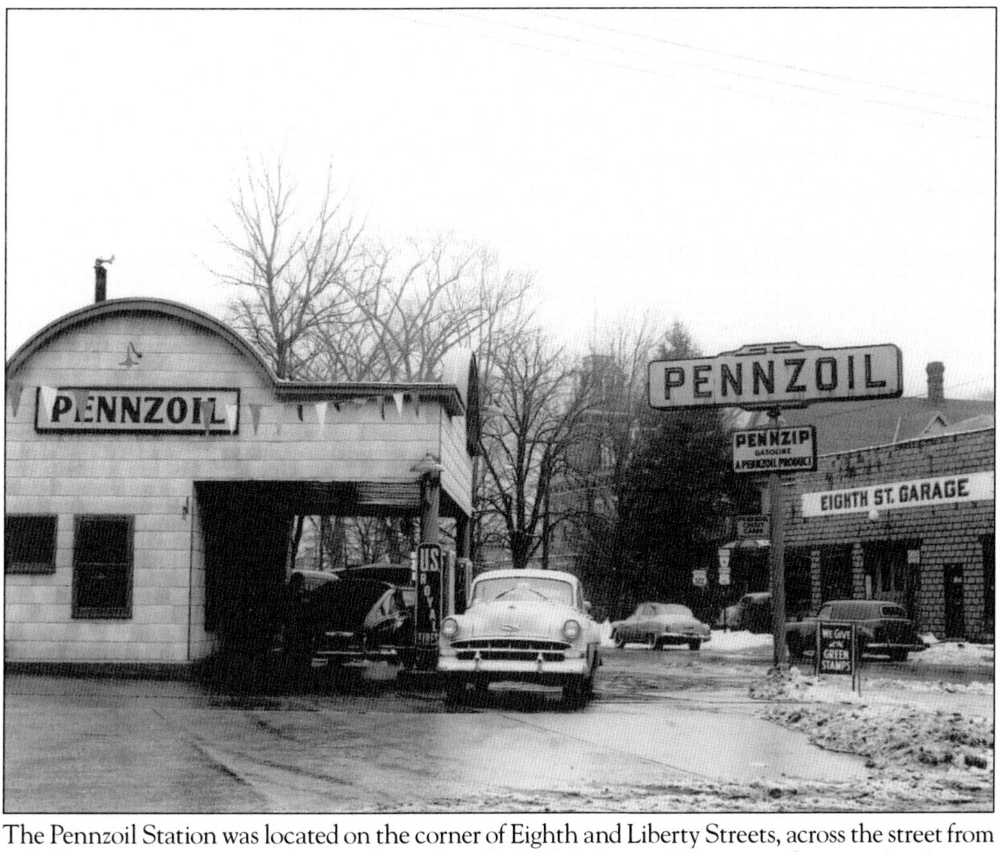

The Pennzoil Station was located on the corner of Eighth and Liberty Streets, across the street from Schiffer Brothers Super Market. On the right is the Eighth Street Garage, now home to StorSecure. The beautiful home in the background is gone and has been replaced by a church owned by the Salvation Army. The Pennzoil Station is now Walz Tire Company. (Courtesy of Peter Solle.)

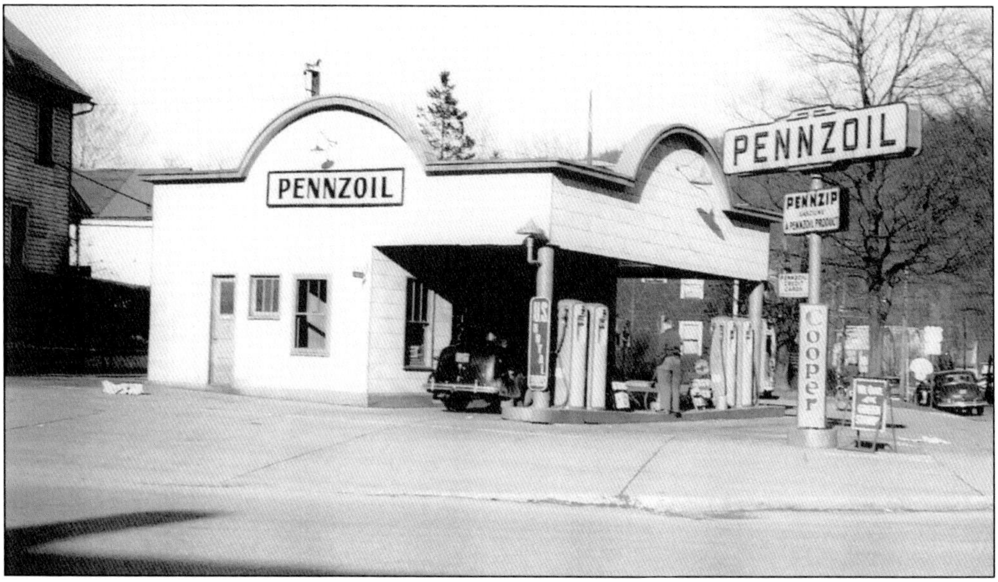

The Pennzoil Station shown here was one of nearly 20 family-owned gas and service stations in Franklin during the mid-1900s. As society progressed and the economy changed, those stations could not compete with the national chains, including Sheetz and Kwik Fill. Only a handful of locally owned automotive service stations are still in business within the city. (Courtesy of Peter Solle.)

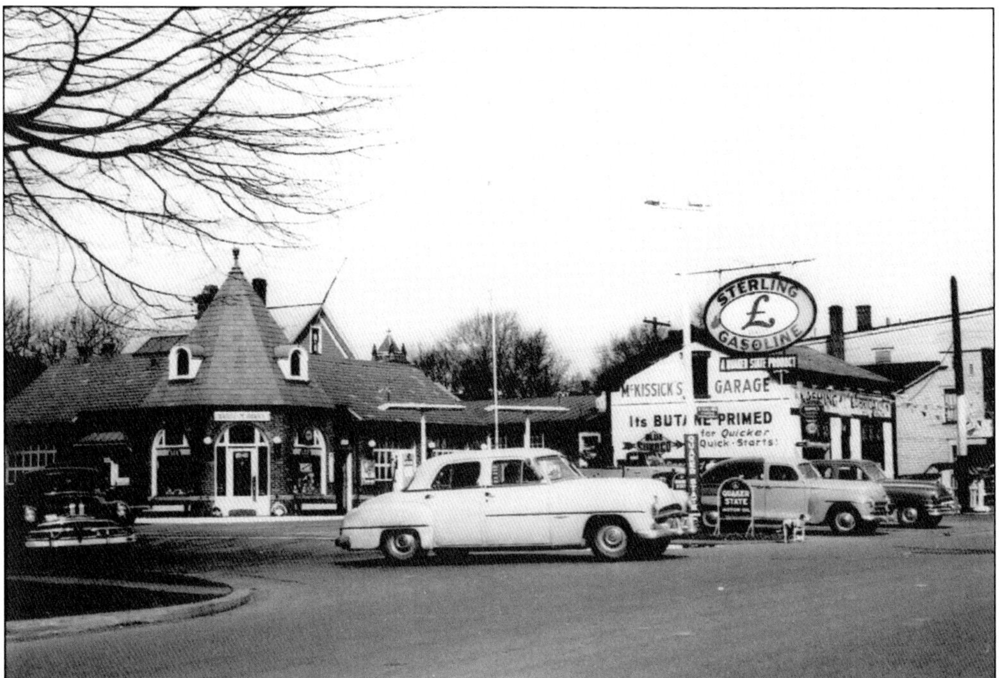

The Sterling Gasoline Station was located on the corner of Eleventh and Liberty Streets. At one time, one could stand at this intersection and count five gas stations on Liberty Street looking toward the downtown area. To the right of the station is McKissick's Garage. The Sterling was remodeled to become a Sheetz. (Courtesy of Peter Solle.)

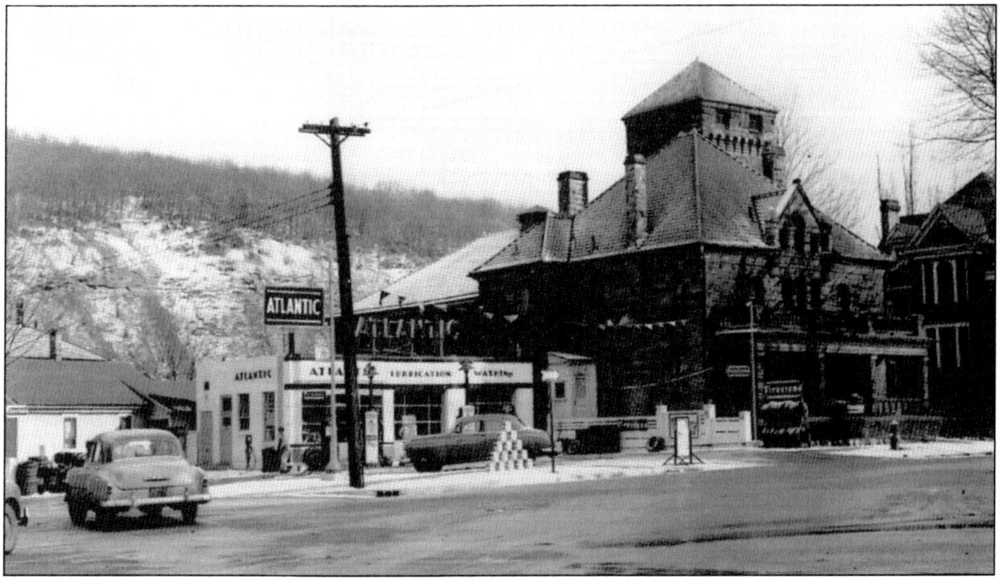

The Atlantic Gas Station stood on the corner of Twelfth and Elk Streets, across the street from the post office. To the right of the station is the Venango County Jail. A new jail building was constructed in 1910 after the former residential-style structure was razed, and it began housing prisoners on May 27, 1911. In 1994, the building was extended back to Otter Street. (Courtesy of Peter Solle.)

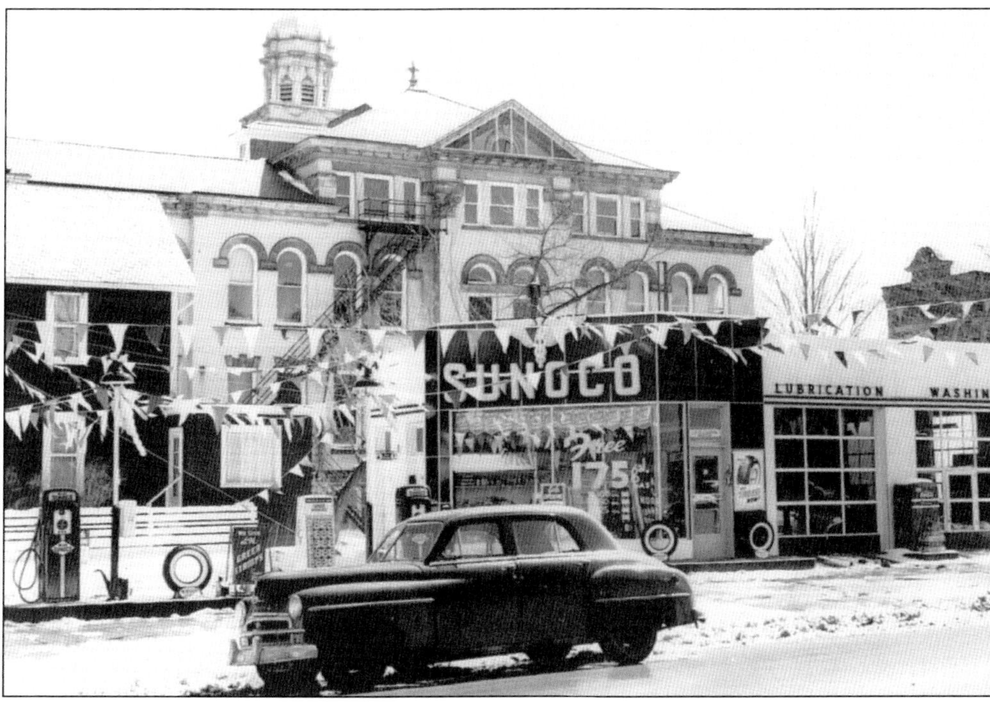

Located right at the corner of Thirteenth and Otter Streets, beside the Franklin Junior-Senior High School complex, was the Sunoco Gas Station owned by Bob Prichard. The gas prices were 25¢ a gallon, 50¢ a gallon, and $1 a gallon. This gas station was eventually torn down, and the Franklin Fire Department was erected on the site in the early 1970s. (Courtesy of Peter Solle.)

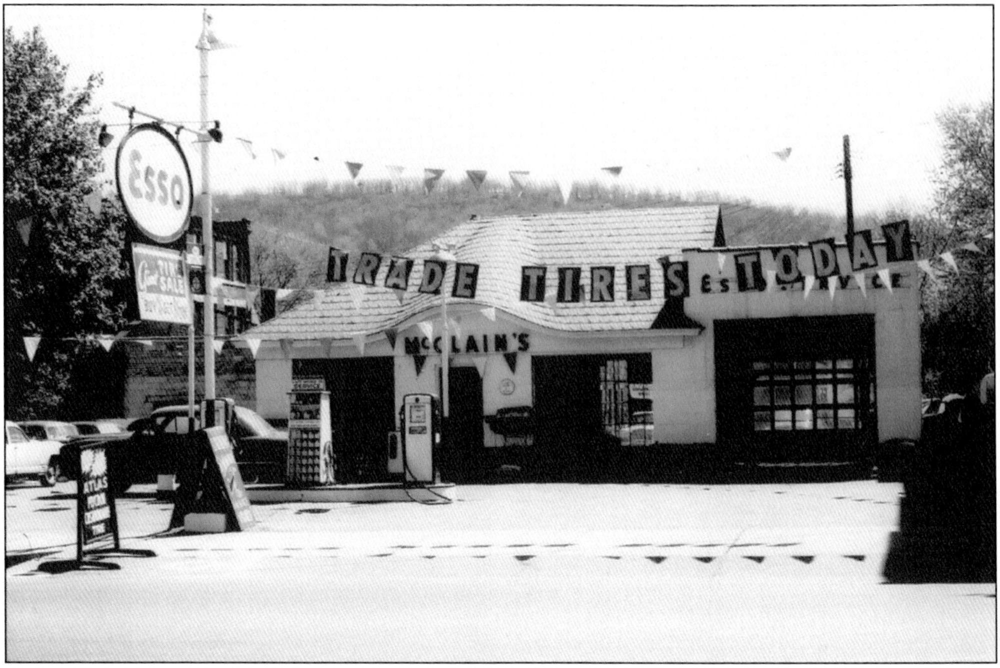

McClain's Esso Station was located in the 200 block of Thirteenth Street, near the intersection with Otter Street. Along with a banner inviting customers to "Trade Tires Today," another sign advertises the service station's "Giant Tire Sale, Buy 2 Get 1 Free." Frank Fleming ran the station during a stretch of time and hired "Baldy" Rice on as an employee. (Courtesy of Peter Solle.)

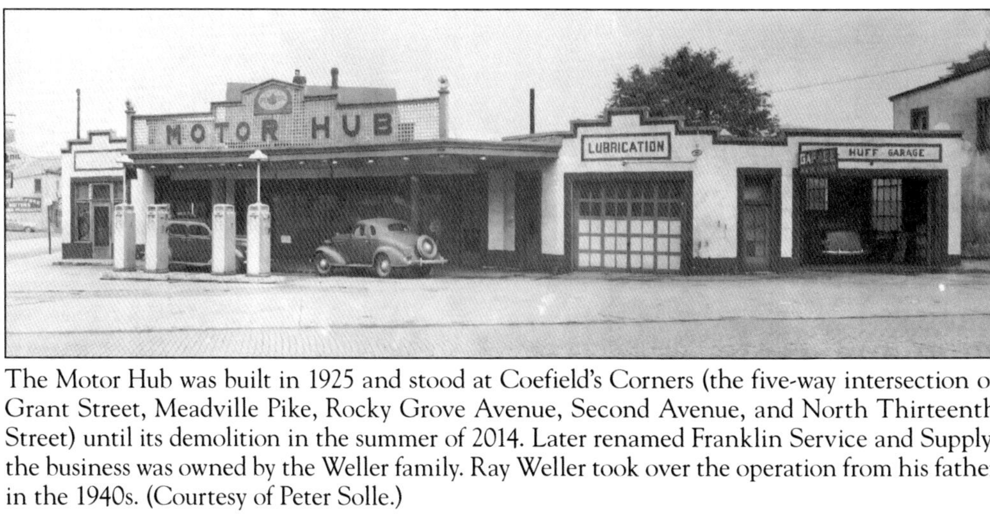

The Motor Hub was built in 1925 and stood at Coefield's Corners (the five-way intersection of Grant Street, Meadville Pike, Rocky Grove Avenue, Second Avenue, and North Thirteenth Street) until its demolition in the summer of 2014. Later renamed Franklin Service and Supply, the business was owned by the Weller family. Ray Weller took over the operation from his father in the 1940s. (Courtesy of Peter Solle.)

Ten

Industrial Franklin

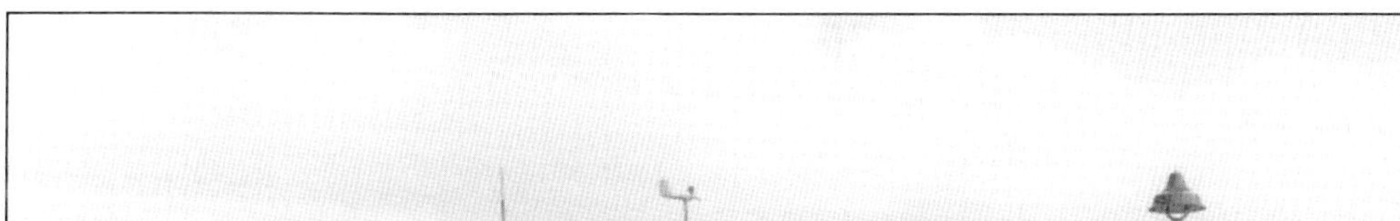

Construction of the Chess Lamberton Airport began in 1950 and was named for J. Robert Lamberton's grandson. Prior to its inception, an airport was used in Sugarcreek Borough from 1929 to 1938, followed by Splane Memorial Airport in Oil City from 1941 to 1950, both of which are now defunct. Today, the airport is known as Venango Regional Airport and offers commuter service to Pittsburgh. (Courtesy of Peter Solle.)

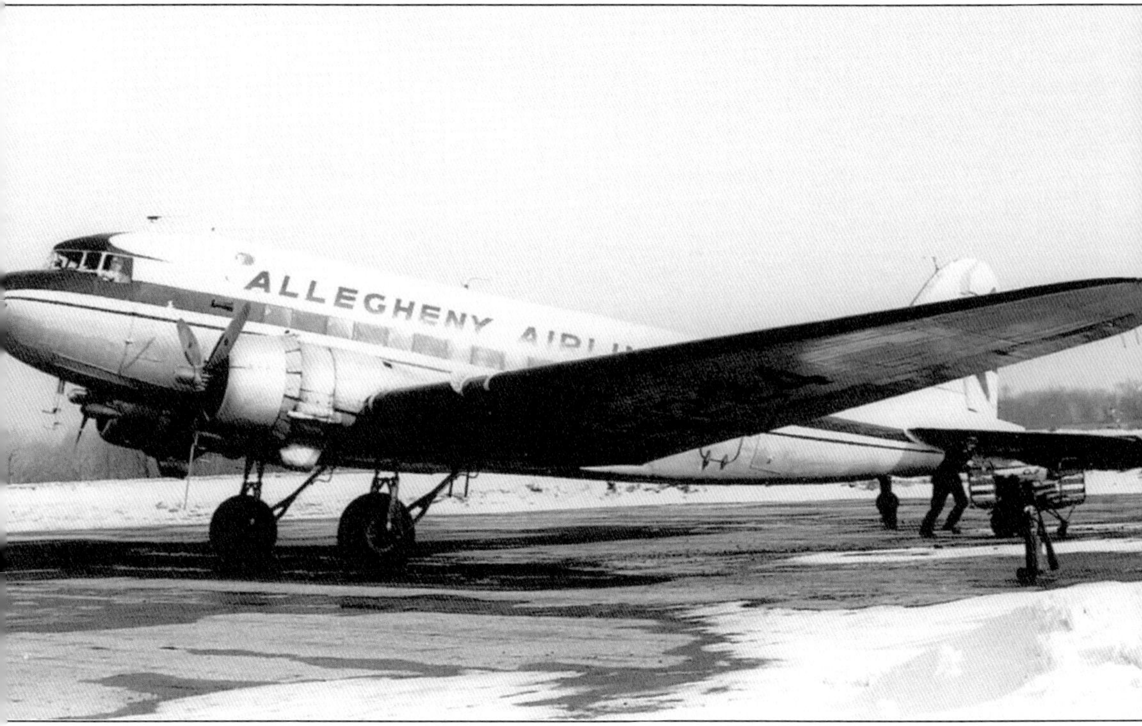

Pictured here is an Allegheny Airlines plane. When Richard C. DuPont and Alexis Felix DuPont Jr. founded the airline in March 1939, it was originally known as the All-American Aviation Company; the name was changed to Allegheny Airlines on January 1, 1953. The company began offering a commuter service the same year. In 1979, the company changed its name again to USAir, then later to US Airways, as it is known today. With the Wright brothers' first flight in 1903, aviation fever hit Franklin hard. In 1930, C.A. Barrow, along with his father W.E. Barrow and J.P. Bauer, created the Franklin Aircraft Corporation and began manufacturing a biplane they called the Franklin Sport. The Oil City Flying Club purchased the first plane built. The last model, the Franklin Sport 90, was built in the fall of 1932. On May 19, 1938, the first airmail flight from Franklin took place. (Courtesy of Peter Solle.)

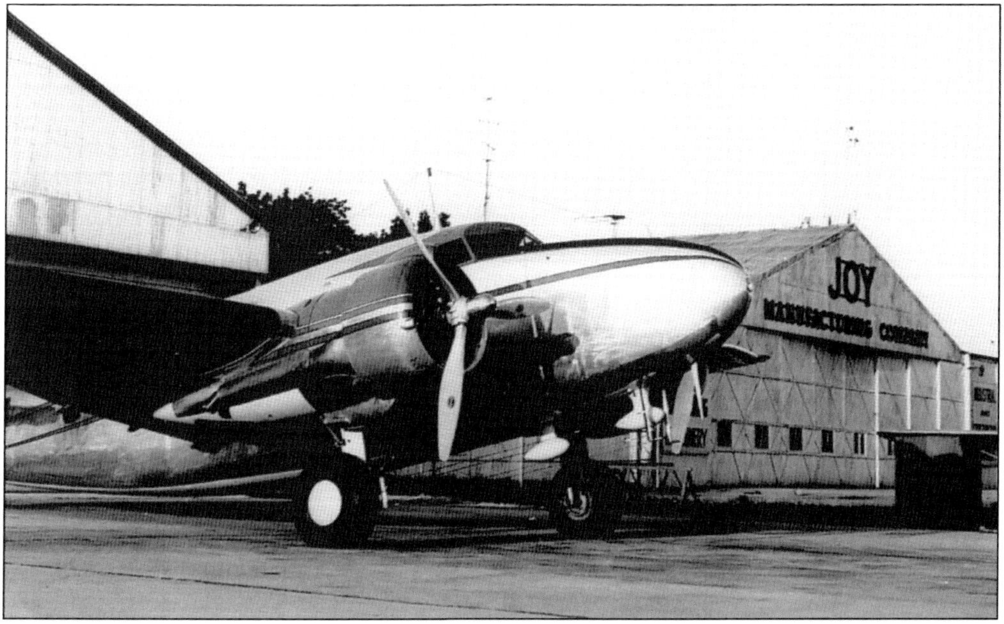

A plane sits outside a hangar at Chess Lamberton Airport in the early 1950s. In the background is the Joy Manufacturing Company hangar. Incorporated in 1919, the company had a very large presence in the community. Founder Joseph Francis Joy was born in Cumberland, Maryland, on September 13, 1883, and went to work in the coal mines at 12 years old. (Courtesy of Peter Solle.)

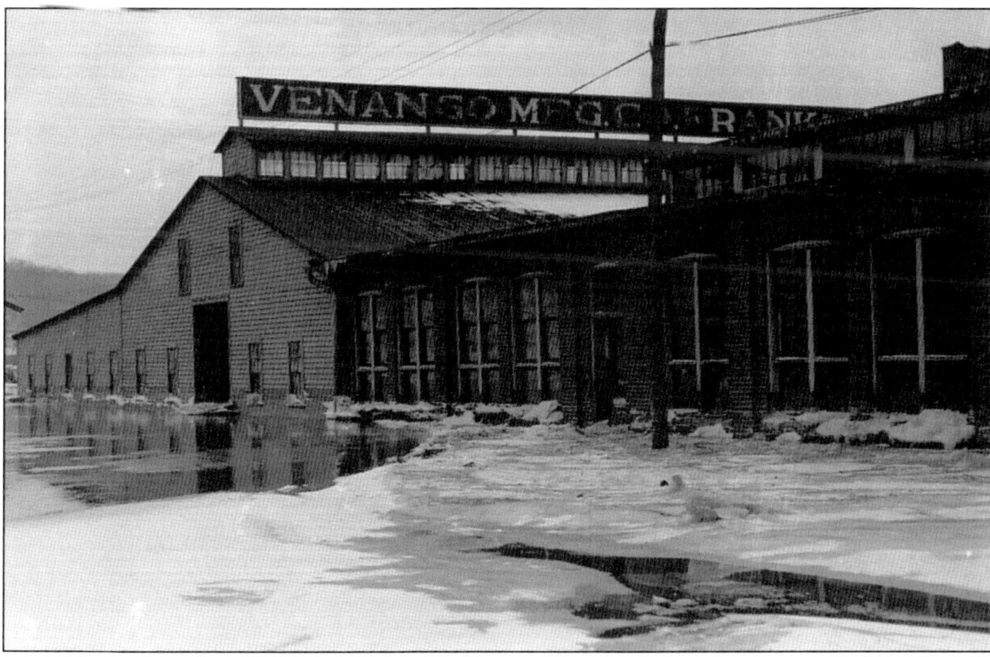

The Venango Manufacturing Company is seen during the flood of 1926. Located on First Street along the Allegheny River, the plant sustained damage due to ice jams. Many houses located in the lower part of town were flooded, some with water as high as their second floors. Many residents reported rugs and carpets frozen to the ceilings of their second stories. (Courtesy of Peter Solle.)

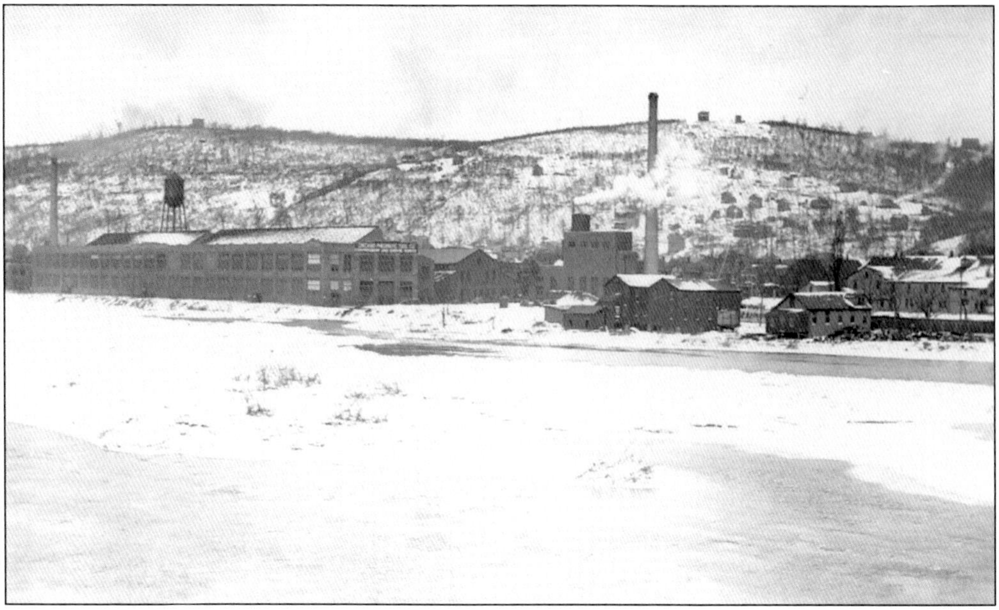

The Chicago Pneumatic Tool Company (CPT) took control of the Grant Company in 1901. The following year, CPT also acquired the Franklin Air Compressor Company, which had financial problems. Both of the author's grandfathers, William E. Ross and Jesse V. Benton, worked for CPT for many years. Ross could remember balling up asbestos and playing catch during breaks. (Courtesy of Peter Solle.)

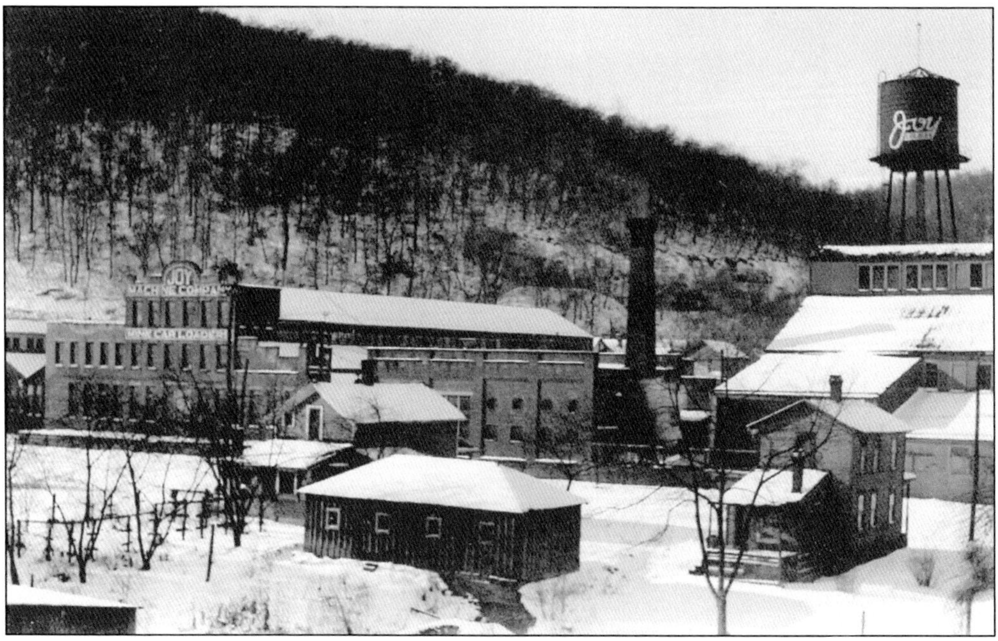

The Franklin Plant of Joy Manufacturing was the first plant to carry the company's name. Presently, the Franklin division is made up of three producing groups and remains the biggest division in the creation of mining equipment within the entire Joy Global corporation. The Franklin branch employs over 270 engineers and serves as the center of engineering for Joy Mining Manufacturing. (Courtesy of Peter Solle.)

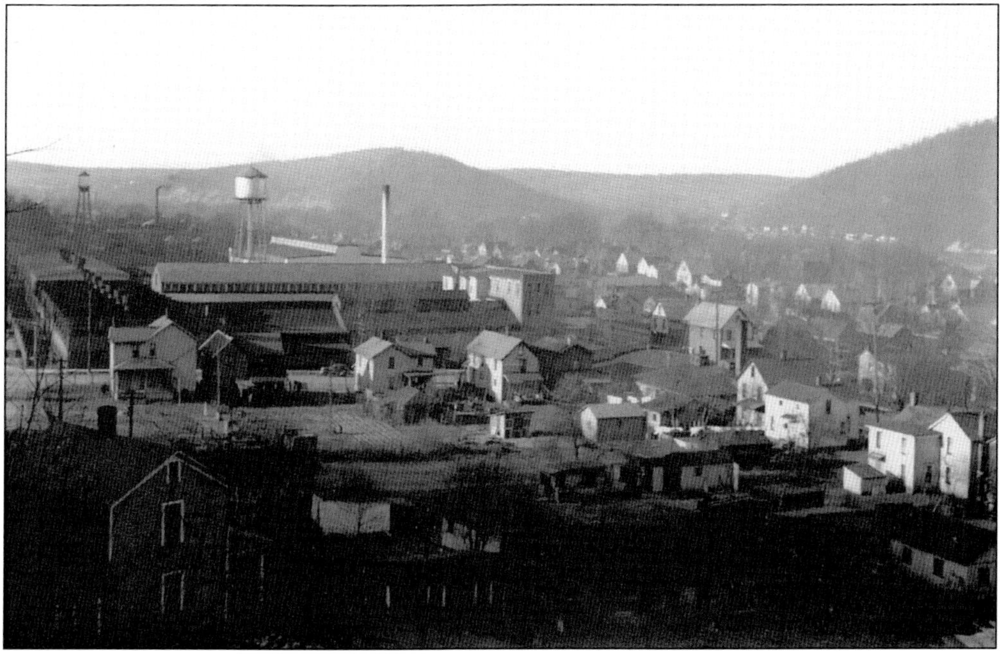

Joy Manufacturing Company's Plant No. 1 is seen in this aerial shot taken from Bully Hill. Currently, Plant No. 1 is the engineering Center of Excellence for continuous miners. The chain plant located in nearby Reno, Pennsylvania, is the top supplier of conveyor, ripperveyor, and crawler chains, as well as bit holding systems, for all portions of business. (Courtesy of Peter Solle.)

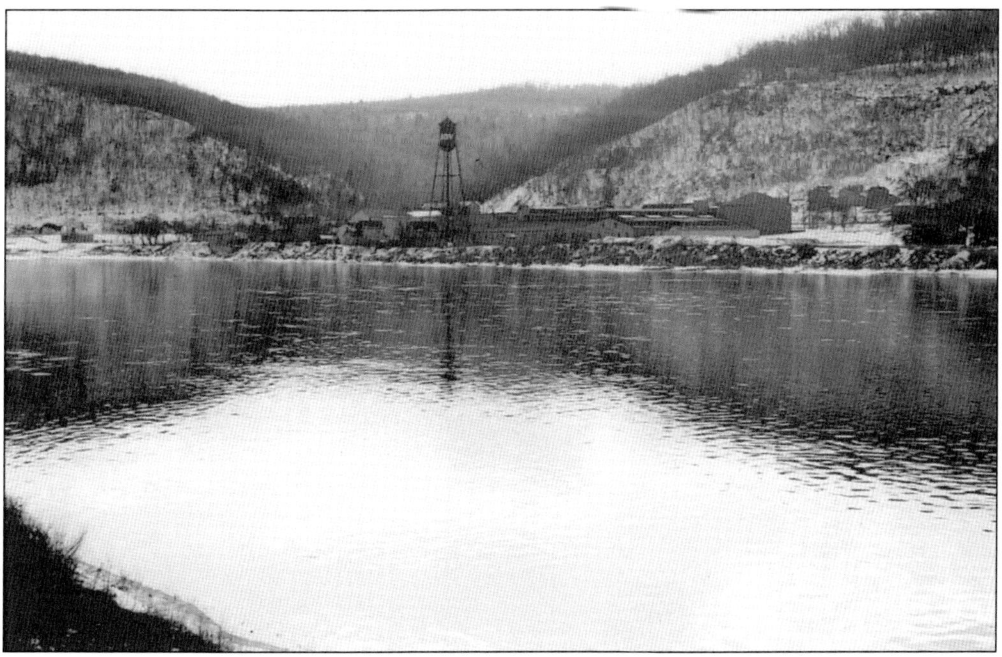

Situated along the Allegheny River at the eastern end of town, Joy Underground Mining, a division of Joy Global, has been a part of Franklin since 1924. The Joy water tower welcomed residents heading west along US Route 322 into the city for decades; however, the tower has since disappeared from the landscape. (Courtesy of Peter Solle.)

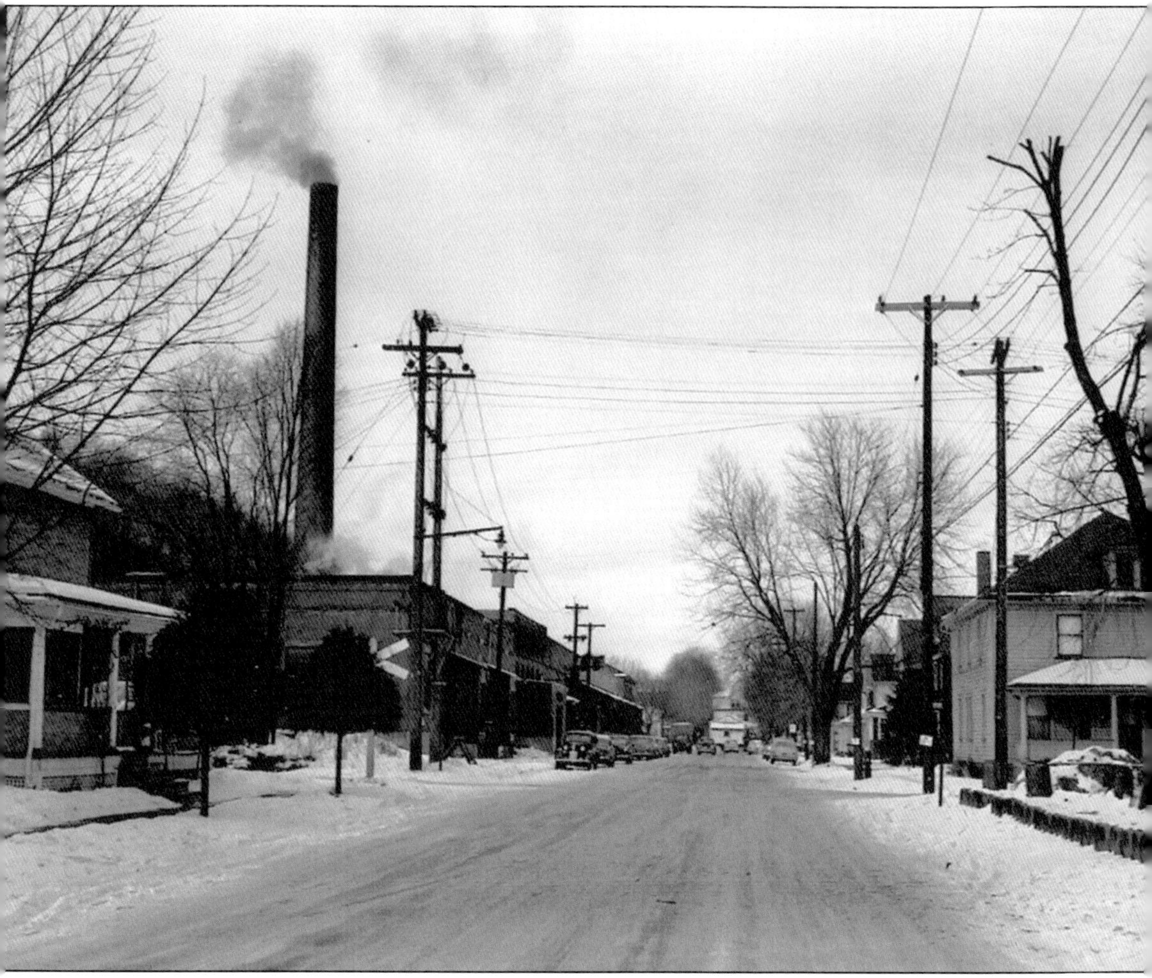

Once located at the intersection of Fifth and Buffalo Streets, the General Manifold and Printing Company (left) was established in 1901. The main office and plant was located in Franklin, while district sales offices were located in Detroit, Pittsburgh, Boston, Philadelphia, Chicago, and New York. The company specialized in commercial, railroad, and industrial printing of all kinds, as well as other specialties. Dr. Franklin H. Johnston was the manager of the General Manifold and Printing Company. Dr. Johnston was born in nearby Canal Township on December 20, 1841. He was a corporal in the Civil War, serving with Company G, the 63rd Regiment of Pennsylvania Volunteers. He began teaching in Cooperstown and studying medicine upon his return home. After graduating from medical school, he moved several places before settling in Butler County and opening his own practice. Dr. Johnston studied shorthand and, due to his expertise in it, was offered a position from Joseph Sibley to work for his Galena Oil Company, which he accepted. (Courtesy of Peter Solle.)

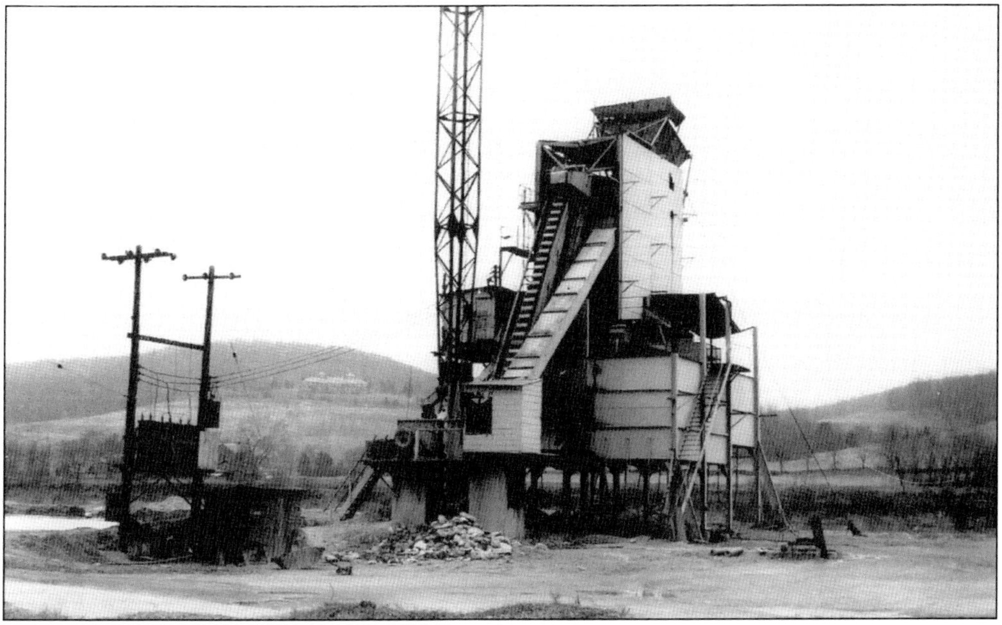

Oil City Sand and Gravel was located along the Allegheny River in Sugarcreek Borough, across Washington Crossing Bridge when heading north toward Oil City on PA Route 8. This was a dangerous business, costing a few workers their lives due to falling off barges. Presently, this is the site of IA Construction Corporation. River Ridge mansion can be seen on the hill in the background. (Courtesy of Peter Solle.)

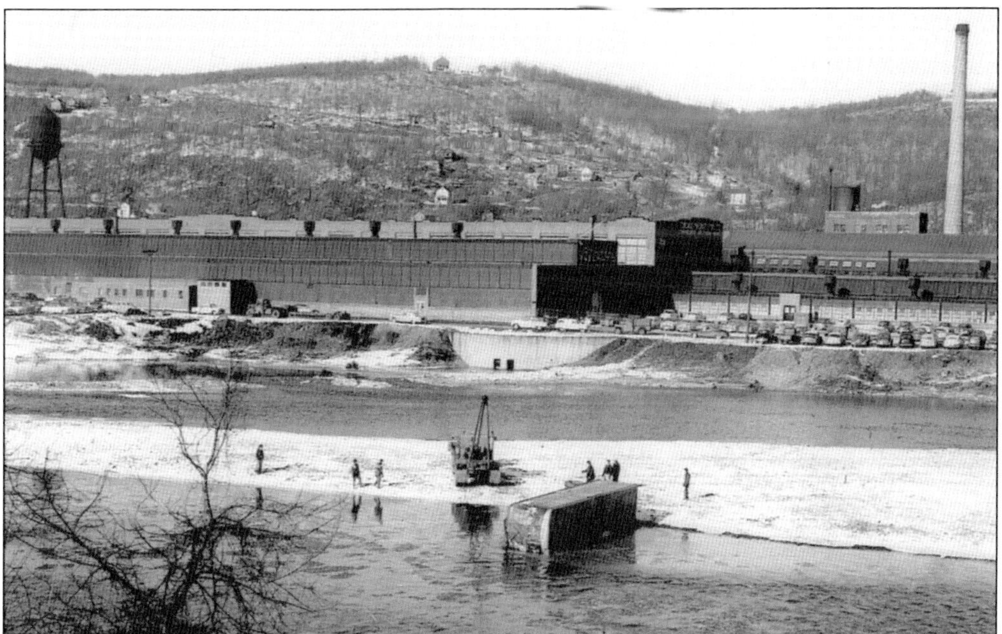

A delivery truck is seen lying in French Creek with a tow truck ready to pull it from the water. Accidents like this have happened a handful of times over the past 100 years when trucks lose their brakes on the steep grade of Fifteenth Street Hill on their way into town. The Chicago Pneumatic Tool Company is shown in the background. (Courtesy of Peter Solle.)

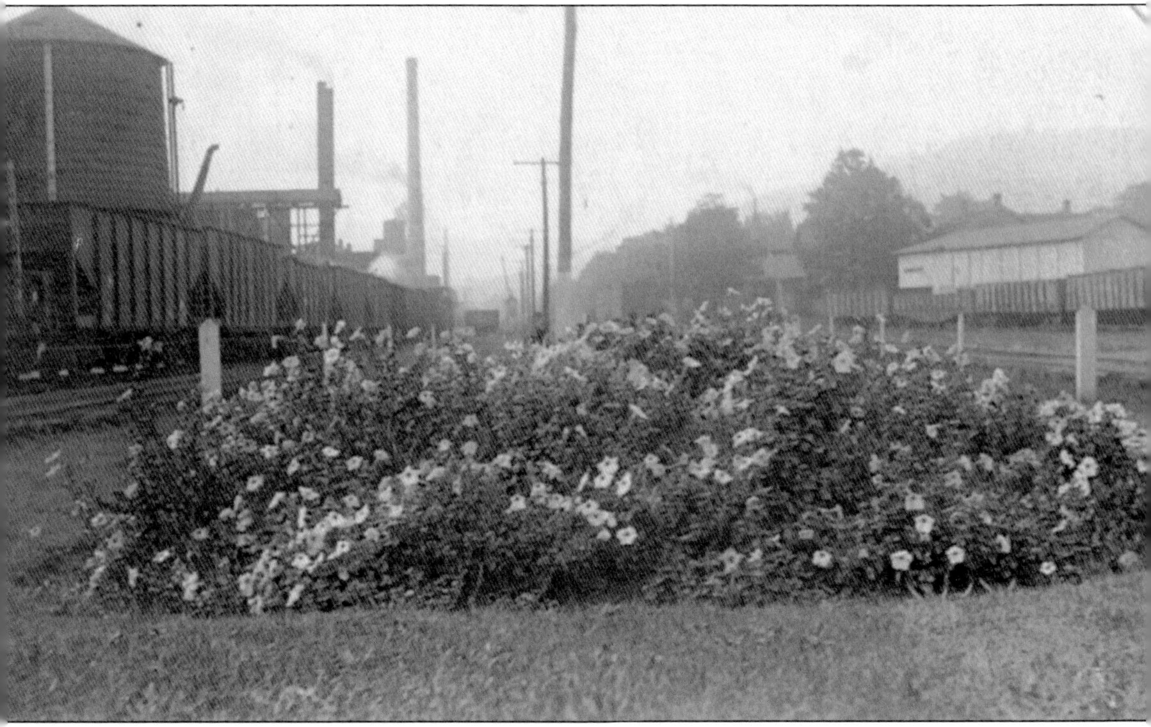

A beautiful flowering bush decorates the rail yards and factories in the Third Ward along the shores of French Creek. Located between the Erie Railroad station and the Chicago Pneumatic Tool Company, this area of the city has always been an industrial complex, which also includes the Franklin Industrial and Commercial Development Authority's incubator as well as Franklin Bronze and Franklin Steel. The Oil Creek & Titusville Railroad (OC&T) began operation on July 18, 1986, and runs to the Rynd Farm area near Oil Creek State Park, just north of Rouseville, to Titusville's Perry Street Station. The train utilizes the tracks built in the 1880s for the now defunct Buffalo, New York & Philadelphia Railroad. The Dunkirk, Allegheny Valley & Pittsburgh Railroad previously owned the tracks used by the OC&T in Titusville. The rail line travels a total distance of 16.5 miles and boasts the only railway post office in service in the United States. (Courtesy of Peter Solle.)

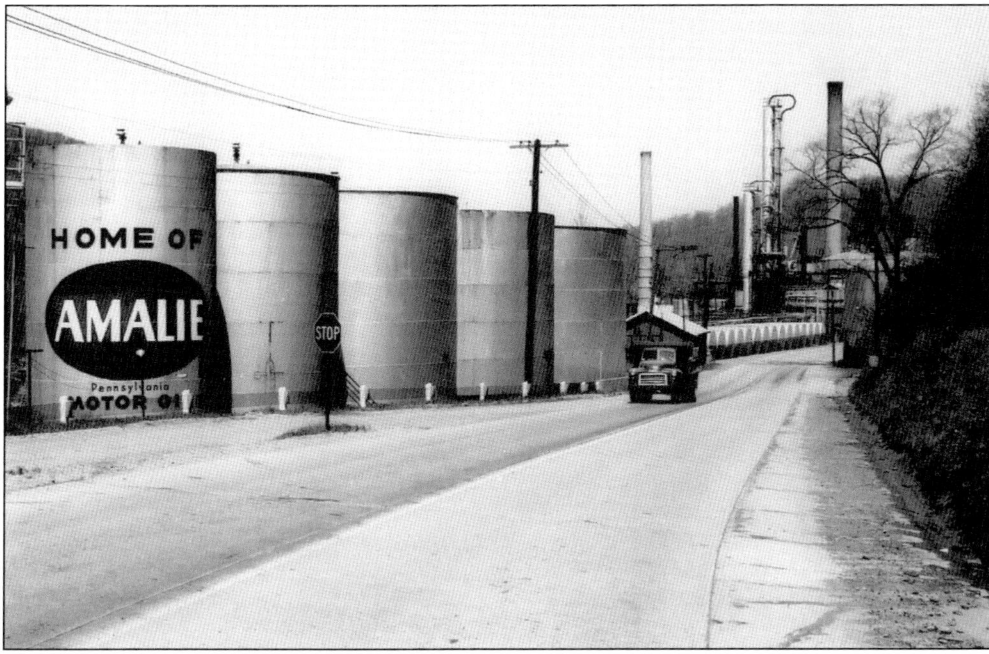

Franklin was the original home of the Amalie Motor Oil Company. Founded in 1903, it was one of the original Pennsylvania crude oil companies. Currently, the company is proud to be the top North American privately owned manufacturer of blended motor oil and lubricants. The company is now based in Tampa Bay, Florida. (Courtesy of Peter Solle.)

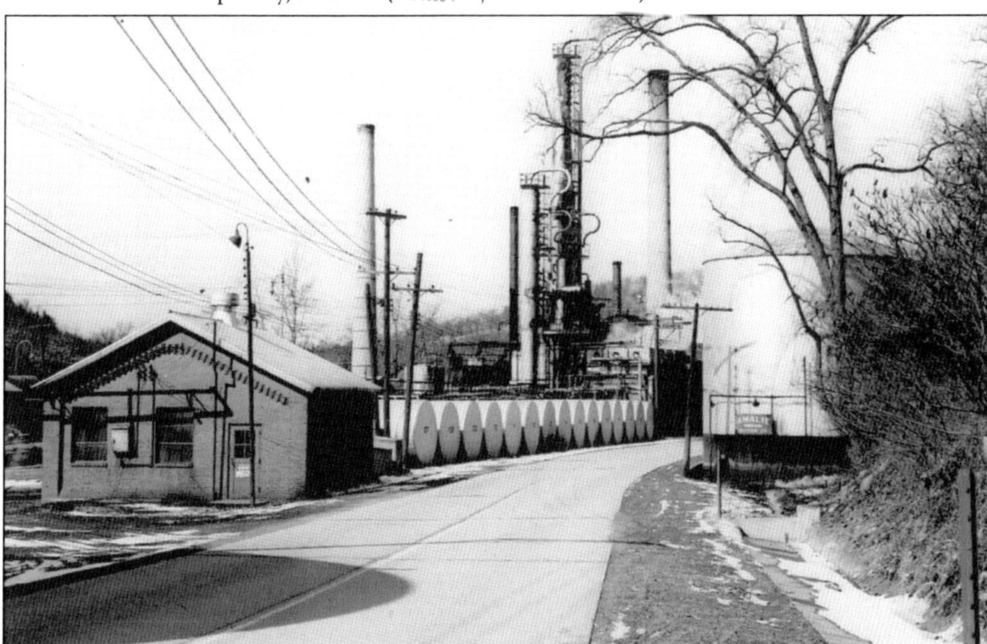

The view at the end of Grant Street (US Route 322) shows the Amalie Motor Oil Company. Founded by the Sonneborn brothers, it was the first oil company to introduce a multigrade motor oil. The plant, built in 1914, was then the Foco Oil Company. The Sonneborns purchased it in 1924. Finally, in 1960, the plant was purchased by Witco. (Courtesy of Peter Solle.)

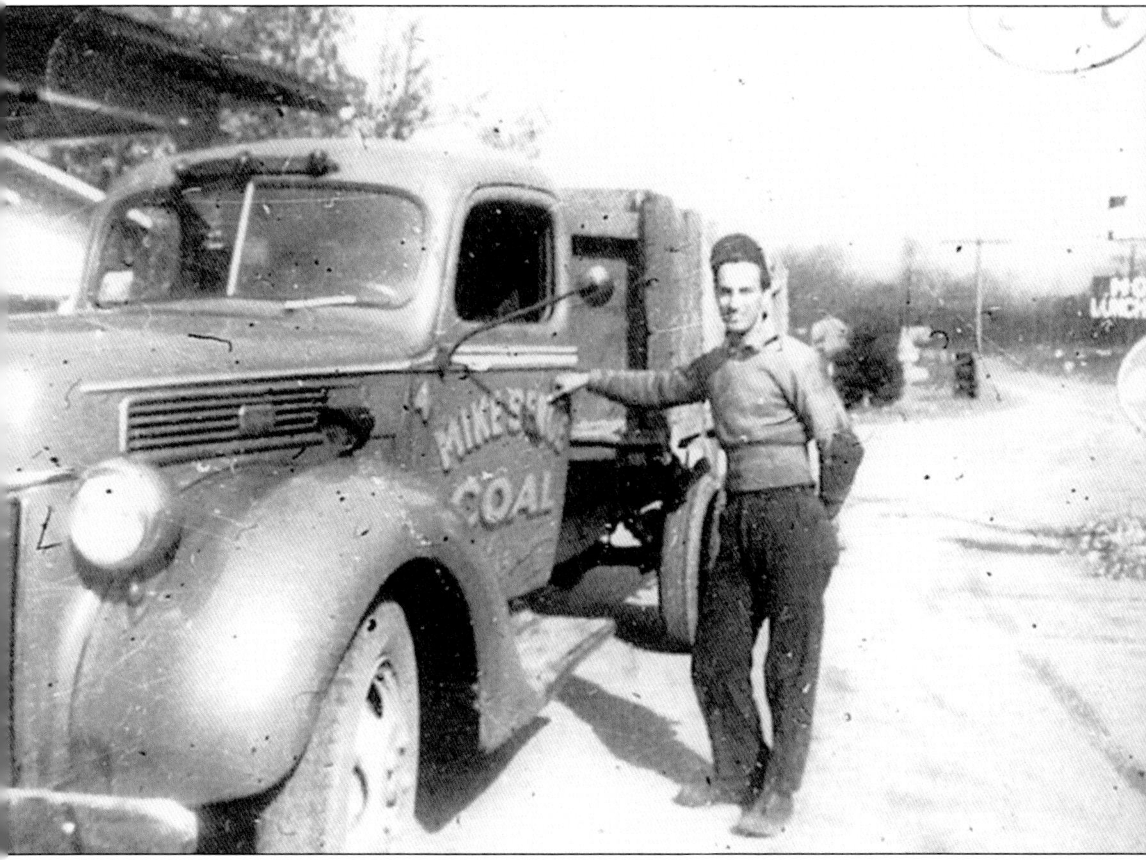

Pat Serge poses beside a Mike Serge Coal truck. The Serge Coal Company was one of a few coal companies that existed in Franklin during the mid-1900s, helping to serve two train stations (the New York Central Railroad and the Erie Railroad Depot), numerous businesses and factories, and homes that used coal as fuel for heat and equipment. Coal is a combustible, dark-colored rock sediment usually found in coal seams or beds. It has been used in industrial environments to assist in refining metals, as well as a source of energy, mainly burned to produce heat and electricity. Because of the high combustibility, coal mining fires are extremely possible and dangerous. Started by a fire at a nearby landfill in 1962, a vein of anthracite was ignited beneath the ground in Centralia, Pennsylvania, near Bloomsburg, in the eastern part of the state. The fire has been burning ever since and is estimated to burn another 250 years. (Courtesy of Frances Serge Eakin.)

Bibliography

Michener, Carolee. *Franklin: A Place in History*. Franklin, PA: Franklin Bicentennial Committee, 1995.

News-Herald, the. *Franklin Pictorial Heritage*. Marceline, MO: Vintage Publications, 1998.

Swetnam, George and Helene Smith. *A Guidebook to Historic Western Pennsylvania*. Pittsburgh, PA: University of Pittsburgh Press, 1976.

Venango County Historical Society. *Venango County Panorama: A Salute to Its People!* Marceline, MO: Walsworth Publishing, 1983.